CW00691095

BSA
PRE-UNIT TWINS
The Complete Story

Other Titles in the Crowood MotoClassics Series

BSA PRE-UNIT TWINS
The Complete Story

Mick Walker

THE CROWOOD PRESS

First published in 2005 by
The Crowood Press Ltd
Ramsbury, Marlborough
Wiltshire SN8 2HR

www.crowood.com

© Mick Walker 2005

All rights reserved. No part of this publication may be reproduced or
transmitted in any form or by any means, electronic or mechanical,
including photocopy, recording, or any information storage and
retrieval system, without permission in writing from the publishers.

British Library Cataloguing-in-Publication Data
A catalogue record for this book is available from the British Library.

ISBN 1 86126 806 8

Typeset and designed by D & N Publishing
Lambourn Woodlands, Hungerford, Berkshire.

Printed and bound in Great Britain by CPI Bath.

Contents

Acknowledgements

When compiling *BSA Pre-Unit Twins – The Complete Story* I was fortunate enough to not only have many close friends within the industry who provided information and shared their own experiences, but I was also able to draw upon my own experiences of BSA ownership – which proved of considerable benefit.

The list of those good people who helped in some way include: John Kendle, Rob Carrick, Fred Pidcock, Owen Wright, Val Emery, Tony Charnock, Sammy Miller, Pat Slinn, Bill Little, Philip Pearson, members of the Gold Star Owners' Club, Pooks Motor Bookshop and Mortons Motorcycle Media. My grateful thanks are extended to them all.

Introduction

For many years BSA (Birmingham Small Arms) promoted itself as 'The Most Popular Motorcycle in the World' – a title which, during the middle of the twentieth century, was absolutely true. The BSA Group was also a vast corporate empire that manufactured a wide and diverse range of products. At various stages this not only included motorcycles, scooters and autocycles from BSA, Ariel, Triumph, Sunbeam and New Hudson, but cars from BSA, Daimler and Lanchester, pedal cycles, guns and rifles, military equipment, agricultural and industrial engines, buses, car bodies (including taxis), machine tools, giant earth-moving equipment, special steels and alloys, even the prestigious Hooper Coachwork concern. At its height there was virtually nothing that BSA could not achieve, and compared with other British motorcycle manufacturers BSA stood head and shoulders above the rest, certainly as regards industrial strength.

As far as its motorcycles were concerned, the name BSA stood for long life, good service from the dealer network, excellent spares availability and in most cases, ease of maintenance. In general, BSA built its reputation upon solid worth rather than outright performance.

BSA Pre-Unit Twins – The Complete Story covers not just the famous A7 and A10 series of post-war parallel twins, but also the not so well remembered ohv and side-valve V-twins that spanned the interwar period of 1919–39.

Although BSA could trace its origins back to 1851, the company did not begin motorcycle production until 1910. However, from then on until the early 1960s the marque enjoyed great sales and profitability. Then came the decline, the reasons for which I have covered in Chapter 10, but suffice to say as a former BSA owner and motorcycle enthusiast, relating what went wrong was a depressing experience. Even so, BSA remains one of the truly great marques in the history of the motorcycle and certainly ranks alongside names such as BMW, Honda and Triumph.

Compiling *BSA Pre-Unit Twins – The Complete Story* was an experience I really enjoyed. And it reminded me of just how great the British motorcycle industry really was, but also, sadly, just how great its fall from power was too.

Mick Walker
Wisbech, Cambridgeshire
March 2005

1 Origins

The origins of Britain's largest motorcycle manufacturer, BSA (Birmingham Small Arms), can be traced all the way back to 1855, when John Dent Goodman was elected as Chairman of the Birmingham Small Arms Trade Association.

The Association is Formed

The forming of this Association came about as a direct result of the Crimean War of 1854–56. Very briefly, the Crimea is a large peninsula, separating the Black Sea from the Sea of Azov and is now part of the Ukraine. The conflict was between Great Britain, France, Turkey and Sardinia on one side, and Imperial Russia on the other.

As my friend Owen Wright says in his book, *BSA – The Complete Story* (The Crowood Press):

> The shortcomings of the Crimean campaign, scandalized by newspaper correspondents, caused an outcry. The manufacture of weapons was then more or less a cottage industry hard pressed to keep up with the huge demand and wastage of early mechanized warfare.

As a result, in 1855 sixteen separate small arms manufacturers in the Birmingham area were recruited by the British government to supply rifles, each gun being patiently and expertly crafted by hand.

However, as the Crimean War dragged on towards its inconclusive ending in April 1856, the Birmingham consortium's position was being overtaken by other manufacturers, notably the Enfield Ordnance Works in North London. This latter organization, instead of handcrafting, was manufacturing its guns by mechanical means.

In the years following the end of the Crimean campaign, the Birmingham gun trade attempted to convince the authorities of the virtues associated with handcrafting weapons. But as the 1860s dawned, they were fast realizing that their cause was lost, so, facing rapidly falling demand, a meeting of the consortium was called on 7 June 1861.

BSA

The result of this meeting was the formation of BSA, with its aim 'to manufacture guns by machinery'. The Birmingham Small Arms Company, to give the new concern its official trading title, elected its inaugural board of directors in September 1863. Several ideas were put forward by interested parties, but the board chose a 25-acre (10ha) site on a green field at Small Heath – this decision being influenced strongly by a promise that Brunel's Great Western Railway was soon to construct a station nearby.

The original planning took in a road linking the new buildings, when constructed, to the main road artery running through the city. Along this road, for one hundred years many millions of guns (and also motorcycles!) would pass. And the name of this road? Well, the very appropriate Armoury Road.

Employing American-made machinery, Birmingham Small Arms strode forward into the new industrial age with considerable

View of BSA's Small Heath works as it was in 1866.

success. This was greatly helped by a combination of astute management, the general international situation (war being good for business!) and a certain amount of good old-fashioned Lady Luck. BSA really hit the jackpot in 1873, when it was given a truly massive order from the Prussian Government for no fewer than forty million cartridge cases. In order to cope with an order of such magnitude, the directors took the highly unusual step of putting the company into voluntary liquidation and relocating its assets into a new enterprise named the Birmingham Small Arms and Metal Company.

However, by the end of that decade, BSA had struck problems and by 1880 was staring at a bleak situation, with little work and no profits. Then that year E.C.F. Otto visited the Small Heath works to exhibit his bicycle. This was to result in the Birmingham company entering into bicycle manufacture. Some one thousand bicycles were built during the early 1880s, before the first BSA Safety Bicycle was constructed in 1884 – rumoured to have been produced from old metal and gun components.

Birth of the Modern Pedal Cycle

Whereas the Otto Bicycle employed two wheels side-by-side in the fashion of a wheel chair, the safety bicycle can be regarded as the forerunner of the modern pedal cycle. It was also in 1880 that the now world-famous 'piled arms' logo was adopted for the first time.

When the company reverted to the trading title Birmingham Small Arms Ltd in 1897, a combination of gun and cycle production had enabled it to survive where many other local commercial operations had been forced to close during the final years of the nineteenth century. But BSA had survived and as the new century dawned it was on the up, with a modernization programme, including fresh working practices and the installation of electric lighting.

The South African Boer War (1899–1902) brought BSA yet more work. But even with these demands, the company maintained its bicycle developments. During 1900, it introduced a free-wheel clutch and back-pedalling rim brake device, both of which proved major sales successes. These, together with developments such as the gents and ladies cycles, the latter with an open step-through frame, and braking improvements, helped BSA to maintain progress in this area.

The Motor Bicycle Arrives

The first years of the twentieth century also saw a rapid succession of new-fangled motor bicycles. Early Midlands-based pioneers of this fledgling industry were Ariel (1902), Norton (1902), Raleigh (1899), Rover (1902), Royal Enfield (1901), Triumph (1902) and Velocette (1904). Watching these companies' progress, BSA began to study the emerging motorcycle industry, at first manufacturing a quantity of special frames and components that it had created for use on motorized bicycles. It should be noted that the term 'bicycle' rather than 'motorcycle' was used, because at that time these early machines were precisely that, a largely standard pedal cycle with a low-powered engine.

The Motorcycle Prototype

Then in 1905 BSA built its first 'motorcycle' prototype, using a bought-in Belgian Minerva power plant. That same year the Eadie Manufacturing Company of Redditch was acquired,

---

BSA Cars

BSA's first involvement with cars came in 1900 when it manufactured component parts for Roots and Venables. But when BSA decided to build its own cars, rather than use the existing Small Heath works, BSA purchased a former government arms factory at Sparkbrook.

The first BSA car was a conventional four-cylinder model with shaft drive. This went into limited production during 1907, but was not to be released to the press or exhibited at shows until 1908. Known as the 18/23, some 150 examples were made, and in 1909 this was joined by the smaller 14/18 and the larger 25/33. Production of these cars continued until 1910, but in December of that year BSA took over Daimler.

As this latter marque was already making a comprehensive range of cars, the existing BSA models were dropped. The only BSA listed for the 1912 season featured a Daimler Knight 13.9hp sleeve-valve engine and a pressed-steel body manufactured at Sparkbrook.

BSA began motorcycle production at its Small Heath factory in 1910. It was not until the early 1920s that the company produced another new car. This was a robust, light car powered by an 1100cc V-twin engine made by Hotchkiss of Coventry. Some 2,500 examples were built between 1922 and 1924, but after this BSA produced badge-engineered Daimler models.

Then in 1929 BSA Cycles Ltd launched a brand new three-wheeler, which was designed by F.W. (Freddie) Hulse and powered by a 1021cc V-twin engine manufactured by BSA. Although lacking the performance of the rival Morgan, the BSA was much easier to drive and more user-friendly. This was even more the case when it received a 1075cc four-cylinder engine in 1933. Both two- and four-cylinder three-wheelers were manufactured until 1936, selling some 5,200 and 1,700 examples respectively. There were also four wheel derivatives, but these were built in very small numbers.

In 1933 a new line of BSA cars was launched. These were based on the existing Lanchester Ten, but with side-valve, instead of ohv, engines. However, Lanchester's fluid flywheel transmission was retained. It is a fact that the BSA 500cc FF (Fluid Flywheel) prototype motorcycle was prompted via the car connection, in this case Lanchester (who had joined the BSA Group in 1931).

But the best-known BSA car of the 1930s was the Scout, which debuted in 1935 and was made by BSA Cycles Ltd (the fluid-flywheel cars were built at the Lanchester factory). A total of 2,700 Scout models was produced up to 1939. Powered by a 1075cc (1203cc from 1936) four-cylinder engine, the Scout was available as a two- or four-seater sports, coupé or two-door saloon.

No BSA cars were manufactured in the post-Second World War period, although both Daimler and Lanchester continued production of their own brands.

Eadie having a close association with the Royal Enfield marque. Albert Eadie had been deeply involved in the history of the bicycle industry, being both an engineer/designer and entrepreneur. Eadie also played a vital role in the design and production of BSA's first 'in-house' motorcycle, the 3½hp single that was unveiled at Olympia, London, in October 1910.

In 1910 BSA also acquired the Coventry-based Daimler Motor Company.

The First All-BSA Motorcycle

The first all-BSA motorcycle had bore and stroke dimensions of 85 × 88mm and displaced 498cc. Besides Albert Eadie, the design team comprised Charles Hyde and pioneer TT rider, Frank Baker (later to manufacture his own brand of motorcycle during the late 1920s). These three men, together with the rest of the production engineers, were based at the BSA Redditch factory (formerly the headquarters of the Eadie Manufacturing Company). And certainly it's a fact that the Redditch team did not simply rest on their laurels, as they were soon displaying their determination to succeed with several notable innovations following this first model.

During 1911, a patented two-speed rear hub was introduced, followed by a three-speed countershaft gearbox. By 1914, a BSA customer was able to order from a number of transmission options. These variations were listed by the company in its official catalogue, using letters from the alphabet. This resulted in Model A, the basic (and cheapest) single speeder; Model B was equipped with the patented BSA cone clutch, and so on. BSA was to retain this method of model designation throughout the entire life of its motorcycle range, until production finally ceased during the 1970s.

Success at Brooklands

BSA's first success at the famous Brooklands racetrack in Surrey was when chief tester,

Kenneth Holden, took a standard 3½hp model to victory (the machine's first) in the spring of 1913. This spurred the Birmingham factory into its initial foray to the Isle of Man for the annual TT races. No fewer than seven specially prepared versions of the production 3½ were entered; however, six retired and the one remaining example came home a lowly seventeenth.

For the 1914 TT, an eight-man BSA team rode the new Model D TT variant. However, race preparation was largely limited to removing the pedalling gear, fitting a larger capacity fuel tank and tuning the engine, which was carried out by S.T. Tessier, formally of the BAT marque. These bikes produced a far better show of reliability, if not speed, by coming home twelfth, twentieth, twenty-third, twenty-eighth, thirty-fourth and forty-fourth, with two retirements – one of which was Frank Baker.

The Line-Up Expands

By now, the BSA model line-up had begun to expand. For example, a 4¼hp, the Model H with fully enclosed all-chain drive, had debuted in the final weeks of 1913. The 557cc engine displacement had been achieved by increasing the stroke to 98mm. Descendants of the '4¼ horse', as it was known, were still listed by BSA until as late as the early 1930s.

Unlike many of its contemporaries in the motorcycle world, BSA did not have to rely on bought-in components. And this applied not just to the major items such as the engine and frame, but even chains, sprockets, bearings and carburettors. Everything seemed rosy, but then came the outbreak of the First World War, following the fatal shooting on a Sarajevo street corner of Archduke Franz Ferdinand of Austria on 28 June 1914.

The following four and a half years were a time of mixed emotions for BSA and its workforce, with the whole country going through the horrors of a truly global conflict. By the time the armistice was signed on 11 November 1918, BSA at Small Heath had upped production of the Lee-Enfield .303 rifles from 135 to a massive 10,000 per week!

But BSA's most notable wartime armament was the renowned Lewis air-cooled machine gun. Many claim this 26lb (11.7kg) gun, which could pump out 500 rounds per minute, was one of the most decisive weapons of this terrible conflict, which claimed over 19 million lives in under 4½ years. Originally designed by Colonel Lewis, a retired American coastguard officer, the Lewis gun was used for both ground and air fighting and was only manufactured by BSA. At the end of the war a total of 145,000 had been constructed in a now purpose-built four-storey factory within the Small Heath complex.

A New Chairman

During the war years, BSA, under the chairmanship of Sir Hallewell Rogers (who had become group chairman in 1906), grew at a rapid pace. By the war's end the company had expanded to five factories employing some 13,000 workers. This huge industrial enterprise built vast amounts of motorcycles, lorries, aero engines, ambulances and various weaponry, including both guns and shells that could weigh anything up to 685lb (310kg).

With the wealth accrued from the war years, BSA invested by purchasing the long-established Sheffield Steel manufacturer, William Jessup & Son Ltd. Again, this move was to benefit significantly BSA's industrial ability to manufacture its own component parts in the post-war era. For the first time, BSA could truly be referred to as an empire – the management of the day realized this and so came a reorganization in readiness for the new challenge and opportunities of a world at peace again.

BSA Cycles Ltd

The production of pedal cycles and motorcycles then came via the BSA Cycles Ltd division, under the management of Charles Hyde,

one of the original trio of the design team at Redditch in pre-war days. However, although the immediate post-war period saw excellent motorcycle and cycle sales, the remainder of the BSA empire was soon struggling. For a start, armaments were an unfashionable commodity in peacetime.

So for the first time, two wheels became the focus of BSA's commercial enterprise. This led to the marque's major entry into the world of motorcycle sport. In 1921, Charles Hyde retired, his place being taken by Commander Godfrey Herbert, who was big and bold both in physique and spirit. Herbert brought with him a desire to win, and, with publicity guru Joe Bryan, set out to put BSA motorcycles on the map.

In many ways the duo succeeded, thanks in no small part to the efforts of one man, Harry S. Perry, who had joined BSA shortly after the war ended. Of all Perry's achievements in the saddle, none is better remembered than his well-publicized climbing of Mount Snowdon in under twenty-five minutes on one of the company's brand new 350cc ohv singles in May 1924.

Problems in Competition

However, BSA did not succeed in one area of motorcycle competition. This disappointment occurred during 1921 and was to blight the company's road racing ambitions for many a long year. The event was the 1921 Senior TT. Until then, the BSA group directors had clung to a dream that the marque could win glory in this, the biggest motorcycle race in the world at that time.

A batch of secret four-valve single-cylinder racing bikes had been constructed, the prototype having already reeled off a number of laps around the Brooklands track in Surrey, in the process displaying considerable promise.

In all, six of these specialist machines were built, at considerable cost, both in terms of materials and working hours. As Owen Wright describes:

The omens were highly encouraging. It was merely a question as to which BSA rider would take the laurels. Eight TT-experienced men were assembled and steeled to the task, all smartly turned out in green and cream jackets.

For their day, the 1921 TT specials were very attractive-looking motorcycles, featuring duplex frames, ohv engines with inclined cylinders and twin-port, four-valve heads. The valve gear was unorthodox in that the rockers operated on a strange V-groove, knife-edge support layout and were operated by square-section coil springs. In contrast with the purpose-built top end, the lower half of the power unit was essentially series-production BSA, but with a specially designed oscillating oil pump.

Everyone at BSA, and the so-called pundits, expected the company to clean up. However, just the reverse happened. Firstly, the Brooklands testing had not exposed the poor handling which the Isle of Man's twisting sections soon revealed. Next came a catalogue of engine problems. These were caused by piston seizures, valve breakages and exhaust manifold glitches. The BSA engineering team attempted to solve the seizure problems by changing the piston material from cast iron to aluminium, but this failed to address the causes fully; if anything it aggravated the situation. But if the practice week was bad, the race itself was a monumental disaster, with not a single works BSA completing the distance! Commander Herbert was so annoyed he vowed BSA would never again take part in the TT. Although this order was eventually overturned, it effectively meant that BSA factory support at the TT was not made again on an official basis for years to come.

Workhorse Rather than Sportster

Instead, BSA proceeded to concentrate on other branches of the sport, in the process building up an excellent reputation for producing mostly affordable, reliable, if rather staid, roadsters. In fact, during most of the

1925 2¼hp ohv single, with forward-mounted magneto, flat tank and hand-change …

… with caliper brake and girder front forks from the same machine.

1929/30 BSA 557cc Sloper; side-valve engine with wet-sump lubrication (oil container at front of crankcase).

interwar years BSA meant workhorse rather than sportster.

So the BSA motorcycle division grew and prospered with machines that suited the majority of the buying public. These were bikes such as the Round Tank and 'the Sloper', both of which sold in their thousands and were much loved by their owners. Such bikes were backed up by a range of singles in varying capacities,

plus the E and G series of V-twins (*see* Chapter 2). The BSA marketing men also came up with a wide range of guises for customers to choose from, including touring, sports and de luxe specifications.

Often BSA motorcycles of the 1920s and early 1930s had features that were advanced for their time, but never to the point where they could be described as innovations. So, unlike

BSA excelled itself with its new and innovative S27 (usually referred to as 'the Sloper'), a 493cc ohv single. Launched in August 1926, this really was a milestone in the Birmingham marque's history, with its saddle tank, wet-sump lubrication and detachable 90-degree valve cylinder head.

smaller firms such as Brough Superior, Excelsior, Chater-Lea, Coventry Eagle, Douglas and Velocette, the BSA models were conventional and practical – all mass-produced but employing manufacturing techniques that were in advance of their rivals, using good materials and an effective quality-control system.

During these austere years motorcyclists loved to talk and read of the sports machines produced by BSA's rivals, but when it came to opening their wallets they opted for a more conventional machine, at which BSA was so adept, one that could take them to work during the week or a ride in the country at weekends. Finally, and most importantly, a BSA-produced product offered the prospect of not only years of reliable service, but a dealer in almost every town.

This policy enabled the Birmingham company to survive the period of the Great Depression, which came in the aftermath of the New York Wall Street stock-market crash of October 1929. With its well-established reputation for service and value-for-money, BSA was able not only to survive, but as things eventually began to brighten up as the 1930s progressed, the company also made an

B30-3 249cc (63 × 80mm) sv single-cylinder engine with oil sump at the front and magneto above; the model ran from 1930 through to 1935.

attempt to render its bikes more visually attractive.

This really began with the introduction of the Blue Star series for the 1932 season. Cleverly, the differences were effected by switching components during assembly, rather than by designing completely new models. This meant that additional glitter and performance could be made at the minimum of cost and without any real disruption to the BSA production line. Even the top super sports versions were little more than attending to components such as pistons, camshafts and providing a competition-type magneto and larger carburettor, with modified porting for the cylinder head. The vertical range of singles, with their compact dimensions (at least compared to their existing Sloper counterparts), wet sump and forward-mounted magneto, were the work of Herbert Perkins, and the specially tuned versions described above were adorned with the six-pointed blue star from which their name was taken.

The FF Prototype

An interesting prototype appeared on the BSA stand at the 1933 London Olympia Show. This was a brand new 500 single, the FF, known because its transmission comprised a fluid flywheel and pre-selector gearbox. The flywheel was formed on the nearside (left) half of the crankshaft, which still retained a sprocket at its outer end. This drove the gearbox, which featured three speeds, pre-selected by the rider via a handlebar lever and engaged by moving a foot pedal. No clutch was needed as the fluid did this job, whilst the kickstarter turned the engine via gears in an extended timing cover. The main reason why this idea was not carried through to production centred around the effect the system had on performance levels.

A Five-Hundred V-Twin

But most important, to this story at least, was the launch, also at Olympia that year, of a new

1934 499cc Blue Star W34-9 twin-port ohv single.

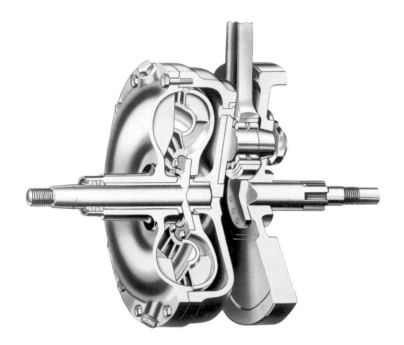

Factory sectional illustration of the experimental BSA Fluid Flywheel transmission of 1934; it never entered production.

five-hundred V-twin, which had originally been designed for the War Department. The full story of this, and the other BSA V-twins of the interwar years, is contained in the following chapter, but, suffice to say, the Model J was a most attractive bike and also showed that at long last BSA was actively engaged in developing new models with more than one cylinder.

The year 1936 was to be important in the history of BSA Cycles Ltd. First, Joe Bryan took over the Managing Director's position after Commander Godfrey Herbert was promoted 'upstairs' to the senior board of the BSA group's directors. The new MD's first act has to be seen as a master stroke. He recruited the man whom many regard as the finest British motorcycle designer ever, Val Page. Together with Herbert Perkins, Page set about creating a range of new and updated models, which, as Owen Wright says: 'were stylish, sensible and right up to date'. Only the V-twins were left alone, the result being a full range of dry sump

lubricated models, with rear-mounted magnetos for the 1937 model year. These consisted of the 249cc and 348cc B series, seven models in all, featuring either ohv or sv, plus the heavier M models, which were largely intended for sidecar duties. This range of singles was also to give birth to the legendary Gold Star – named because, in June 1937, a specially prepared 496cc ohv M23 Blue Star circulated the famous Brooklands circuit at over 100mph, thus winning the 'Gold Star' awarded by the Surrey circuit for this achievement.

The Speed Twin Arrives

But it was the launch in July 1937 of Edward Turner's Triumph Speed Twin that really caused BSA to realize that it had to build a parallel twin. Here at a stroke was a new breed of motorcycle. And as with all great designs, the Speed Twin was essentially simple. Amazingly, the engine was actually lighter and narrower

The Motor Cycle, November 8th, 1934.

BSA
LEADERS IN THE INDUSTRY

OFFER YOU THE
FINEST PROGRAMME
AND THE
BIGGEST RANGE
WITH THE
BIGGEST SALES

Stand No.30.
OLYMPIA

'BSA Leaders in the Industry' advertisement, November 1934.

than the existing Triumph Tiger 90 five-hundred single of the same era.

Housed in the familiar Tiger 90 chassis, the Speed Twin was able to sell at a highly competitive price. And so BSA, together with every major British motorcycle manufacturer, knew immediately that it had no option but to follow Triumph's lead. So BSA set to and managed to build a couple of prototype parallel twins before the outbreak of war in September 1939. One was overhead valve, the other overhead camshaft. BSA pursued two very different lines of thought with these two prototypes – one was intended to be sporting enough to challenge even the Tiger 100, which Triumph had launched in 1938, whilst the other was clearly a much more staid and sedate bike that Small Heath management considered would appeal to the traditional 'value-for-money' BSA buyer.

BSA staff with one of the original M24 Gold Star singles in spring 1939, and a foreign customer who is just taking delivery of his new bike at the Birmingham factory.

The 1938–39 Prototypes

Following the shock arrival of the Triumph Speed Twin in mid-1937, BSA suddenly found itself needing to produce its own parallel twin. For many years, like the rest of the British industry, the Birmingham company had considered that the long-running V-twin concept was all that buyers needed – and then mainly to haul a sidecar rather than as a sporting solo.

Also, it has to be borne in mind that BSA had, in the main, tended to be conservative when it came to motorcycle design. And, unlike many of its rivals, it had been successful because of this policy. In other words, let others take the risk of innovative, new technology. As fellow author Roy Bacon once put it:

BSA existed for half a century with a reputation for producing reliable, unexciting motorcycles with stolid performance and little to fire the imagination. They knew better than most that their first need was to stay in business and make a profit, and that however much motorcyclists of those times clamoured in the press for exotic specifications, they went out and bought the well known and reliable singles and vee-twins they trusted. The history of motorcycling is littered with names of companies who were foolish enough to provide what was requested, only to find that the conservative public always waited for someone else to buy first in case there were problems.

So, in attempting to come up with a creditable challenger to the Triumph design, BSA was

BUY

YOUR B·S·A FROM
THE LARGEST B·S·A DEALERS IN THE HOME COUNTIES——

PAY WHILE YOU RIDE THE WHITBY WAY

250 c.c. O.H.V. Empire Star £50

OVER 100 B·S·A's IN STOCK

1938 MODELS AND PRICES.

Model	Price		Model	Price
250 c.c. S.V. Tourer	£43 0 0		600 c.c. S.V. Tourer	£63 10 0
250 c.c. O.H.V. Sports	£45 15 0		500 c.c. O.H.V. Sports	£65 0 0
350 c.c. S.V. Tourer	£47 0 0		500 c.c. O.H.V. Empire Star	£70 0 0
350 c.c. O.H.V. Empire Star	£55 15 0		500 c.c. O.H.V. Gold Star	£85 0 0
350 c.c. O.H.V. Competition	£62 10 0		750 c.c. O.H.V. Vee-Twin	£82 0 0
350 c.c. O.H.V. Sports	£49 15 0		1,000 c.c. S.V. Vee-Twin	£82 0 0
350 c.c. O.H.V. De Luxe	£63 0 0		All prices include electric lighting, electric	
500 c.c. S.V. Tourer	£61 17 6		horn and licence holder.	

WHITBYS
OF ACTON

A Special Offer Awaits You, So SEND THIS COUPON RIGHT AWAY!

To WHITBYS,
273, The Vale,
Acton, W.3

I am interested in a B.S.A.

Model..................................

I have a........Year.....................

Model...

NAME ....

ADDRESS................. ....

WE are the largest B.S.A. Dealers in the Home Counties and can give you the benefit of over 30 years' experience with B.S.A. productions.

You will do best by getting your B.S.A. from us, as our organisation is complete and up to date in every way.

If deferred terms are desired, here we can be of particular assistance to you—you can purchase a new B.S.A. "The Whitby Way" over any period up to two years, and we believe that our method is the easiest yet evolved.

Thousands of riders have bought their B.S.A.'s from Whitbys, a large percentage on a paid exchange basis, which is in itself proof positive of our claim to give the highest possible allowances. By the way, there is a coupon on this page for the use of readers who are unable to call at our Showrooms which are open on week days from 9 a.m. till 9 p.m.

Immediate delivery can be given of 1938 Models. They are all here, taxed and ready to drive away.

273. THE VALE, ACTON, W.3.

Phone : SHEpherds Bush 5355/6.

During the late 1930s BSA were the most popular of all British motorcycles. The 1938 range included fourteen motorcycles ranging from the 250cc Side-Valve Tourer through to the mighty 1000cc V-Twin.

21

faced with a choice of glamour or dependability, price or performance, innovation or proven ideas. However, the new parallel twin was something that was largely unknown at the time. Certainly, there had been a few earlier designs with this format, but in reality Turner's Speed Twin was the first truly successful, modern and commercially viable example.

Much earlier, during the first half of the 1920s, BSA engineers had built a number of prototype twin-cylinder engines (discounting their existing vee layout). One was a flat twin, with the cylinders across the frame (like BMW) and featuring side valves and an in-unit gearbox. The second was an overhead cam inline design with a unit construction gearbox bolted to the rear of the engine. Finally, the third power unit was a vertical twin-cylinder two-stroke with a displacement of 150cc. None of these designs was destined to reach production status; instead, at that time BSA chose to stick with its tried and tested side-valve single and V-twins. There is no doubt that the company's disastrous experience during the 1921 TT played into the hands of those within the company who wished to stick with old-fashioned but reliable layouts. This policy survived for many years, but the arrival of the Triumph Speed Twin, and to a lesser extent BSA's own Gold Star sporting single (both in 1937), showed there was serious demand for faster, more glamorous designs.

BSA followed two entirely different paths when it created the two parallel-twin prototypes in the months leading up to the outbreak of the Second World War. One, with an overhead camshaft and 100mph+ (160km/h+) potential displaced 500cc, could have matched the Tiger 100; in fact, it would have scored over the Triumph due to having ohc rather than ohv.

The single-overhead camshaft was driven by a shaft and two pairs of bevel gears on the offside (right) of the cylinder block. It looked a purposeful assembly with comprehensive finning for both head and barrel, these being retained by long through bolts. The cylinder head was cast in aluminium, with the cambox integral and sealed by large valve-inspection covers at the front and rear. There was also another cover, just above the bevel shaft, which provided access to the bevel gears and camshaft. The valves were operated by hairpin springs, with the entire cambox being lubricated by internal oilways. In traditional British fashion the aluminium crankcases were split vertically; outboard of the timing case were the gears for not only driving the camshaft, but also the twin oil pumps and the magdyno assembly.

This advanced engine was mounted in an existing Silver Star rigid frame with M series cycle parts and girder forks. A heavy duty four-speed, foot-change gearbox was specified, together with a conventional separate oil tank on the offside for the dry sump lubrication system.

A failing of the ohc twin was an extremely narrow power band, although it was something which the BSA engineering team believed they could have cured with further development. Two of these engines were also used in experiments with the Aspin rotary valve. However, as with other similar designs, the rotary valve proved to have an Achille's heel – well, two actually – lubrication and heat.

The other prototype design was a 350cc-class ohv. The bottom end of this was very similar to the post-war Ariel KH500 twin. At the top, the valve gear was enclosed by a single, almost square aluminium cover. Otherwise it was a remarkably simple design with nothing of particular interest. It must be said that except for having twin cylinders it did not appear to offer any real advance over the existing ohv singles, certainly not from the performance viewpoint.

However, the fate of these prototypes was sealed by Mr Hitler's war and instead of offering a challenge to Triumph in the parallel twin stakes, BSA instead found itself switching its production to producing thousands upon thousands of side-valve M20 singles for the British War Office.

And when peace finally returned some 5½ years later, the parallel twin which BSA put into production during 1946 was not based on either pre-war design.

2   V-Twins

Long before the parallel twin became fashionable from the late 1930s onwards, any motorcycle having more than one cylinder was likely to be a V-twin. Why? Well, as Owen Wright says in *BSA – The Complete Story:* 'Ever since the days of Gottlieb Daimler and his *zweizylindermotor* of 1889, two cylinders joined on a common crankpin in a single longitudinal plane has been one of the most enduring methods of providing plenty of sidecar pulling power.' Before the advent of the small affordable car, the only practical means of transporting a family on a budget was with a motorcycle and sidecar, something that was to remain a feature of the world's highways until the late 1950s.

Although BSA only entered production of motorcycles in 1910, it was not long after this that the company realized that besides its range of single-cylinder machines in various capacities, it needed a V-twin for sidecar duties. A V-twin is, of course, basically a pair of single cylinders on a common crankcase, hence its near ideal pulling power for sidecar use.

The V-Twin Project

In the months leading up to the outbreak of the First World War in August 1914, BSA engineers had worked on their own V-twin project. However, with the coming of the conflict peaceful priorities obviously had to give way to military requirements. So it was not until 1920 that the first BSA V-twin was manufactured. Initially known as the Model A, this was soon changed to the E prefix.

The engineering team chose a 50-degree angle for its vee, this providing enough distance between the cylinders for cooling, but at the same time not extending the wheelbase too much – as would have been the case if the perfect 90-degree layout had been employed.

The BSA side-valve V-twin debuted in 1920. This is the 986cc model from 1924.

The Model A became the Model E in 1921 and proved a good seller throughout the 1920s.

A Side-Valve Layout

The design was a side-valve with a displacement of 771cc and bore and stroke dimensions of 76 × 85mm. As the engine's foremost requirement was that of sidecar duties, the main need was not only for great pulling power, but also reliability and ease of maintenance.

In total, some three years had been taken up with the design's development. And BSA was confident that its vee would be a match for the competition, certainly in its robust nature and engineering standards. In this, the Birmingham company was to be proved right, as not only did the E remain on production until as late as 1931, but it spawned a whole family of V-twins, which eventually ranged from 498cc to 986cc and ran up to the outbreak of the Second World War in 1939.

Mechanical Features

With long service in mind, mechanical features included interchangeable valves, roller big-end bearings, H-section connecting rods, long-skirted pistons, a mechanical oil pump back-up with an additional hand-operated plunger device, aluminium chaincases and a three-speed, hand-operated countershaft gearbox. The period-style flat tank was mounted by way of three lugs on the top frame tube.

The valves benefited from advances made in this field during the war, and the Model E was equipped with high temperature nickel alloy steel components. As for the timing gear, this employed the external cam method, with the contact area between cam lobe and tappet being more than adequate to give long life, even under the most harsh conditions.

1930 E30-14 Specifications

Engine	Air-cooled, side-valve 50-degree V-twin, interchangeable valves, roller big-end bearings, H section connecting rods, long-skirted pistons, vertically split aluminium crankcases
Bore	76mm
Stroke	85mm
Displacement	771cc
Compression ratio	4.5:1
Lubrication	Mechanical pump, backed up by a hand-operated plunger
Ignition	Magneto
Carburettor	Amal
Primary drive	Chain
Final drive	Chain
Gearbox	Three-speed, countershaft hand-change
Frame	Steel, tubular; welded and bolted-up construction
Front suspension	Girder forks
Rear suspension	Rigid
Front brake	Dummy belt rim
Rear brake	Internal expanding
Tyres	26 × 3 front and rear

General Specifications

Wheelbase	65in (1,650mm)
Ground clearance	N/A
Seat height	N/A
Fuel tank capacity	2½gal (11.4ltr)
Dry weight	320lb (145kg)
Maximum power	6/7hp (ACU rating)
Top speed	57mph (92km/h)

The First Updates

The first updates to the design occurred for the 1923 model year. They were introduced more to improve production methods than to meet mechanical needs. The early 1920s was a period when production costs were being reviewed in light of profit margins, as a result of the production line techniques introduced by Henry Ford in America. In addition, the recent war had shown that savings could be made and production speeded up – without sacrificing engineering standards.

The 1923 changes are listed below:

- The crankcases were revised, providing a more oval shape. Originally, these were virtually circular.
- The fuel tank was given a rounded front nose section, with an increase in the size of the filler caps.
- The outer magneto drive cover was given a convex shape, providing additional clearance for the drive chain.
- The exhaust was revised, now having a detachable header pipe instead of the previous cast-in pinch-bolt set-up, the latter having been prone to breakage in service.
- The gear-change gate at the side of the tank was revised from its original upright position to a forward angle of some 45 degrees.

Also for 1923 BSA included the Light 6 Twin. This was a budget version of the standard E (now referred to as the de luxe), with new, slimmer mudguards, a pressed steel (instead of alloy) fixed drive cover and other cost-cutting measures. However, because of its reduced weight it was equally suitable for solo or side-car work. In fact, the Light 6 was to outlive its de luxe brother by a couple of years (1931 against 1929).

The Taxi Cab

During the 1920s the motorcycle was used for a large number of commercial purposes – transporting everything from milk to people. And so the Model E 'taxi cab' was born, arriving in 1922 and leading to the Model F with a larger 986cc (80 × 98mm) engine. Just the thing for heavy loads that demanded what is today referred to as 'torque in abundance'.

The arrival of this bigger engine model also opened up export opportunities, which as we will see was ultimately to transform into one of the greatest ever motorcycle sales achievements, when a pair of the 'Colonial' version of the big vee, coded 'G', took part in a fantastic 'around-the-globe' tour that began in 1926 and ended two years later.

The World Tour

What Owen Wright describes as 'the ultimate test for this colossal Birmingham Dray' came in 1926 when the company constructed a couple of heavy duty Model G Colonial outfits for what was accurately described as 'The World Tour'. That it took two years and covered 23,000 miles (37,000km) over largely unsurfaced roads with few mechanical problems says a lot for the sheer reliability and robust nature of the big BSA V-twins. The men who undertook this heroic venture were BSA salesman Bertram Cathrick and *The Motor Cycle* journalist, John Castley.

This venture – adventure is probably a more appropriate word – began and ended in Birmingham and took in twenty-five countries. In the process, the pair did more than probably anyone in establishing sales outlets in many far-flung areas of the globe. What better way of proving the product could there have been in those pioneering days of the two-wheel industry than showing the locals the actual product! As a mark of their achievement, BSA even listed a Model G World Tour version for several years thereafter.

Model G Development

Drum brakes had appeared in 1926, then in 1927 came a lower seat height, together with improved cylinder head cooling (achieved by increasing the fin area, which now extended onto the exhaust manifold). Valve inspection covers arrived in 1930, together with a 3gal (13.6ltr) saddle tank (to replace the old-fashioned flat tank). This new tank came complete with an integral oil supply.

Then came the recession of the early 1930s, caused by the Wall Street stock-market crash of October 1929, with BSA surviving thanks to its wide range of products throughout the group. Motorcycles played an important part. For

Nearside view of the 1935 498cc ohv V-twin, showing the single carb between the cylinders, and a front-mounted mag/dyno.

example, even in 1928 BSA Cycles Ltd listed a wide range of models with engine sizes of: 174cc, 249cc, 349cc, 493cc, 557cc, 770cc and 986cc, together with a number of sidecars. There was a BSA for everyone except the sporting rider, the company catering very much for the bread-and-butter commuter and touring market. And with the coming of the austere days caused by the recession this played into BSA's hands. It was not until late 1932 that any real sign of an upturn was forthcoming, and even then things didn't improve overnight.

BSA advertisement of March 1928, promoting the wide dealer base.

The 1933 Model Year

With the last of the Model E 771cc V-twins being built during 1931, the only vee to continue into 1932 was the G, now coded 32-10. When the 1933 BSA model range was announced at the end of September 1932, there was an additional version of the 986cc side-valve twin, which had been introduced primarily, so

the factory stated, 'to meet police requirements overseas'. The engine of the latter model, BSA sources revealed, had been given 'racing cams, special alloy steel exhaust valves, and detachable high compression cylinder heads', whilst a 'larger bore carburettor is fitted with an air cleaner'. Transmission was via a heavy duty four-speed gearbox, and the clutch was provided with both foot and hand controls.

The frame had also been revised to give a slightly shorter wheelbase, and was provided with right- or left-hand sidecar lugs and interchangeable wheels with 27 × 4in tyres. Following BSA practice at the time, the brakes were interconnected, whilst both drums were of 7in (178mm) diameter – however, the width of the front was 1in (25mm) compared

to that of the rear 1⅜in (35mm). Folding foot boards were specified for overseas machines. The motorcycle was 'intended for speeds up to 75mph (120km/h) with sidecar'. As for prices, in September 1932 BSA listed the British market G33 12 (Light) at £60, whereas the export G33 13 (WT) was £62.

New, Smaller Vee for War Office Order

In April 1933, first news was released of an entirely new ohv V-twin, supplies of which had already been delivered to the War Office. This order was placed after a prototype had undergone a 10,000-mile (16,090km) test, which included 5,000 miles (8,045km) over the British Army test-ground at Farnborough, Hampshire, where, as *The Motor Cycle* reported, 'there are sandy knolls, severe hills, watersplashes, bogs, and a 1 in 2 test hill.' The remaining 5,000 miles were conducted in Wales. Full details appeared later, when the 'Advance Details of 1934 Models' was published in *The Motor Cycle*, dated 21 September 1933.

With bore and stroke dimensions of 63 × 80mm respectively, the newcomer had a capacity of 498cc. The cylinders were set at a narrow 45 degrees, whilst the valves in the detachable heads formed an angle of 75 degrees.

The news that BSA had decided to offer the new five-hundred twin to civilian customers was generally well received by press and public alike. And there is no disputing that the 'J', as it was known, had the looks to please any enthusiast of the era.

Engine Design
The J34-11 featured dual-taper-section tubular pushrods, and each pair lay side-by-side within a large diameter tubular cover; the rockers, also, were enclosed as far as the outer arm.

There were two camshafts, each carrying the inlet and exhaust cam lobe for one cylinder, the rockers themselves being interposed between the cams and the pushrods. No tappets

1933 G33-13 Specifications

Engine	Air-cooled, side-valve 50-degree V-twin, double roller big-ends, H-section connecting rods, aluminium alloy pistons (new cylinder design with detachable heads), vertically split aluminium crankcases
Bore	80mm
Stroke	98mm
Displacement	986cc
Compression ratio	N/A
Lubrication	By mechanical pump; oil compartment in section of fuel tank
Ignition	Magneto
Carburettor	Amal
Primary drive	Chain
Final drive	Chain
Gearbox	Three-speed, hand-change
Frame	All-steel tubular construction, with sidecar lugs
Front suspension	BSA girder forks with adjustable shock absorbers
Rear suspension	Rigid
Front brake	7in (178mm)
Rear brake	7in (178mm)
Tyres	27 × 4 or 28 × 3.5 front and rear

General Specifications

Wheelbase	N/A
Ground clearance	N/A
Seat height	N/A
Fuel tank capacity	3gal (13.6ltr)
Dry weight	425lb (193kg)
Maximum power	23bhp
Top speed	64mph (103km/h)

Originally conceived for a government specification, the J12 featured a 498cc 50-degree V-twin engine with overhead valves. It made its public bow at Olympia in November 1933 and went on sale to the public in 1934.

were employed. Between the forward camshaft and the magneto driving gear was a single idler.

Two compression rings were fitted to each of the light alloy pistons, and the compression ratio was 6:1. Double-row roller bearings were fitted to each big-end, and were mounted side-by-side on a large diameter crankpin. As the cylinders were set in the same line, the connecting rods were slightly offset, but their H-section formation was described by one journalist of the day as being 'especially rigid'.

The Lubrication System

Below and behind the crankshaft timing pinion was a gear wheel that was employed to drive the twin gear-type oil pumps. These pumps were always submerged, as they lay in a pocket in the timing chest, thus forming an oil trap and ensuring priming of the pumps and thorough lubrication of the gear train.

Oil was drawn from an external tank and delivered to the big-ends; thereafter it was thrown out to feed all moving parts. The scavenging pump returned the surplus lubricant to the tank from a pocket behind the crankcase, and thus a full dry system was used. An oil-pressure gauge was fitted to the tank top (some machines had this gauge in the instrument panel – if the latter fitting was desired). There were also oilways to each inlet valve stem from the roller boxes.

The Transmission

From the engine-shaft shock absorber, power was transmitted to the dry-plate clutch via a 0.5in × 0.305in primary chain enclosed by the usual BSA system and incorporating an oil container. A four-speed gearbox was fitted, with a choice of hand or foot operation.

1934 J34-11 Specifications

Engine	Air-cooled, ohv 45-degree V-twin, valves in detachable heads with 75-degree angle, dual-taper-section tubular pushrods, two camshafts, piston with two compression rings, one oil scraper, exposed coil valve springs*, double-row roller-bearing big-ends
Bore	63mm
Stroke	80mm
Displacement	499cc
Compression ratio	5.5:1
Lubrication	Twin mechanical oil pumps; dry sump
Ignition	Magneto
Carburettor	Amal 276 1in (25.4mm)
Primary drive	Chain
Final drive	Chain
Gearbox	Four-speed; choice of hand or foot operation
Frame	Forged steel, BSA backbone type
Front suspension	BSA girder forks
Rear suspension	Rigid
Front brake	7in (178mm)
Rear brake	7in (178mm)
Tyres	26 × 3.25 front and rear

General Specifications

Wheelbase	N/A
Ground clearance	N/A
Seat height	N/A
Fuel tank capacity	3¾gal (17ltr)
Dry weight	N/A
Maximum power	22bhp @ 5,000rpm
Top speed	72mph (116km/h)

* Later models have enclosed valve gear.

The frame was of the forged steel BSA backbone type and almost identical to the then current Blue Star single-cylinder models, but a shade longer in order to accommodate the engine and electrical equipment within the frame members.

In addition to the normal rear chain guard, the J34-11 also featured protection for the lower chain run. One of the latest three-peg type QD rear wheels was also fitted (previously this was by way of studs), with brake diameters front and rear of 7in (178mm). Tyre size was 26 × 3.25 front and rear, whilst both silencers were carried on the offside (right) of the machine. *The Motor Cycle* described the Model J's performance in the following terms:

Although this machine was designed in the first place as a sturdy and reliable touring mount, the question of high speed has not been overlooked, and its performance is said to run well into the eighties. It runs smoothly and quietly, and should prove to be an ideal fast touring mount with the addition of just that trait of flexibility and smoothness which is lacking in some otherwise excellent singles.

Although the big-twin, the G, remained virtually unchanged for the 1934 season, there was a further BSA development that year which concerned the entire range of twins and singles. For the first time, all the machines were to be marketed with full electric equipment, including an electric horn, and this equipment was included in the prices, together with a licence holder.

An Olympia Show Debut

Although the new five-hundred vee had already appeared in the press, it was not until the Olympia Show in late November 1933 that the public got to see it in the metal, so to speak. BSA claimed a power output of 22bhp at 5,000rpm, which it claimed was sufficient to propel the 350lb (158kg) machine along up to 80mph (130km/h).

Improvements for 1935

A year later, when the 1935 BSA range was announced, the five-hundred V-twin benefited by way of improvements introduced on what BSA described as its 'medium capacity group of machines'. This saw all the ohv models (with the exception of the 595cc Sloper) have the inlet valve springs enclosed, whereas the exhaust valve springs were left exposed.

There was also a new front fork in which stronger links were used and the linkage so arranged that the wheelbase remained constant throughout the entire range of fork deflection. Yet another change was new 'shock-insulated' (basically rubber-mounted) handlebars.

The Model J also received a modification to its oiling system, with a certain amount of oil being bypassed to the overhead rockers in such a way that the main stream of oil was not robbed and the supply to the big-ends and other working components was not affected.

The 986cc Model G side-valve vee was again largely unchanged.

A New 750 Ohv V-Twin

When BSA published details of its 1936 model range, there were not only the new long-stroke side- and overhead-valve singles of 348 and 496cc, but, more importantly as regards this book, a 748cc ohv V-twin. Together with the existing 498cc J12 and 986cc G14, the latter of which had, as BSA said, been 'Modernized in appearance', there was now a total of three V-twin models of different

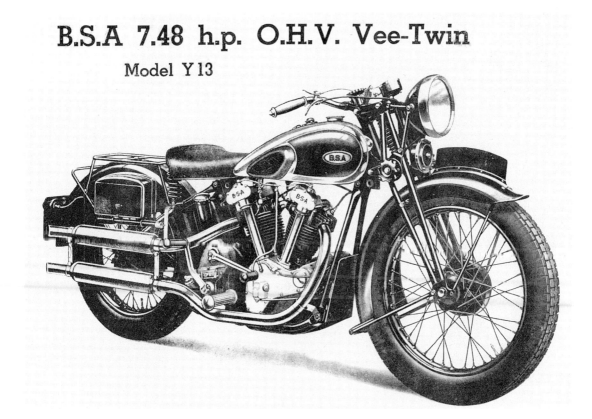

B.S.A 7.48 h.p. O.H.V. Vee-Twin
Model Y13

The larger capacity Y13, with 748cc engine, was launched in time for the 1936 model year. Capable of 90mph (145km/h), it was a much underrated machine.

31

1936 Y13 Specifications	
Engine	Air-cooled, ohv 45-degree V-twin, cast-iron cylinder heads and barrels, forked connecting rod layout, two rows of rollers on crankpin, twin main bearings on drive side, exposed exhaust valve springs, enclosed inlet valve mechanism, vertically split aluminium crankcases
Bore	71mm
Stroke	94.5mm
Displacement	748cc
Compression ratio	5.5:1
Lubrication	Double, gear pumps, dry sump
Ignition	Magdyno, Lucas 6V
Carburettor	Amal 276 1⅛in (28.5mm)
Primary drive	Chain
Final drive	Chain
Gearbox	BSA four-speed, foot-change
Frame	Duplex cradle with forged steel backbone and integral sidecar lugs
Front suspension	Constant wheelbase forks, with adjustable shock absorber and steering damper
Rear suspension	Rigid
Front brake	7in (178mm)
Rear brake	7in (178mm)
Tyres	4.00 × 18 front and rear

General Specifications

Wheelbase	N/A
Ground clearance	N/A
Seat height	N/A
Fuel tank capacity	3¾gal (17ltr)
Dry weight	N/A
Maximum power	29bhp
Top speed	85mph (137km/h)

capacities, the first time this had occurred in the BSA line-up.

The newcomer, the Y13, was built on similar lines to the existing five-hundred ohv J12 vee, with its 748cc (71 × 94.5mm) engine set at the same 45 degrees. *The Motor Cycle* described the crank unit as being 'remarkably sturdy' and having 'twin bearings on the drive side'. The big-end arrangement was notable, because instead of the bearings being placed side by side, as in the smaller V-twin, a forked connecting rod was employed. There were two rows of ½in (13mm) rollers on the crankpin, shrouded by a hardened-steel sleeve that was pressed into the eyes of the forked rod. On this sleeve was a bronze bush, mounted in the central rod. The forked rod was webbed, and the forks joined round the periphery with a gap only large enough for convenience when building up and to provide room for the small swing of the central rod. This system, and indeed the entire engine, had proved to be entirely satisfactory under prolonged testing. Both exhaust valve springs were exposed and the inlets were fully enclosed. Some 1,500 examples were subsequently produced, many of these being exported abroad to police forces around the world.

Bringing the G Big Twin up to Date

Another feature of the 1935 model year programme was the attempt to bring the Model G big twin up to date. Like the majority of the BSA range that year it had been provided with a backbone frame. There was also a neater exhaust system, whilst the machine now had a separate oil tank located under the seat. The new slotted rings were fitted to the pistons, although the old-fashioned twin pilgrim oil pump system had been retained. Although not widespread, the changes made had given the machine a much smarter and modern appearance, and were the first serious update for many years to this, the largest of the BSA V-twin family.

The prices of the 1935 V-twin range as published in October 1935 were as follows:

- J12 498cc ohv £70
- Y13 748cc ohv £75
- G14 986cc sv £75.

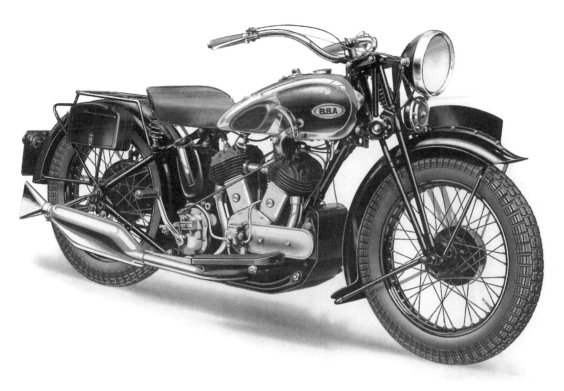

1937 986cc Model G14, a development of the design that had debuted back in 1926.

1936 G14 Specifications

Engine	Air-cooled, side-valve 50-degree V-twin, double roller big-ends, H-section connecting rods, aluminium alloy pistons with slotted scraper oil control rings, detachable cylinder heads, vertically split aluminium crankcases	Frame	Duplex cradle with forged steel backbone and integral sidecar lugs
		Front suspension	Girder forks with adjustable shock absorber
		Rear suspension	Rigid
		Front brake	7in (178mm)
		Rear brake	7in (178mm)
Bore	80mm	Tyres	4.00 × 18 front and rear
Stroke	98mm		
Displacement	986cc	*General Specifications*	
Compression ratio	4.5:1		
Lubrication	Double mechanical pump, dry sump	Wheelbase	63in (1,600mm)
		Ground clearance	N/A
		Seat height	N/A
Ignition	Lucas 6V magdyno	Fuel tank capacity	3¾gal (17ltr)
Carburettor	Amal 76	Dry weight	420lb (190kg)
Primary drive	Chain	Maximum power	25bhp @ 3,800rpm
Final drive	Chain	Top speed	65mph (105km/h)
Gearbox	Four-speed, hand-change		

Model G14 with Watsonian family sidecar, c. 1938.

The Smaller Vees are Axed

The next moves saw the axing first of the J12 five-hundred in mid-1936, with the Y13 seven-fifty following in mid-1938, leaving only the long-serving one-litre G14 still listed. The only real change, and then only applicable to the G14, came in September 1938. This saw a new corporate BSA colour scheme adopted. Out went the familiar green and in its place came a mixture of chromium and silver with red and black lines. The frame components remained black in either case.

During 1939 BSA was, like Norton, fully occupied building motorcycles for military rather than civilian use. The British armed forces, notably the RAF, had small quantities of the E15 (coded J12 in the civilian market) during the mid-1930s, but the main wartime contracts went to the M20 side-valve single. However, BSA did build some G14s for military service in 1939 and the early days of the war itself. As for the civilian G14, the last (1940 model) year was listed at £82. And so the BSA V-twin passed into history. Its place was taken

1937 G14 V-twin with factory-fitted leg shields.

post-war by the A7 and later A10 vertical twins. But the V-twin played an important role in BSA's history, as the company's first multi-cylinder motorcycle series.

3 A7 Mark 1

The BSA overhead-valve parallel twin that entered series production after the Second World War in 1946 as the A7 was the end result of several men's design work over a number of years – and various prototypes built between 1938 and 1945.

First came Val Page (*see* box overleaf), to whom the basic design layout can be contributed, then Joe Craig, who had left Norton to join BSA (he was also at AMC) before returning to the Norton works at Bracebridge Street; even Edward Turner was involved at one stage. Craig had left Norton where he was in charge of the works racing team because Norton did not enter a race team in 1939. Craig rejoined Norton after the conflict, retiring at the end of 1955. But the really detailed work that preceded the production itself was the responsibility of Herbert Perkins, assisted by David Munro.

The A7 Arrives

As for the definitive motorcycle that reached production status in mid–1946, this was, in many ways, an excellent machine, features of which were still to be found when the last of the unit A65s were being built during the early 1970s. Fellow author Steve Wilson went even further in his 1983 *British Motor Cycles Since 1950 Volume 2* (Patrick Stephens Ltd), saying:

> I will probably immediately make enemies but I must declare an interest – for me the A7/A10 parallel twins are the definitive British motorcycles of this period, and possibly of all time.

But, as Steve points out, they were 'not, of course, the original', Edward Turner's trend-setting 500cc Speed Twin of 1938 having already taken that title.

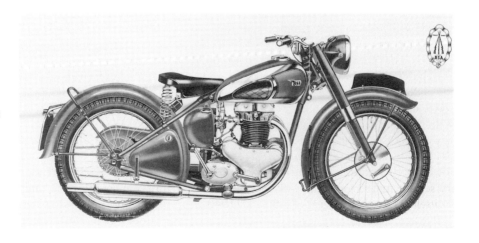

The first series A7 model as it appeared upon its debut in September 1946 with telescopic forks and rigid frame. Most of the design work was by Herbert Perkins.

The A7 engine was of semi-unit construction design and differed considerably from the 'Mark 2' produced from the early 1950s onwards.

The Engine Design

At the heart of the A7 was a vertical twin-cylinder engine, with four pushrods operated by a single camshaft carried in the rear of the crankcase. The latter was made of aluminium and vertically split in the traditional British manner. The engine was arranged with the crankpins in line, that is, the pistons rising and descending together (360 degrees), with one power stroke every revolution of the crankshaft. With bore and stroke dimensions of 62 × 82mm respectively, the displacement was 495cc. Official BSA sources at the launch in September 1946 stated a maximum power of 26bhp at 6,000rpm – which BSA said was 'equivalent to 90mph with a solo top gear of 5.1 to 1'.

The crankshaft assembly was unusual. There were three main parts:

- a 7in (178mm), 2in (50mm)-wide high-tensile steel central flywheel-cum-bobweight;
- two forged-steel members, each comprising a mainshaft, crank cheek and crankpin.

Tapered holes were provided in the central flywheel and there were equivalent, case-hardened tapered portions extending from the crankpins. But the crankshaft was, as *The Motor Cycle* described, 'of no ordinary built-up construction'. It is therefore worthwhile to describe this in some detail.

The tapers were pulled up by the differential action of two different-pitch screw threads cut on the single central securing bolt or, as BSA described, 'the differential thread locking bolt'. The thread in the nearside (left) crank cheek number was twelve per inch, and that in the other twenty per inch. BSA said 'An ordinary box spanner is used for locking purposes, and the whole assembly can be built up by even a novice, since there are $\frac{7}{16}$in diameter alignment holes in all three parts – the central flywheel and the crank cheeks.'

The actual procedure was as follows. After being smeared with heavy grease, the securing bolt was screwed into the offside (right) crank cheek until the bolt stood proud of the cheek by between ½ to $\frac{33}{64}$in (12.7 to 13mm). Next, the entire assembly was fitted together and a $\frac{7}{16}$in (11mm) rod passed through the three holes. Finally, the bolt was screwed into the second crank cheek, the operator ensuring that the thread started immediately. After tightening, it was necessary to check that there was the required 0.015in (0.4mm) clearance laterally at the big-ends and that the overall dimension was 5.492in (140mm) maximum, which resulted in the assembly fitting in the crankcase with 0.005in (0.127mm) clearance after the appropriate shim had been fitted.

About the only areas to watch, said BSA, were cleanliness and the position of the oil hole in the nearside (left) big-end – a bleed that threw oil inwards to lubricate the inner cylinder wall. How satisfactory this arrangement had been was borne out by BSA pulling

Val Page – Design Genius

Born in London during 1892, Val Page began his working life by serving an apprenticeship with a south coast automobile dealer. This was to be the start of a lifetime of involvement with the internal combustion engine.

Aged sixteen, the young Page displayed his future direction by constructing his own motorcycle. The combination of this, together with his working experience in automobile engineering, was enough to see him recruited by the north London-based J.A. Prestwich in the drawing office. At that time JAP was at the very forefront of motorcycle engine development, supplying companies in Britain and all over Europe with proprietary engines for fitment into locally produced frames.

Then followed a period of gradual promotion – on merit – until, in 1920, Val Page was appointed chief development engineer and chief designer for the London firm. It should be remembered that this was at a time when the JAP V-twin engine was very much the dominant power unit at Brooklands and in many of the speed records that were a feature of the immediate post-war era.

Page was recruited by Jack Sangster, owner of the Ariel marque, during the mid-1920s. With Vic Mole he was responsible for revitalizing Ariel's flagging fortunes. Ariel was based in Selly Oak, Birmingham. Page's next appointment was at the Coventry-based Triumph concern (which was at the time also owned by Sangster). Here he was responsible for the Triumph 6/1, a 650cc ohv parallel twin that debuted in 1933 and preceded the Edward Turner Speed Twin from the same company by several years.

In 1936 Page was on the move again, this time to BSA. Here he created the B, M and C ranges of singles – which were to form the mainstay of the Birmingham marque's motorcycle production for many years.

Although Val Page left Small Heath in early 1939 never to return – going back to Ariel – his importance in the BSA story cannot be underestimated. And in any case, when Jack Sangster sold out to the BSA group during the Second World War, the BSA family connection was maintained.

But, most importantly, from the BSA pre-unit twins' history, it had been Page who had worked on the original design, which was to emerge as the A7 twin, during his last months in the BSA design office in 1938. And in the immediate post-Second World War era Page was responsible for the Ariel 500 twin, which bore more than a passing resemblance to the A7.

Sadly, Page's post-war period with Ariel was badly affected by BSA management interference, which meant he was at many times deeply frustrated. In fact, only a few of his ideas actually received the green light and reached production status. One was the Ariel Leader. This futuristic machine was awarded the prestigious *Motor Cycle News* 'Machine of the Year' for two years running in the late 1950s. The Leader, a twin-cylinder 250cc two-stroke, was subsequently 'undressed' to become the Arrow.

But Val Page's greatest post-war design was a 700cc ohv inline four, with shaft final drive. Its cylinder block was laid horizontally, as in the BMW K100 of the 1980s. But BSA group politics, notably the overbearing presence in later years of the dreaded cost accountants, finally killed off this potentially great project. With that, Val Page had had enough; he cleared his desk and drawing board and quit the motorcycle design world altogether. He died in 1978, aged eighty-five.

down a crankshaft and reassembling it again no fewer than sixty times.

The crankshaft assembly was located by the nearside main bearing, a deep-groove ball race. On the offside there was a steel white-metal-lined main bearing. The big-end bearings, which thanks to the built-up crank construction were not split, were steel-backed lead-bronze – 1½in (38mm) diameter and 13⁄16in (20.6mm) wide. A rib ran around the big-end eye of the one-piece steel connecting rods.

Silicone alloy was used for the three-ring solid skirt pistons. There were two compression rings and a single oil scraper for each piston. As was usual practice with BSA, the taper-bore 11⁄16in (17.5mm) diameter gudgeon pins were fully floating and retained by circlips. The flat-top pistons, which were cut away for valve clearance, gave a compression ratio of 7:1 – this, of course, was the period when only low octane 'pool' petrol was available to British users.

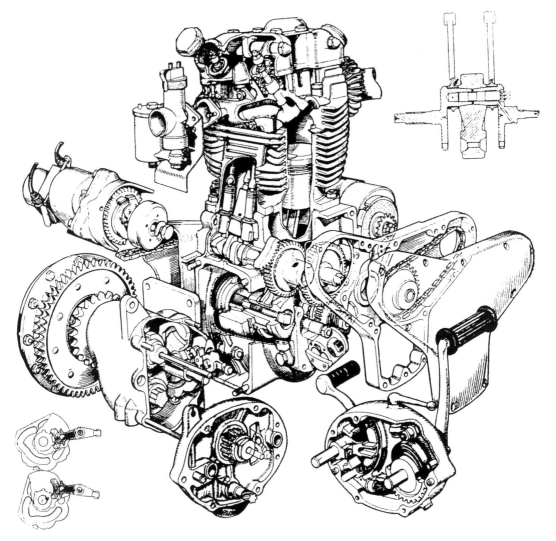

The original 495cc (62 × 82mm) semi-unit A7 engine and gearbox: single carb, chain-driven dynamo, magneto ignition and bolt-up gearbox.

A Monobloc Cylinder Head

BSA described the cylinder head as being 'monobloc'. It had been designed to provide 'an excellent air passage between the inlet and exhaust sides; there is also a good flow between the cylinders'. Air flowed rearwards to both the sides and centre of the two barrels and out again rearwards; centrally, this rearward air flow passed either side of the equally centrally located pushrod tunnel – this being possible

not only by clever layout, but also the fact that the engine's single camshaft was mounted at the rear of the crankcase.

The combustion head was what is best described as slightly less than a hemisphere – in other words, as described by *The Motor Cycle*, a hemisphere 'with a slice removed from the bottom'.

The inlet valves were inclined at 43 degrees and the exhausts at 38. The latter were of austenitic steel and 3 per cent nickel for the inlet valves. The location of the valves permitted straight-line operation of the rockers and space between the inlet and exhaust rocker boxes. Nickel-chrome iron was employed for the valve guides. Washers were provided beneath the dual (inner and outer) coil valve springs.

The rocker boxes, one for the two exhaust and one for the two inlet valves, were held down by five bolts each. Each valve had its own large circular aluminium rocker box inspection caps (one per valve), which showed Edward Turner's influence on the design.

The cylinder head (a one-piece casting) featured seven bolts and two studs to provide the fixing; the gasket for the hand/barrel joint was a single copper/asbestos one. The bolt for the middle of the head, which was slackened first and tightened last, was set at an angle for ease of access. No cylinder head bolt passed through the rocker boxes, so the tightening of the cylinder head was straightforward. An example of the ease with which this could be achieved was the employment of the two aforementioned studs. These were at the rear and had the surrounding cooling fins cut away for ready access to the nuts.

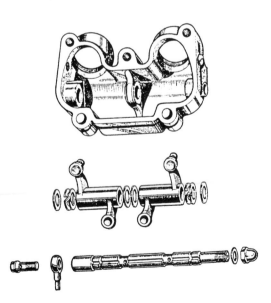

The rocker box, rockers, rocker shaft and associated components.

Inner and Outer Timing Covers

Both inner and outer timing gear covers were fitted. This was done to avoid flooding of the chain drive to the separate dynamo – no oil exuded when the dynamo was removed. Above the timing pinion on the mainshaft was the half-time pinion, which was supported on each side and carried on the outside of the sprocket for the dynamo drive. A reverse thread was provided at the end of the outer bush to retain oil in the inner timing chest – the half-time pinion dipping in the oil. From this pinion the drive went to the camshaft, which ran on the trio of phosphor-bronze bushes, and thence to the magneto (either Lucas or BTH). In either case the magneto was equipped with automatic advance.

The camshaft was located by its offside (right) bearing. At the end of the camshaft was a mechanical breather, the end of which was shrouded so as to prevent oil escaping.

Chain adjustment for the dynamo, which had a domed casing over the commutator end, involved slackening a single nut.

Tappets and Tappet Guides

The case-hardened tappets had a deposit of hard chromium on their feet, and the outer tappet guides, which were not of split construction like the middle pair, were provided with an external screw thread for ease of extraction. There was a single locking strip for all four tappet guides. The tappets were drilled so that oil passing down the pushrod housing lubricated the cams; in addition the direction of rotation of the engine resulted in oil mist being driven upwards.

Lubrication

A submerged twin gear-type pump was fitted. This was driven by skew gears from the end of the crankshaft. A ball-valve with what BSA described as 'a knife-edge seating' prevented lubricant siphoning into the engine. From the pump, oil travelled via a release valve working at 50lb/sq in when the lubricant was hot. This too, had the 'knife-edge type' of seating to prevent problems such as grit and was accessible from the front side of the timing chest. Oil was fed by the timing-side main bearing to the big-end bearings and passed on, in the form of oil mist, to lubricate the remainder of the engine. There were no external oil pipes other than the delivery and return pipes linking the oil tank to the timing chest.

The oil pump had a delivery rate of 3.5gal (16ltr) an hour and on the scavenge side a capacity of some 5gal (23ltr) an hour.

A Bolted-Up Gearbox

What is best described as a bolted-up form of unit construction is the term best used to describe the engine and gearbox. There was a new four-speed foot-change 'box. This featured a flat, machined face on its forward side that was bolted directly to a matching machined face on the rear of the crankcase. As *The Motor Cycle* described, 'Thus there is, in effect, one rigid unit with a fixed centre distance between the engine shaft and the gearbox mainshaft.' The primary chain was an endless ⅜in (9.5mm) duplex, which could be adjusted by a special case-hardened slipper fitted in the primary chaincase immediately below the bottom run of the chain. The contact surface of this slipper was hard chromium, a deposit which BSA claimed offered both a low frictional resistance and good durability. Adjustment was effected by a single screw locked by a Simmonds nut. A spring-loaded damper for the slipper was mounted on the inner half of the chaincase. On the engine shaft there was a newly conceived two-cam, spring-loaded cush drive. Motorcycles were dispatched from the Small Heath works with a special mixture of grease and oil in the chaincase, and all the owner had to do was to replace this occasionally with ordinary engine oil.

Ratios of 5.1, 6.2, 9 and 13.2 to 1 were provided for solo work, and 5.4, 6.6, 9.5 and 14 to 1 where a sidecar was fitted.

At the time of the A7's launch, BSA claimed that the new gearbox was both lighter and more compact and also provided a lighter and

sweeter gear change. *The Motor Cycle*, in describing the newcomer in its 19 September 1946 issue, said 'A delightfully simple form of change-speed mechanism has been devised.' The gearbox had been positioned with the layshaft submerged and was lubricated by oil, not grease. At the gearbox mainshaft there was an oil seal. Additionally, there was a shroud over the five-plate Ferodo-lined clutch, with an oil flinger incorporated on the back; the actual clutch mechanism was within the gearbox. Access to this was gained through an endplate, which doubled up as the gearbox oil filler. A drain plug was provided at the rear of the gearbox housing, where there was also a level-plug.

The Cycle Parts

The power unit was housed in a duplex downtube (the front tubes were 1in (25mm) in

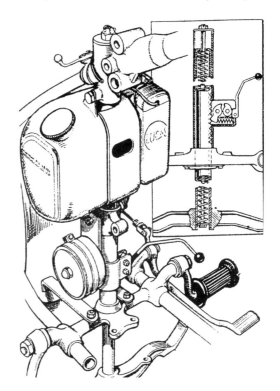

The rigid-framed A7 seat stay, air filter, battery, horn and choke lever, plus ingenious stand operation – this latter feature was soon discontinued.

Telescopic Forks

In the British motorcycle industry Matchless was the first manufacturer to fit telescopic front forks to a series production motorcycle, with the wartime G3/L three-fifty military model. But with the war almost at an end during the spring of 1945, peacetime loomed. BSA realized that besides its new civilian post-war models – headed by the new five-hundred twin that would be launched in around eighteen months' time – the other need was to present a more modern appearance, especially in the light of AMC's successful Teledraulic sprung telescopic forks (modelled on ones that the German BMW concern had introduced in the late 1930s). As *The Motor Cycle* said in February 1946, 'simplicity and strength' were the keynotes of BSA's hydraulically damped telescopic spring fork.

The fork legs comprised a pair of fixed tubes, over the lower sections of which were two sliding tubes. Welded to the base of the sliding tubes were legs that carried the front-wheel spindle. The fixed tubes were bridged by 'two cross members, triangular in shape, with their apexes connected to the top and bottom of the steering column', as described by *The Motor Cycle*, but which in more modern terms would simply be referred to as top and bottom yokes.

Of high tensile steel, the main (fixed) member of each fork leg was constant throughout the tube's inner length. The outer tube section featured a gradual taper above and below the position of the lower cross member, with the greatest wall thickness occurring where the cross member was clamped to the tube by means of a clip lug. At its top end, the tube had a more pronounced taper where it located into a taper hole of the upper cross-member, which was locked by a large cap nut. Below the lower cross-member the gradual taper extended for a certain distance only; below that the fixed tube was ground parallel on its outside diameter over the full distance of travel between the extremes of fork deflection. Each of the sliding tubes was also of high-tensile steel, with a ground bore.

Lightly pressed over the lower end of the fixed tube was a white-metal-coated steel bush with oil-retaining grooves round its outer periphery. This bush was clamped in position by a special gland nut that screwed into the bottom end of the tube.

In similar fashion, a white-metal-lined steel bush was pressed into the top end of the sliding member and retained by a spring ring. This bush had oil grooves round its bore, as it operated on the outside diameter of the fixed tube.

At the upper end of the sliding member a short sleeve was brazed in position, accommodating an oil-seal gland that operated on the fixed tube. Screwed to this sleeve was another short sleeve which located, and provided abutment for, the lower end of a compression spring. The upper abutment for the spring was provided by the clip lug of the lower cross-member (bottom yoke).

Attached to the lower abutment sleeve was a light metal shroud that enclosed the lower portion of the spring. Another shroud enclosed the entire upper portion of the fork leg and overlapped the lower shroud by some 4in (100mm) with the fork in its static position (this upper shroud also doubled up as a headlamp bracket). Thus the spring and fixed tube (stanchion) were shielded from the elements throughout the entire range of fork deflection of nearly 6in (150mm).

Before the hydraulic damping action is described here, other items should be noted. These are: the graduated taper plug attached to the top of the wheel spindle lug; the hole up through the centre of the gland nut that secured the lower bearing; and an oil transfer hole provided through one side of the fixed tube (stanchion) near its lower section.

Oil was carried in the base of the fork leg. With the fork in its static position, the oil level was approximately between the bottom chamber of the sliding member. The inside of the fixed tube was through a comparatively large hole in the gland nut; from there oil flowed by way of the transfer hole to the annular space between the fixed tube (stanchion) and the bore of the sliding member. When the fork was deflected upwards, the volume of the bottom chamber decreased, forcing oil through the gland nut orifice to the interior of the fixed tube.

At the same time, the annular space between fixed and sliding members increased; thus oil was forced through the transfer hole into the annular space by air pressure. Increased upward movement caused the top of the taper plug to enter the gland nut hole, thereby restricting the orifice and increasing the degree of damping. With further upward movement of the plug, the damping was rapidly progressive until, at extreme upward deflection, there was a virtual cut-off of the air flow, with consequent hydraulic buffer effect.

On the rebound, the damping was progressively reduced until the plug had moved out of the hole, when the damping again became constant. At extreme downward deflection the top bearing covered the transfer hole; in such circumstances, the oil remaining in the annual space between the transfer hole formed a hydraulic buffer between the upper and lower bearings.

The first models to be fitted with the new fork assembly were the B31 and B32 Competition models, whilst right from day one all the new twin-cylinder models were so equipped.

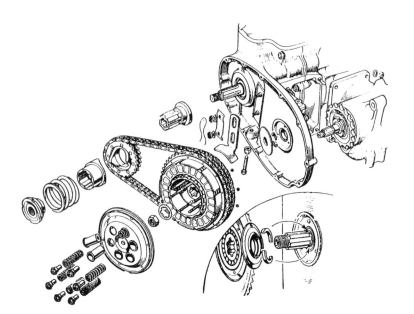

The primary side of the A7 Mark 1 with bolted-up gearbox. Details include crank-mounted shock absorber, duplex primary chain, multi-plate clutch and chain tensioner.

diameter) cradle frame of brazed construction, with a rigid rear end. It should be noted that this frame was not simply a case of utilizing the existing B31 single-cylinder component, as the latter at that time only had a single front downtube and was not of the full cradle type at that stage. However, the new twin did share the recently introduced BSA-made telescopic front forks with the singles. Both brakes were 7in (178mm) single leading shoe, single-sided devices with 1⅛in (28.5mm) wide drum operating area.

An unusual feature was the vertical seat tube – this was vertical so that it could also act as the outer member of what *The Motor Cycle* described as 'the ingenious telescopic stand'. This was operated by pressing down the foot of this spring-controlled central stand and automatically, without any effort – the motorcycle was supported on the bottom T-shaped member – the operator just kept the foot there and raised the rear of the machine, with the result that the back wheel was then held off the ground. For the stand to spring upwards it was only necessary to operate a small hand control, which released the ratchet lock.

The Quietest, If Not the Fastest

The 1946 A7 might not have been the fastest British vertical twin of its era, but it was most certainly the quietest mechanically. Why? Well, for a start it had only a single camshaft (instead of Triumph's two) and timing gears instead of chains (Ariel and Royal Enfield for example). Inner and outer timing covers also helped to keep down internal noises, with the minimum of whine or clatter.

Durability and oil-tightness were other virtues of particular note. It is also worth pointing out that the early (Mark 1) A7 engine type, which was used until the end of 1950, differed in considerable detail from the 'Mark 2' that replaced it, the latter sharing much with the then newly introduced A10 Golden Flash. Notable differences included bore and stroke dimensions, engine displacement, rocker box and cylinder head design and many, many smaller features.

The semi-unit design of gearbox – bolted to the rear of the crankcase, and one that was to remain in the Mark 2 A7 and the A10 series – was an unusual feature in 1946, when the vast majority of manufacturers built the gearbox as a separate unit to be mounted at the rear of the engine in plates, thus allowing it to be moved for primary chain adjustment.

Even though it had 19in wheels, the 1946 A7 was blessed with the low seat height of 29.5in (749mm) and a dry weight of 365lb (166kg), which made for reasonable ease both under motion and when stationary. Both wheels were quickly detachable and inter-changeable. *The Motor Cycle* described how easy they were to detach: 'It is only necessary to insert a tommy bar in the hole at the end of the rear spindle, unscrew and pull out the spin-dle, remove the distance piece and the wheel comes out. A special form of tooth has been developed for engagement purposes; this is a cross between a spline and a gear tooth.'

Other details of interest were as follows:

- double-butted wheel spokes, running in a dead straight line from hub to rim;
- deep-groove journal bearings on both wheels;
- hinged rear mudguard;
- front wheel stand (bottom mudguard stay);
- carrier/pillion seat available to special order;
- fully adjustable rider's footrests;
- air-control (choke) lever mounted below the rider's seat;
- 8in (203mm) headlamp; 6V system;
- voltage control unit carried on rear mud-guard, front section, under the rider's seat;
- handlebars adjustable for angle;
- Smith's speedometer (cost option);
- 3gal (13.6ltr) fuel tank;
- Speedo drive from gearbox;
- ½gal (2.3ltr) oil tank, with built-in filter;
- single Amal 276 carburettor ¹⁵⁄₁₆in (24mm).

The 1947 model year A7 was finished in Devon Red and chromium or in black and chrome, with black lined with gold.

The official September 1946 launch price structure was as follows: £135 plus £36 9s purchase tax in Britain; the speedometer was £4 (purchase tax £1 1s 7d). First deliveries to customers came at the end of November 1946.

1946 A7 Specifications	
Engine	Air-cooled, ohv vertical twin, 360-degree crank, single camshaft at rear of crankcase, cast-iron cylinder head and barrel, screw-in rocker box caps, vertically split aluminium crankcases, coil valve springs
Bore	62mm
Stroke	82mm
Displacement	495cc
Compression ratio	6.6:1
Lubrication	Dry sump, with oil pump featuring worm drive; a pressure relief valve screwed into the crankcase
Ignition	Magneto
Carburettor	Amal 276 ¹⁵⁄₁₆in (24mm)
Primary drive	Duplex chain
Final drive	Chain
Gearbox	Bolt-up, four-speed, foot-change
Frame	All-steel construction, double front downtube
Front suspension	BSA telescopic, oil-damped forks
Rear suspension	Rigid
Front brake	7in drum (178mm), SLS
Rear brake	7in drum (178mm), SLS
Tyres	Front 3.25 × 19; rear 3.50 × 19

General Specifications

Wheelbase	54.5in (1,384mm)
Ground clearance	6.5in (165mm)
Seat height	29.5in (749mm)
Fuel tank capacity	3gal (13.6ltr)
Dry weight	365lb (166kg)
Maximum power	26bhp @ 6,000rpm
Top speed	85mph (137km/h)

First Change – A New Crankshaft

Almost as soon as production had got under way, the A7 crankshaft design was superseded by a revised assembly. The original type, as already described, was built-up, held together by a differential thread locking bolt.

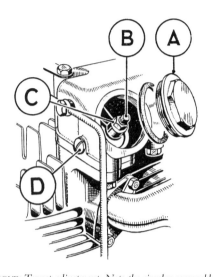

To facilitate manufacture and servicing, a redesigned crankshaft was introduced at the very end of 1946 and was reported in the 2 January 1947 issue of *The Motor Cycle*. The new one was interchangeable with the original; in other words, the new one-piece crank and connecting rods could be replaced, without modification, in lieu of the old type.

The new unit comprised the two main-shafts, two webs and, between them, the big-end journals and the flywheel flange. This was now in one piece and machined from what

ABOVE: *Tappet adjustment. Note the circular, removable inspection cap; not a feature on the later Mark 2 version.*

BELOW: *The top half of the 1947 model year A7, showing air flow around the pushrods.*

The lubrication system, with details including the pump and pressure relief valve.

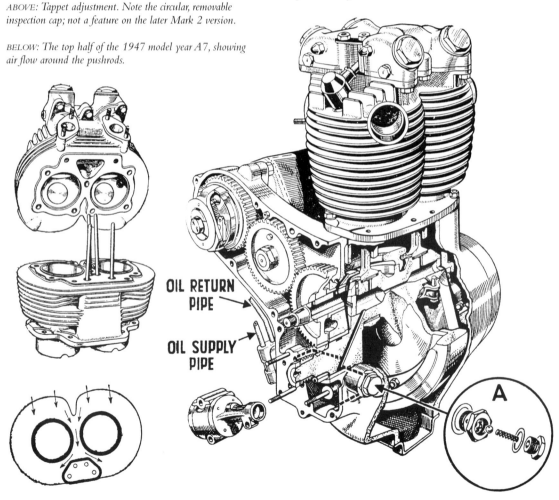

OIL RETURN PIPE

OIL SUPPLY PIPE

was described by BSA sources as 'a high-grade steel forging'. Six bolts held the forged steel flywheel to the crankshaft flange; there was a cutaway in the inner edge of the flywheel to clear the crank web during assembly.

Incorporated in the flywheel and in the crank webs were bobweights for balancing. In this way, the balancing forces were evenly distributed throughout the crankshaft.

In place of the original one-piece connecting rods were rods (still in steel) with conventional split big-ends (and thus two-piece rods), the bolts of which were in high tensile nickel-chrome steel. The bearing linings of the big-ends were steel-backed, indium-flashed lead-bronze.

Testing the A7

With virtually all production going overseas, the first the British public got to know about what the A7 was actually like to ride came via a road test published in *The Motor Cycle*, dated 3 April 1947. The test began by saying:

> Absolutely new post-war models are as yet rare. Of those recently announced, the BSA model A7 proves on test to vindicate the promise of its design features. The 495cc engine is a good example of the vertical twin type. The straightforward duplex cradle frame, in conjunction with the hydraulically damped telescopic forks, endows the machine with first-class steering and road-holding qualities, and the compactness of the whole machine means more than a trim, business-like appearance; it means a five-hundred which has the feel of a three-fifty – until the grip is twisted.

The tester went on:

> The last is perhaps the greatest charm of the new BSA. In appearance and in feel on first acquaintance, it gives the impression of smallness. When manoeuvred in the garage or when ridden at walking-pace speeds there is the inescapable sensation of handling a small, light machine with sedate performance. But when the vivacious engine is given

its head the machine becomes a full-blooded five-hundred in the best sense of the term.

In fact, from personal experience, the author can verify this feeling of compactness, having ridden a 1947 A7 and having owned a 1959 example. The 1947 bike weighed in at 365lb (166kg), whereas the later A7 tipped the scales at a portly 425lb (193kg). And the more compact nature of the earlier model is shown by its wheelbase of 54½in (1,384mm), compared to 56in (1,422mm) of the later bike.

Easy Starting

The tester found that 'Starting the engine is very easy indeed.' He even went as far as saying 'Such is the kickstarter leverage and gearing that it might be thought the engine has poor compression – so light is the weight necessary to depress the pedal.'

Particular mention was made of the low level of mechanical and exhaust noise: 'Mechanically, the engine was quiet; at idling speeds the valve gear was audible, but there was a noticeable absence of intake hiss thanks to the Vokes air filter concealed between the oil tank and the battery. Exhaust noise was subdued enough for the nippy performance of the machine to be used in towns without embarrassment.'

The riding position was found to be of the 'sit up and beg' style. With the handlebars 'well upswept and wider than average – 29in from tip to tip'.

On-Road Performance

The tester felt that the on-road performance of the 1947 test A7 'approaches ideal'. He went on to say:

> At low speeds it is as smooth and tractable as only good even-firing twins can be. The engine-shaft shock absorber is up to its job, and the clutch is light to operate and sure in action. The clutch frees perfectly, and bottom gear can be engaged from neutral without noise. Gear-changing with the new positive-stop mechanism is absolutely positive, but a slowish movement of the pedal is

required to obtain clean engagement. The gear ratios suit the characteristics of the engine admirably and a really sparkling performance can be obtained from the A7 in the intermediate ratios.

The test continued:

> On the open road at highish speeds the smoothness of the engine is unimpaired. There is no vibration period – not even when the engine is revved to the point of valve float. Another attractive characteristic is that the engine is so 'happy' in all circumstances that there is no cruising speed which might be termed the best. If one aimed to keep the speedometer needle at 50, 60, 70 or even 80mph as often as possible, the engine responded without flagging and without fuss.

Besides the bike 'holding its line without pitch or tail wag', *The Motor Cycle* tester had special praise for the telescopic forks, saying they: 'have a soft, long action, but were never bottomed throughout the test; they seem admirably suited to the frame, and steering is first class.' And: 'really good averages can be maintained without effort and zestful mile-gobbling and acceleration achieved in undulating country by making good use of the close third gear.'

Common-Sense Features

As the tester pointed out: 'There are so many common-sense riders' points on the A7 that only a long list would include them all. But mention must be made of the really good lock, which would be envied on a specially prepared trials machine,' and 'of the filter-cum-drain plug in the base of the oil tank, with plenty of air around it so that a spanner can easily be used on the hexagon and a funnel placed underneath; of the really quickly detachable wheels.' Plus, 'the well tucked-in exhaust system'.

The test concluded by saying 'The BSA model A7 is an outstandingly attractive machine. It is assured of a brilliant future among discriminating riders – those who can evaluate genuine, worthwhile features.' The maximum speeds obtained were as follows:

- first: 38mph (61km/h)
- second: 59mph (95km/h)
- third: 75mph (120km/h)
- top (fourth): 82mph (132km/h).

Minimum non-snatch speed in top gear was 12mph (19km/h). All of the performance figures were obtained in high winds and rain, with the rider 'in bulky, all-weather garb'.

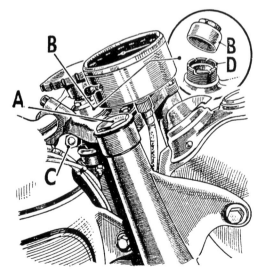

The front fork and steering head details of a 1948-on A7.

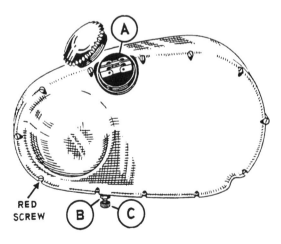

The short primary chaincase as fitted to A7 Mark 1 machines. This was continued into the Mark 2 versions, prior to the introduction of the swinging frame.

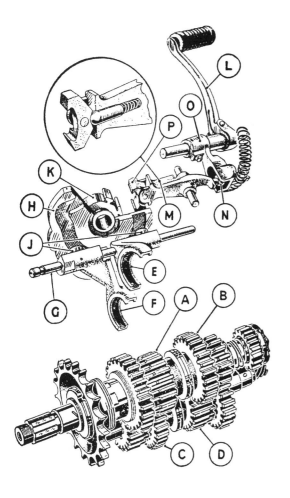

Changes for the 1948 Season

When the 1948 BSA programme was announced in December 1947 there were what BSA sources described 'a certain amount of rider's improvements'. On the A7 these amounted to the following:

- the speedometer transferred from its original tank top mounting to a new position on the top of the front forks;
- the steering damper modification: now fitted with Ferodo friction damper discs – to cure a previous tendency to swell in the wet and warp in the heat;
- new domed headlamp glass;
- new flatter handlebars (common to the whole range);
- the air-control (choke) lever transferred from under the seat to a more accessible position on the right handlebar;
- the telescopic seat-tube stand discontinued in favour of a conventional, central, spring-up type;
- oil fed direct to the valve gear (previously had relied on oil mist). This, BSA claimed, increased mechanical quietness still further;
- a drain plug fitted for oil tanks and at ends of the telescopic forks.

ABOVE: The four-speed foot-change gearbox internals and selector mechanism.

RIGHT: A 1948 A7. Changes that year were speedo relocation, steering damper modification, domed headlamp glass, flatter handlebars, conventional centre stand, direct oil feed to valve gear, and drain plug for oil tank and ends of telescopic forks.

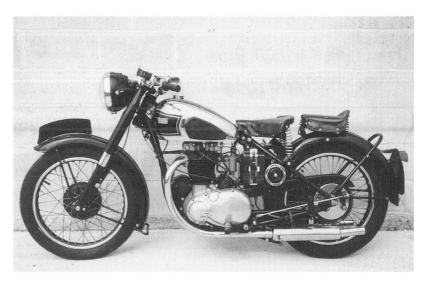

47

The price had increased to £177 16s including British taxes (£140 basic, that is, export).

Side-Valve Military Prototype

In 1948 a prototype military twin also made its public appearance for the first time, after several months of development. Essentially it was a side-valve, but based on the existing A7. As with the TRW Triumph and a 602cc flat-twin Douglas, all three were entered by the Ministry of Supply in the Scottish Six Days Trial in May 1948. Details of the BSA included valves in front of the engine, and a dust-and water-proofed single Solex carburettor (incorporating a bi-starter device). A three-speed foot-operated gearbox

September 1948 advertisement proclaiming the virtues of the BSA vertical twin: 'Single Camshaft Engine; Cooler Running; Simplified Timing Gear; Cleanliness; Easier Maintenance.'

1948 A7 in original 'ex factory' finish, with rigid frame. The speedometer had now been transferred from the tank top to a new position on top of the front forks.

was employed. The frame was of the straightforward duplex cradle type, but an unusual feature was that the rear spindle was fixed instead of adjustable. The final drive chain (like the other two machines) was fully enclosed, but whereas on the Douglas and Triumph the chain adjustment was carried out in the conventional manner, on the BSA it was by an eccentric jockey sprocket. The rear chaincase was of aluminium, not steel.

In the Scottish, the three military prototypes were ridden by Captain H.R. Little (Douglas), Staff Sergeant J. Hird (Triumph) and Sergeant T.A. Tracey (BSA). However, as the 13 May 1948 issue of *The Motor Cycle* reported: 'these were never at ease and they all lost many marks'. The Douglas retired on the third day. The BSA in fact came out best, with Tracey winning a Second Class Award (with 253 points lost), compared to the Triumph ridden by Hird who gained a Third Class Award (with 286 points against him).

But this didn't stop Triumph ultimately winning the military contract, which saw batches of the TRW built for service, mainly with the Royal Air Force, examples remaining in service until well into the 1970s.

The 1949 Programme

When the 1949 programme was announced in early November 1948 there were several important items of news concerning the five-hundred twin-cylinder design. These included not only a brand new model, the Star Twin, with twin carburettors and a new plunger frame as standard, but also a number of important changes to the standard A7.

Duralumin pushrods, with specially shaped steel ends, were now fitted with an oil supply to the two overhead rocker spindles. As a result, BSA claimed, the engines on the twins were quieter mechanically. There was also a new, longer Lucas dynamo with increased output.

At the base of each telescopic, oil-damped fork leg were now two separate lugs (instead of one) for securing the front mudguard stays. In the interests of standardization, a single type of front fork and wheel was now used on all A, B and M group models.

Positions of the float chamber and fuel pipe had been modified so that, if the carburettor should flood, no petrol could drip onto the dynamo or magneto.

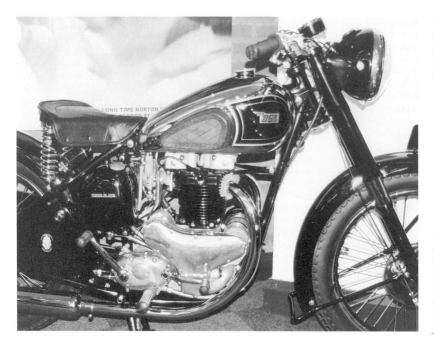

The 1949 model (launched autumn 1948). It could be supplied with either a rigid or plunger frame, the latter at additional cost.

BELOW: *The Star Twin was a more highly tuned 'sports' version of the standard A7. Besides its higher performance it featured plunger rear suspension as standard, and (shown) the powerful 8in front brake.*

The Star Twin

Essentially the same as the A7, the new Star Twin featured a specially tuned engine with high compression (7:1) pistons, twin (Amal 275) ⅞in (22mm) carburettors and a racing-type magneto.

The Star Twin was fitted with the new plunger-type rear suspension, which embodied rebound as well as compression springs. Deflection was given as 1½in (38mm) and rebound ¾in (19mm), a total movement of 2¼in (57mm). The only other BSA model to feature the plunger suspension as standard was the 348cc B32 Special ohv single.

However, it was possible for the spring frame to be specified for the A7 at an additional £10 (£12 14s including British taxes). The standard A7 remained unchanged in price at £177 16s (including taxes), whilst the new Star Twin cost £180 basic and £203 4s including taxes. A maroon finish could be had instead of the standard black enamel on the A7, whereas the Star Twin (in common with the Gold Star models) had a fuel tank enamelled with silver sheen panels, centred on which was

a special BSA transfer. It is also worth noting that the rear springing was the first in BSA's history.

50

1949 Star Twin	
Engine	Air-cooled, ohv vertical twin, 360-degree crank, single camshaft at rear of crankcase; cast-iron cylinder head and barrel, screw-in rocker box caps; vertically split aluminium crankcases; coil valve springs
Bore	62mm
Stroke	82mm
Displacement	495cc
Compression ratio	7.5:1*
Lubrication	Dry sump, with oil pump featuring worm drive; a pressure relief valve screwed into the crankcase
Ignition	Magneto
Carburettor	2 × Amal 275⅞in
Primary drive	Duplex chain
Final drive	Chain
Gearbox	Bolt-up, four-speed, foot-change
Frame	All-steel construction, double front downtube
Front suspension	BSA telescopic, oil-damped forks
Rear suspension	Plunger
Front brake	7in (178mm) drum, SLS
Rear brake	7in (178mm) drum, SLS
Tyres	Front 3.25 × 19; rear 3.50 × 19

General Specifications

Wheelbase	55in (1,397mm)
Ground clearance	5in (127mm)
Seat height	31in (787mm)
Fuel tank capacity	3½gal (16ltr)
Dry weight	382lb (173kg)
Maximum power	31bhp @ 6,000rpm
Top speed	91mph (146km/h)

* Some machines for export 8.6:1.

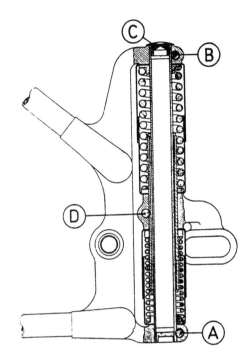

The plunger rear suspension was a standard feature of the higher performance twin carb Star Twin, which debuted at the 1948 Earls Court Show.

The Earls Court Show

As usual, the BSA stand (number 32) was in a centrally placed position at the annual Earls Court Show held in mid-November 1948. And show goers were able to view a sectioned working model of the new Star Twin. In describing the BSA stand in its Show Report issue dated 25 November, *The Motor Cycle* said:

> what must be one of the most comprehensive ranges ever staged by one maker. First, there was the new 125cc two-stroke, the unit-construction Bantam, then a group of side-valve and ohv 250cc models. Next was the B group, the largest in the range, comprising 350cc and 500cc sports and competition models; and following them the M group (500cc and 600cc side-valve and 500cc ohv types suitable for sidecar work and with integral sidecar lugs in their frames).

And finally of course, the A7 and new Star Twin. It was also reported: 'Among overseas buyers the two extreme models, the two-stroke Bantam and the vertical twin A7, appeared to be the most attractive types.'

The Star Twin Tested

As *The Motor Cycle* had done just under a year previously with the standard A7, the magazine tested the new Star Twin in early spring 1949, the test results being published in the 10 March issue. Obviously, in many ways the two tests were similar, with engine quietness, ease of starting, riding position (still of the 'sit up and beg' variety), excellent steering lock, power delivery and oil tightness all coming in for praise. Of the new rear suspension, the tester commented, 'it can be that it was unobtrusive – apparent only by the marked absence of wheel hop. One of the most telling tests for suspension systems lies in riding the machine over the regularly placed, tram-track inspection covers, set in cobbles. Even in these circumstances the suspension earned full marks.'

And in fact the frame and suspension was singled out for praise right at the beginning of the test: 'The combination of sturdy, full duplex cradle frame, oil-damped telescopic forks and road-holding were second to none. Indeed, the general handling properties of the BSA, and the compactness of the model, are among its especially appealing features. It is a five-hundred that can be swept round corners and bends with the facility of a racing mount.'

Although a customer complaint concerning the Star Twin in everyday service was centred upon problems met in keeping carburation settings, this was not experienced in the 500 mile (800km) test. *The Motor Cycle* said: 'At low traffic speeds the engine is as quiet and tractable as that of almost any twin of today. The two carburettors, in delivery tune, were perfectly synchronized to give a clean, rapid pick-up from idling speeds at full throttle.' But the tester did go as far as commenting, 'A tick-over that was slow, smooth, and 100 per cent reliable was, however, never achieved.'

Interestingly, performance, if compared to the earlier A7 test, was largely unchanged, with figures:

- first: 37mph   (60km/h)
- second: 57mph   (92km/h)
- third: 75mph   (120km/h)
- top (fourth):   84mph   (135km/h).

Minimum non-snatch speed in top gear 19mph (31km/h).

The A7 Series Engine Examined

In August 1949 *The Motor Cycle* examined the A7 engine in its 'Modern Engines' series. Harry Louis, then the Assistant Editor, had visited the Birmingham factory, where he met with Bert Hopwood (Chief Designer), Herbert Perkins (Assistant Chief Designer) and David Munro (Technical Department). Right from the outset Hopwood had told Louis that the A7 engine

1949 Star Twin. It could approach 100mph and was a rival to Triumph's popular Tiger 100.

was 'Mr Perkins' baby'. Besides discussing features of the design, together with reasons why this and that had been done, the reader was provided with some of the reasons that had influenced important priorities. These included that the vertical twin had been chosen because it offered a multi-cylinder engine which 'is neat and compact and will fit comfortably in a conventional frame; it can be cooled adequately and gives good accessibility for maintenance'.

Asked about the semi-unit construction achieved by bolting the gearbox to the rear of the crankcase, Herbert Perkins replied: 'That arrangement gives a compact unit' and 'makes for the utmost rigidity. Hence there are lower mechanical losses in the primary drive.' Bert Hopwood went further: 'There is also the attraction of weight saving by the elimination of engine plates between crankcase and gearbox and by the reduction in the frame member lugs. Louis also added that: 'Maintenance was easier because a primary chain adjustment could be made very quickly by resetting a slipper, which did not mean the rear chain had afterwards to be readjusted as with a separate gearbox design.'

Another area discussed in detail was that of oil tightness. Herbert Perkins had this to say:

> We wanted a really effective breather and we were prepared to go to some trouble to get it. Not only was the A7 to be a smooth, quiet engine, but also it was to be clean, which means oil tightness. How far we succeeded with this breather can be gauged from the fact that even at maximum crankshaft revolutions, there is still a depression in the crankcase – something of an achievement.

Then there was the matter of the separate chain dynamo drive. This drive was enclosed by the outer timing chest cover and was remote from the timing chest proper with its camshaft and magneto drive pinions. Herbert Perkins answered:

> With a high performance engine such as the A7, the precisely accurate timing given by gear drive is desirable for camshaft and magneto. The same

accuracy is not necessary for driving the dynamo. To have employed gear drive for the dynamo would have increased the chance of operating noise in a design in which considerable pains to secure silence had been expended. Another point is that the chain is lubricated by grease, and thus the possibility of oil from a timing chest reaching the dynamo is eliminated.

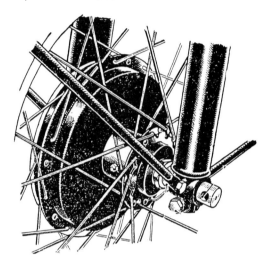

Single-sided drum brake from the original A7 model.

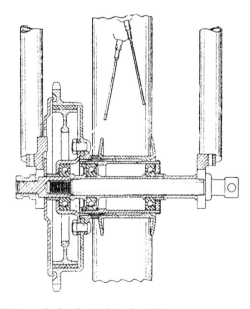

QD rear wheel with straight spokes. This was generally agreed to have been an excellent design.

A Larger Engine

The big news when the 1950 BSA model range was announced in early October 1949 was a new 650cc model, the A10 Golden Flash (*see* Chapter 6). Though the new twin bore a strong resemblance to the by now firmly established A7, the engine had numerous wide departures from current A7 practice. For the present time the existing A7 and Star Twin remained unchanged. However, it was perhaps to be expected that the BSA engineering team would wish to streamline production and so by October 1950, when the 1951 range was presented to the public for the first time, a new A7 based around the newly introduced six-fifty was seen to have replaced the model that had run since the end of 1946. Not only did the

new smaller twin share its engineering with the larger model, but the new A7 changed from 495cc (62 × 82mm) to 497cc (66 × 72.6mm). The full story of this, the 'Mark 2' A7, is fully covered in the following chapter.

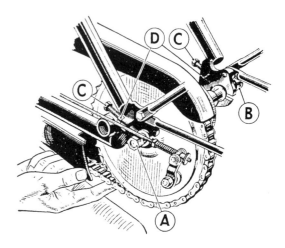

Chain adjustment for the rigid-frame model.

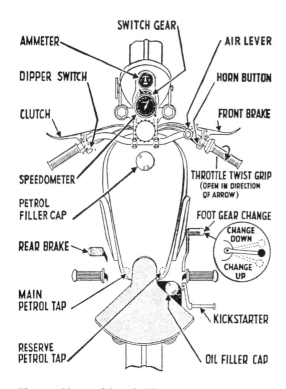

The control layout of the early A7 series.

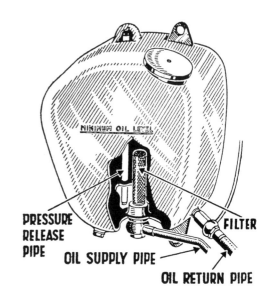

The oil tank, showing the internal filter and external connecting pipes.

4 A7 Mark 2

In October 1950, when the 1951 BSA pro-gramme was announced, a major feature was the arrival of what *The Motor Cycle* described as 'An entirely new engine and gearbox for the A7 twin.' This was not, however, strictly true, as the new A7 was in reality very much a small-er brother to the six-fifty A10 Golden Flash.

The A7 Mark 2 Engine

Revised Bore and Stroke Dimensions

With new bore and stroke dimensions of 66 × 72.6mm (as opposed to 62 × 82mm) the engine displacement was lifted from 495 to 497cc. Increased bore size meant, of course, a shallower combustion chamber. The narrow angle valve geometry was identical with that of the A10 (*see* Chapter 6), and had been adopted also with a view to ensuring efficient combus-tion chamber design and the use of high com-pression ratios with flat-top pistons. The stan-dard compression ratio was 6.7:1, with pistons giving 7.2:1 ratio being available to order. BSA realized that not only did the export market, notably the USA, have access to higher octane fuel, but also that even the austere Britain of the 1940s was rapidly giving way to a new, less restrictive regime as the 1950s dawned.

Sharing Bits with the A10

Both the crankcase and crankshaft were basi-cally similar to those of the A10. Indeed, as *The Motor Cycle* of 19 October 1950 reported: 'the majority of the parts are identical and about 95 per cent are interchangeable'. The crankshaft was an extremely rigid one-piece design with a bolted-on central flywheel. It was a high-grade steel forging comprising two mainshafts, the two crank webs, the big-end journals and the flywheel flange. Bobweights for balancing purposes were incorporated in the flywheel and crank webs. As on the original A7, a ball journal supported the crankshaft on the drive side, with a plain bearing on the timing side. The journals of the plain bearings were induc-tion-hardened, ground and polished.

H-section, light alloy (instead of steel, as pre-viously) connecting rods with conventional split big-end shells were employed. These shells were steel-backed, lead-bronze with indium flash, a material which BSA sources said 'has a very high load capacity and which develops an excellent bearing surface'. The big-end track was 1.460in (37mm) wide. The small ends were bushed and, as before, the taper-bored gudgeon pins were fully floating, and retained by circlips.

Semi-Split Skirt Piston Design

The new 66mm pistons were produced from silicon alloy. These were of split-skirt design, or rather, as *The Motor Cycle* said, 'of semi-split skirt design, for the "splits" extend upward only as far as the centre line through the gudgeon pin bosses'. An unusual feature was that, cut parallel to the internal webs that ran from the base of the gudgeon-pin bosses up to the crown, there were what one observer called four 'heat gaps', ³⁄₁₆in wide by ⁷⁄₈in long (5mm by 22mm) slots; these extended from the centre line through the gudgeon pin to just below the oil control ring. Each pair of these 'heat gaps' was joined at the top ends by a ¹⁄₁₆in (1.6mm) wide horizontal slot, across the piston thrust faces, parallel to the scraper ring. The object was to keep as much heat as possible away from the piston skirt and to allow the skirt to have a certain amount of flexibility. BSA also stated that it had been possible, thanks to these new pistons, 'to reduce the clearances to half those required previously'. This, they claimed, had 'resulted in piston slap having almost entirely been eliminated'.

The Cylinder Head

The cylinder head design of the new (Mark 2) A7 was identical with that of the A10 so far as its contour and airflow layout.

Austentic steel (G2) was used for both the inlet and exhaust valves, whilst the stems were stellite tipped – thus eliminating the need for separate, hardened-steel caps. The diameter of the exhaust valve throat measured 1³⁄₁₆in (30mm) diameter; the inlet 1½in (26mm).

The cylinder head was retained by nine studs to secure it to the crankcase. As in the earlier A7 engine, the one-piece cylinder barrel incorporated an integral pushrod tunnel running up the rear of the barrel. And as usual on a BSA parallel twin, a single camshaft was housed at the rear of the crankcase. As before, this was a one-piece affair with integral cam lobes, which provided 0.3in (7.6mm) valve lift. Drive to the camshaft

was from the mainshaft via an idler spur pinion. Width of the timing pinion was ⅓in (7.6mm). The camshaft drove a magneto fibre pinion that incorporated the automatic advance-and-retard unit. Carried alongside the idler pinion, but as before in a separate compartment, was the chain sprocket, which operated the dynamo through an 8mm simplex roller chain.

Dynamo speed was 1.1 times engine speed. As before, the object behind the isolating of

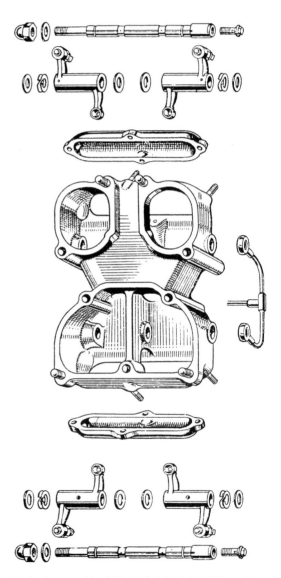

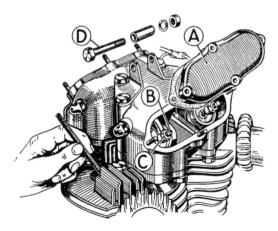

A major difference between the Mark 1 and the Mark 2 A7 model was the rocker covers. On the Mk1 there were four circular tappet inspection covers, on the Mark 2 only two much larger elongated ones.

Rocker box assembly of A7 Mark 2 (and also A10 series).

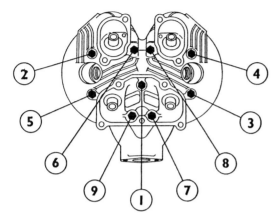

The sequence for tightening down cylinder head bolts.

the dynamo chain was to ensure against oil reaching the dynamo. The gear-type oil pump was driven from a worm carried on an extension on the crankshaft. Pump capacity was a nominal 76 pints (43ltr) per hour at 3,000rpm.

Revising the Lubrication System

With orthodox lubrication systems, the pump capacity, of course, is much bigger than that required by the big-ends and so there is a vast waste of lubricant, which drains back into the crankcase before returning to the tank. In the system used by the Mark 2 A7 (and on A10s from that time), provision had been made for making use of what had, in the past, been surplus.

From the end of 1950, the oil was now passed, via a small relief valve in the timing chest, through a drilled oilway diagonally upward and rearward; thence into a horizontal passage, and then diagonally rearward until it met a transverse passage running across the crankcase to the rear of, and slightly below, the centreline through the camshaft. From an orifice in the transverse oilway, the oil was fed forward and upward to the camshaft, draining into what BSA described as a 'trough'. From there it 'spilled' onto the big-end bearings, which flung it upward onto the cylinder bores. The trough under the camshaft was so positioned that the camshaft was, in fact, running in an oil bath.

To replace the excess oil which was formerly led into the timing chest, there was now a controlled oil feed to the idler and mainshaft pinions. Owing to the improved oil distribution, BSA sources said that 'crankcase bias has been eliminated and the drive-side cylinder receives much more oil than it did previously'.

Retaining the Bolted-Up Gearbox

As with the original A7, and on the existing A10, the bolted-up gearbox (to the four locating points on the crankcases) was retained. The primary chain was again by an endless ⅜in (9.5mm) pitch flat-backed duplex type, tensioned by a case-hardened slipper fitted in the case.

A New Gearbox

Although gear selection continued to be carried out by a cam-type mechanism, the gearbox was hugely different. BSA also claimed that the 'gear change was greatly improved'. This new gearbox had come into production when the A10 was launched and from now on would be fitted to the five-hundreds as well.

The dogging arrangement had been redesigned so that there was a two-stage tooth engagement on the mainshaft and a complete dog engagement on the layshaft. The two-stage engagement on the mainshaft had been done by removing, first of all, each alternate tooth on the fixed pinions and relieving the alternate 'pillars' on the sliding dogs back to ⅟₁₆in (1.6mm). The same method was applied to the remaining pair of gears – the mainshaft sliding pinion and the clutch sleeve pinion.

The system of the layshaft was, BSA said, 'quite new and altered completely from a tooth to a dog-type engagement'. Additionally, the layshaft fixed pinion now had a set of six external dogs meshing on widely relieved internal dogs on one of the sliding pinions; on the other sliding pinion there were external dogs, and the low-gear pinion with which it meshed had, of course, internal dogs. The actual dimensions of the shafts and pinions remained unaltered. Gear ratios (solo) were: 5.1, 6.2, 9 and 13.2:1.

Single Carburettor of the 1951 Star Twin

Besides the standard A7, there was still the higher performance Star Twin, with its tuned engine. This had also received the details and

1950 A7 Specifications	
Engine	Air-cooled, ohv vertical twin, 360-degree crank, single camshaft at rear of crankcase, cast-iron cylinder head and barrel, bolt-on rocker box covers, vertically split aluminium crankcases, coil valve springs
Bore	66mm
Stroke	72.6mm
Displacement	497cc
Compression ratio	6.6:1
Lubrication	Dry sump, with oil pump featuring worm drive; a pressure relief valve screwed into the crankcase
Ignition	Magneto
Carburettor	Amal 276 ¹⁵⁄₁₆in (24mm)
Primary drive	Duplex chain
Final drive	Chain
Gearbox	Bolt-up, four-speed, foot-change
Frame	All-steel construction, double front downtube
Front suspension	BSA telescopic, oil-damped forks
Rear suspension	Rigid or plunger
Front brake	7in (178mm) drum, SLS
Rear brake	7in (178mm) drum, SLS
Tyres	Front 3.25 × 19; rear 3.50 × 19

General Specifications

Wheelbase	55in (1,397mm)
Ground clearance	4.5in (114mm)
Seat height	30in (762mm)
Fuel tank capacity	3.6gal (16ltr)
Dry weight	375lb (170kg)*
Maximum power	27bhp @ 5,800rpm
Top speed	86mph (138km/h)

* 400lb (181kg) with plunger suspension.

modifications outlined above for the 1951 season. The more sporty model had rear springing (plunger-frame) as standard (on the A7 it was still a cost option) and a silver and chrome tank with its own motif. Earlier Star Twins had had twin carburettors, but the latest version was now fitted with only one Amal carburettor – a 276 1in (25mm) with a 160 main jet. Why had what seemed a retrograde step been taken? Well, it had been discovered that even for road racing, a single carburettor set-up offered just as much performance as a twin carb one. And, certainly, it was a lot less hassle to maintain and keep running at as near 100 per cent efficiency as possible. The official 1951 BSA price list of 19 October 1950 for the A7/Star Twin series was as follows:

- 497cc A7 basic – £144 (with UK taxes £182 17s 8d);
- 497cc Star Twin basic – £164 (with UK taxes £208 5s 8d);
- plunger frame for standard A7 basic – £10 (with UK taxes £12 4s);
- side stand for basic – 15s (with UK taxes 19s 1d).

A final item concerning the specification of the A7 (and A10) for the 1951 model year was that sidecar lugs were now incorporated on both sides of the motorcycle.

Road Tests

Both *The Motor Cycle* (8 February) and *Motor Cycling* (10 May) published tests during the first half of 1951, of the latest A7 and Star Twin models respectively.

The Motor Cycle's A7 test results began with the headline: 'Latest Edition of an Established High-performance Five-hundred: An Enthralling Machine' and continued:

The original 495cc A7 BSA was introduced to an eager, war-weary market in 1946 and retained its basic and detail design almost without change until the end of last year. Though even to an experienced eye the 1951 engine and gearbox exteriors are largely unchanged, both units are, in fact, new and almost identical in internal design with those of the already illustrious Golden Flash model. The result of the changeover is such that many will immediately class the new A7 as being the best 500cc BSA yet; in terms of all round engine performance, handling, braking and gear change – particularly the last – the new A7 is without doubt one of the best of two, or, perhaps, three machines in its particular capacity class.

During the February 1951 A7 road test, *The Motor Cycle* stated 'the BSA was generally driven in a manner calculated to bring to light – and quickly – any indication that the engine might "fuss" or tire'. To put it another way, the engine was revved very hard in the indirect gears, and speeds wherever possible were just as high as road conditions permitted. On one particular occasion a run of 150 miles (240km) in Warwickshire and Shropshire was completed in a few minutes over three hours!

The Motor Cycle tester went on to explain that: 'Speeds on the main roads were regularly in the 70–75mph [113–120km/h] region, and 80mph [130km/h] was maintained and held effortlessly on several occasions – this by a heavily garbed rider sitting in an orthodox position.' A further revelation came with the following statement: 'When the machine was stopped after several miles on full bore, a hand could be placed on the cylinder finning.'

As before, a particular mention was made that, 'Throughout the entire test the engine and gearbox remained absolutely oil-tight.' However, it was also noted that 'The near chain tended to run dry.'

A Lack of Vibration

British verticals are not renowned for being particularly quiet, but the word vibration is used far too often. The original A7 had been generally regarded as having less vibes than most. And the 'Mark 2' continued this trend.

According to *The Motor Cycle* test: 'From 50mph [80km/h] onwards, high-frequency vibration could be felt at the handlebar, but it was slight and would not worry even fastidious riders. Vibration was marked only when the engine was revved to the point of valve float.'

Other features of the A7 that gained praise were 'A slow, reliable tick-over' and 'the engine was beautifully quiet mechanically'. The test ended by saying 'Engine starting from cold (during some of the coldest weather experienced this winter) was certain at the third or fourth dig on the kick-starter' and 'required commendably little physical effort or knack'. Performance, compared to the April 1947 test by the same magazine (*see* Chapter 3) was improved, with a maximum speed of 98mph (158km/h) in top (fourth) gear and 78mph (126km/h) in third; these were improvements in the region of 5 per cent. The mean speed at the end of the quarter-mile (0.4km) from rest was 76mph (122km/h) – and the same distance from a standing start was 17.6 seconds.

Over 90mph

Motor Cycling's Star Twin test in the 10 May 1951 issue carried the headline: 'A Sporting "Multi", Easy to Handle and Having a Maximum speed of over 90mph' and began:

It was with no little eagerness that a *Motor Cycling* staff man recently piloted a 1951 BSA Star Twin through the main gates of the Small Heath factory on the initial stage of a road test which had been keenly awaited. The standard touring edition, the 497cc ohv vertical twin model A7 had already shown a performance more than adequate for the majority of riders and it was anticipated that the Star Twin, with its additional tuning and special specification, would prove to be outstanding in this respect. The anticipation was fulfilled and on several occasions during the subsequent fortnight on the road, memories of the excellent 650cc Golden Flash were conjured up by its smaller brother.

Detail Rather than Major Changes

When the BSA range for 1952 was announced in late October 1951 it was seen that detail modification rather than major design changes had been made. *The Motor Cycle* commented: 'Though no radical changes are announced for 1952, and there are no new models, there are many minor modifications to engines and cycle parts applying almost throughout the entire range. Few of these changes, it may be added, have been made because of previous bothers.'

Amongst the modifications applying to all three A series twin-cylinder models for 1952 was the provision of a special spring-loaded synthetic rubber oil seal on the gearbox main-shaft. The engine breather on the twins, it should be remembered, was of a ported, timed design, the theory behind this being that because of its high rotational speed (it was driven from the camshaft), it would pass out air but not oil. However, with the original system oil could drip into the outlet passage when the engine was idling at low engine revolutions. To prevent this occurring, a circular shroud had been cast round the breather on the inside of the timing cover to act as a baffle.

Improved Front Fork Action

The damping on the telescopic front forks had been further improved – achieved by the simple expedient of lengthening the fork bushes.

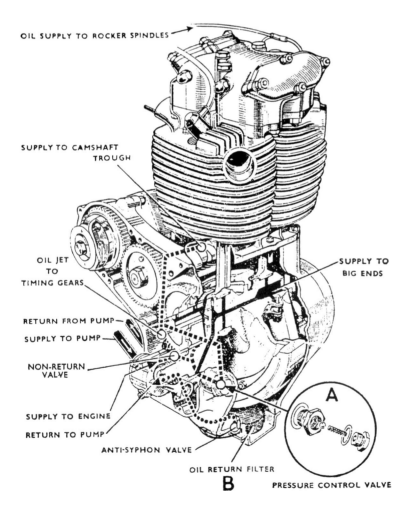

A 497cc (66 × 72.6mm) Mark 2 engine, showing lubrication system, timing gears and revised cylinder head details.

As *The Motor Cycle* pointed out in its 1 November 1951 issue: 'In the case of the BSA fork, the oil reservoir is, in fact, the annular space between the bushes – there is no separate damping element as with some telescopic forks.'

All 1952 BSA twins were supplied with the plunger-type rear springing as standard equipment.

To provide increased clearance under the wheels when the bike was parked, the centre stand had been redesigned. The revised stand was essentially similar to the one being superseded, but was narrower across the bridge section and came up further when not in use. On the nearside toe of the stand there was an extension to clear the nearside (left) silencer.

Although brake diameter sizes remained unchanged, the operation had, BSA said, been 'improved by the stiffening up of the fulcrum pin and cam bearing'.

In order to satisfy customer requests, manual ignition control was now available for the latest 1952 model year Star Twin.

A Dual Seat

As with other British motorcycle manufacturers, the period saw the one-piece dual seat come to the fore. In BSA's case, this arrived in time for the 1952 programme and was made available not only for the twins, but also the B and M group singles. Measuring some 25in (635mm) in length, the new seat was covered in Vynide. The base was a shaped, steel pressing, which supported a Dunlopillo cushion. *The Motor Cycle* commented 'staff have proved that the seat will comfortably accommodate two larger-than-average people'. However, the new dual seat was a cost option at an additional £3 (£3 16s 8d including UK taxes).

As for prices, on 1 November 1951, the latest 1952 specification five-hundred twins were priced as follows:

- A7 basic £168 (with UK taxes £214 13s 4d);
- Star Twin basic £174 (with UK taxes £222 6s 8d).

The plunger rear suspension of the A7. Even though it was to be ultimately succeeded by a new swinging-arm frame, the plunger model continued to be popular with the sidecar brigade.

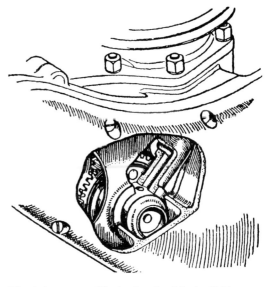

The timing cover modification introduced for the 1952 season to improve engine breathing (on both the A7 and A10).

Because of material shortages, and the restrictions on the use of nickel, BSA, like other British manufacturers, was not always able to adhere to what it described as 'the types of finish hitherto associated with our machines', but that the 'basic colours and highest quality possible will be maintained'. However, in March 1952 BSA announced that the A7, together with other machines over 250cc – with the exception of the Star Twin, A10 Golden Flash and Gold Star single – would be fitted with a new metal tank badge. This was a development of the wing seen in the letter B of BSA, finished in yellow and chrome and retained by screws.

'Brighter-than-ever BSAs'

The Motor Cycle dated 25 September 1952 carried details of the 1953 models, with the headline 'Brighter-than-ever BSAs' and going on to report:

> Keynote of the BSA range for 1953 is attractive appearance and refinement of detail. It has been found possible to reintroduce chromium plating for tanks and wheel rims; add to this the fact that several new colour schemes have been developed, and it is not difficult to foresee that the new BSAs will be amongst the brightest and smartest machines ever to be exhibited at the London Show.

Headlamp and Speedometer Cowl

A brand new headlamp and speedometer cowl (which could also be described as a nacelle) had been introduced for the twins and all models except the 125 Bantam and 250 four-stroke singles. The switch and ammeter were also housed in this cowling. At the same time, a degree of swivel adjustment had been retained for the headlamp itself. Contact between the lamp shell and cowling was by means of a thick rubber beading.

Another change was that of a revised rear number plate incorporating a newly designed

Lucas stop/tail light assembly. Again, this was introduced across the BSA range, excluding the Bantam.

All of the twins featured a new tank mounting that employed a horizontal through-bolt at each end. The set-up incorporated two rubber bushes that were placed under a predetermined amount of compression.

Front Brakes

Front brakes of 8in (203mm) diameter were now specified for all the four-series twins (previously these had only been on the A10 and the Star Twin). The rear brake diameter remained unchanged at 7in (178mm) on all three machines. Two minor modifications were finned collars for the exhaust header pipes and the side (prop) stand lugs brazed on the frame (thus eliminating the previous clip-on stand type).

The Star Twin had been given a completely new dual-green paint job. This comprised a polychromatic mist-green finish for the mudguards, fork and tank, dark green enamel for the frame. The tank panels were, as before, chrome-plated and they bore a Star Twin plastic badge in green. Previously, the Star Twin had been finished in silver/chrome (tank); the remainder of the motorcycle frame and suspension was black, while the exhaust and wheel rims were chromium.

The London Show

During the early 1950s, BSA claimed its machines to be 'The Most Popular Motor Cycle in the World'. And there is no doubt this was probably true, certainly if one included the other group members including Ariel, Triumph, New Hudson and Sunbeam. And BSA usually had a most impressive stand at that showpiece of the British two-wheel industry, Earls Court. The 1952 show was held in mid-November, with pride of place on Stand 37 going to one of the three production Star Twins that had won for BSA the coveted Maudes Trophy. The bike was displayed in the

1953 Star Twin Specifications

Engine	Air-cooled, ohv vertical twin, 360-degree crank, single camshaft at rear of crankcase, alloy cylinder head, cast-iron barrel, bolt-on rocker box covers	Frame	All-steel construction, double front downtube
		Front suspension	BSA telescopic, oil-damped forks
		Rear suspension	Plunger
		Front brake	8in (203mm)
Bore	66mm	Rear brake	7in (178mm)
Stroke	72.6mm	Tyres	Front 3.25 × 19; rear 3.50 × 19
Displacement	497cc		
Compression ratio	7.5:1	*General Specifications*	
Lubrication	Dry sump, with oil pump featuring worm drive; a pressure relief valve screwed into the crankcase	Wheelbase	55in (1,397mm)
		Ground clearance	4.5in (114mm)
		Seat height	30in (762mm)
		Fuel tank capacity	3.5gal (16ltr)
Ignition	Magneto	Dry weight	401lb (182kg)
Carburettor	Amal TT9 1⅟₁₆in (27mm)	Maximum power	31bhp @ 6,000rpm
Primary drive	Duplex chain	Top speed	90mph (145km/h)
Final drive	Chain		
Gearbox	Bolt-up, four-speed, foot-change		

condition in which it had returned from its strenuous 5,000-mile (8,045km) test through Europe and the International Six Days Trial. Also on the stand was the Maudes Trophy itself – which had often been referred to as the 'Oscar of the motorcycling world'. The full story of this magnificent achievement is recounted in Chapter 5, and it is a story to make any BSA enthusiast proud.

A Swinging Arm

The big news for the 1954 A7 five-hundred twin-cylinder family was the introduction of a swinging-arm frame and a new sportster with an alloy cylinder head, the Shooting Star.

The standard A7 was now to be offered in either plunger or swinging-arm frame guises, the Star Twin with only the plunger set-up and the new Shooting Star with the swinging-arm

The last of the line, the 1953 Star Twin, now in two-tone green – dark for the frame; pale polychromatic green for forks, mudguards, oil and petrol tanks. The latter came with chrome panels and circular star badges.

1954 plunger-framed A7, with all-maroon finish, chrome tank panels and 8in (203mm) front brake.

LEFT: *The final version of the Star Twin continued to use a tuned A7 engine (with iron head), in a plunger frame with dark green frame and lighter body components (tanks, chainguard, head lamps, etc.).*

BELOW: *The nacelle was a feature of the 1953 Star Twin (also to be found on the A7 and A10 of the era).*

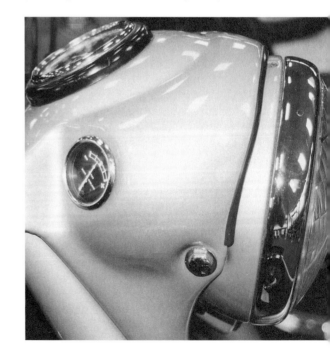

frame only. Most notably, the adoption of the new frame had led to a major redesign concerning the mounting of the gearbox and the gear ratios. Where plunger-frame rear springing was used (as with the original rigid frame, now discarded), the gearbox was built in semi-unit with the engine. But the new pivoted fork (swinging-arm) models employed an entirely separate gearbox, the crankcase shape having been modified to suit as part of the re-design. It also meant that the separate gearbox was adjustable to provide correct chain tension.

Different Gear Ratios

Gear ratios on bikes equipped with the swinging-arm suspension were slightly different. The new ratios were: 5.28, 6.38, 9.28 and 13.62:1. It should be noted that these are different from the swinging-arm A10 introduced at the same time.

A minor modification to all A series twins was that the finning on the cast-iron cylinder barrels and heads had been extended, thus

ABOVE: BSA factory tester Reg Slinn, seated on a prototype swinging-arm A7 sports model; Isle of Man c.1953.

BELOW: The swinging-arm frame arrived for the 1954 season. One of the first of the new Shooting Star models is shown, with its owner.

increasing the cooling area – and giving the engine a more chunky appearance.

On the models with the swinging-arm frame, there was an oil tank of an entirely new shape, together with a matching toolbox. Both were of a triangular appearance with rounded corners, and effectively filled the area from the rear of the petrol tank/front of the dual seat rearward to the lug for mounting the rear shock absorber, ending, downwards, to the aft of the new, longer aluminium primary chaincase. The battery was carried on a platform located centrally between the toolbox and oil tank.

The price structure for the 1954 models was as follows:

- A7 (plunger) basic £172 10s (with UK taxes £207);
- A7 (swinging-arm) basic £177 10s (with UK taxes £213);
- Star Twin basic £180 (with UK taxes £216);

- Shooting Star basic £187 10s (with UK taxes £225).

The cost extras were:

- legshields basic £2 10s (with UK taxes £3);
- pillion seat basic £1 1s (with UK taxes £1 5s 3d);
- carrier basic £1 1s (with UK taxes £1 5s 3d);
- BSA dual seat basic £3 (with UK taxes £3 12s);
- pillion footrests basic 10s (with UK taxes 12s);
- prop stand basic 15s (with UK taxes 18s).

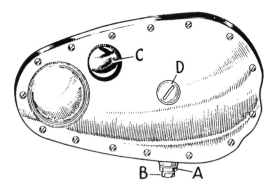

The primary chaincase from the swinging-arm machine was considerably longer than that of earlier A7 models with either rigid or plunger frames.

Another change for the swinging-arm frame A7 was a Simplex 0.5 × 0.305in primary chain.

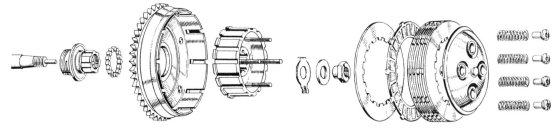

An exploded view of the clutch on the swinging-arm A7. Note four clutch springs in place of six on the rigid/plunger models.

The finishes were:

- A7: dark maroon enamel with chromium-plated tank panels;
- Star Twin and Shooting Star: dual green comprising polychromatic mist green and dark green enamel; the tanks had chromium-plated panels and carried three-dimensional plastic badges.

The Star Twin is Axed

By the time the 1955 range was announced in mid-October 1954, it was seen that BSA had not only discontinued the Star Twin, but that also the A7 was now only to be sold in swinging-arm guise (buyers still having a choice of plunger or swinging-arm on the larger A10).

The 1955 model year A7 was priced at £219 12s (£183 basic) and the Shooting Star £231 12s (£193 basic). As for technical changes, these were relatively few. In line with certain other models, all A series twins now included a steering-head lock. There was also a redesigned engine shock absorber, whilst the new Amal Monobloc carburettor had been standardized on the A7/Shooting Star models, which also had a one-piece valanced mudguard (swinging-arm frame). This resulted in a more horizontal position of the dual seat, and thus, said BSA, 'in an improved riding position'. A new one-piece, valanced front mudguard was fitted to the A7 (and A10), but not the Shooting Star. It is also worth noting that buyers of the swinging-arm framed model had the choice of three different spring ratings – 90, 110 and 130lb – for the rear shock absorbers. But, generally, most machines were supplied with 110lb springs.

Testing the Shooting Star

The 16 December 1954 edition of *The Motor Cycle* noted that the Shooting Star was 'basically a Star Twin with various modifications, including a light alloy cylinder head and the latest BSA pivoted-fork rear springing'. The

1955 Shooting Star Specifications	
Engine	Air-cooled, ohv vertical twin, 360-degree crank, single camshaft at rear of crankcase, alloy cylinder head, cast-iron barrel, bolt-on rocker box covers, aluminium vertically split crankcases
Bore	66mm
Stroke	72.6mm
Displacement	497cc
Compression ratio	7.25:1
Lubrication	Dry sump, with oil pump featuring worm drive; a pressure relief valve screwed into crankcase
Ignition	Magneto
Carburettor	Amal 376 Monobloc 1in (25mm)
Primary drive	Simplex chain
Final drive	Chain
Gearbox	Separate, four-speed, foot-change
Frame	All-steel tubular construction, duplex
Front suspension	BSA telescopic, oil-damped forks
Rear suspension	Swinging arm, twin Girling shock absorbers
Front brake	8in (203mm)
Rear brake	7in (178mm)
Tyres	Front 3.25 × 19; rear 3.50 × 19

General Specifications

Wheelbase	56in (1,422mm)
Ground clearance	6in (152mm)
Seat height	30in (762mm)
Fuel tank capacity	4gal (18ltr)
Dry weight	416lb (189kg)
Maximum power	32bhp @ 6,250rpm
Top speed	93mph (150km/h)

tester was enthusiastic about the latest BSA sporting five-hundred twin, saying:

To a remarkable degree the makers have succeeded in combining tractability, excellent traffic manners and relatively low fuel consumption with

1956 A7 Specifications	
Engine	Air-cooled, ohv vertical twin, 360-degree crank, single camshaft at rear of crankcase, cast-iron cylinder head and barrel, bolt-on rocker box covers, aluminium vertically split crankcases
Bore	66mm
Stroke	72.6mm
Displacement	497cc
Compression ratio	6.6:1
Lubrication	Dry sump, with oil pump featuring worm drive, a pressure relief valve screwed into the crankcase
Ignition	Magneto
Carburettor	Amal 376 Monobloc 1in (25mm)
Primary drive	Simplex chain
Final drive	Chain
Gearbox	Separate, four-speed, foot-change
Frame	All-steel tubular construction, duplex
Front suspension	BSA telescopic, oil-damped forks
Rear suspension	Swinging-arm, twin Girling shock absorbers
Front brake	Ariel 7in (178mm) alloy full-width hub, SLS
Rear brake	Ariel 7in (178mm) alloy full-width hub, SLS
Tyres	Front 3.25 × 19; rear 3.50 × 19

General Specifications

Wheelbase	56in (1,422mm)
Ground clearance	6in (152mm)
Seat height	30in (762mm)
Fuel tank capacity	4gal (18ltr)
Dry weight	425lb (193kg)
Maximum power	28bhp @ 5,800rpm
Top speed	88mph (142km/h)

an open-road potential in the best traditions of the modern sporting five-hundred. Ease of handling, sweet transmission and smooth low-speed pulling make the Shooting Star a delightful machine to ride in traffic, while zestful acceleration in all gears,

a tireless engine and superb braking and steering cater admirably for the rider who wants something out of the ordinary in 500cc performance.

Manual ignition control and a long level permitted accurate setting to be achieved – borne out by the fact that by retarding the ignition the minimum non-snatch speed was 13mph (21km/h) in top gear, which *The Motor Cycle* said was 'a remarkable figure for a sporting five-hundred twin'. Also, it was noted that:

Engine vibration was virtually non-existent below 70mph [110km/h] in top gear. Above this speed a slight tremor was detectable at the petrol tank and handlebar, but was not of sufficient magnitude to warrant criticism. Only when the engine was revved to the point of valve float in bottom and second gears did vibration become pronounced – through the footrests.

As for performance figures, although these were no better than the Star Twin, 'some qualification of the performance figures' was needed, due to the conditions prevailing when these were carried out. These were described as 'extremely unfavourable' and that 'a gale force wind, reported to have a maximum velocity of 70mph blew across the machine's path'.

Mean maximum speed:

- first   43mph (69km/h);
- second   63mph (101km/h);
- third   88mph (142km/h);
- fourth   90mph (145km/h).

Ariel Full-Width Hubs

An innovation for the twins for the 1956 model range (announced in mid-October 1955) was the introduction of Ariel-type full-width brake hubs to both wheels. These featured centrally disposed brakes and were of cast aluminium with integral spoke flanges, each hub being ribbed externally for brake cooling and webbed internally for rigidity. Cast-in steel bearing housings and iron brake liners were incorporated.

LEFT: *Ariel type 7in full-width alloy hubs were used front and rear on the 1956–57 swinging-arm A7 and A10 models. Optional rear chain enclosure was also fitted on this machine.*

BELOW: *BSA rear chaincase. Not only could the rear section be removed, but there were rubber plugs to give quicker access for chain tension checks.*

The brake shoes and shoe backplates were aluminium die castings. The brake linings were 1½in (38mm) wide, whilst the brake diameter was 7in (178mm); the same for both wheels. A ratchet-type fulcrum adjustment for the brake shoes was a feature of the design.

Front and rear hubs differed from one another only in that the rear hub carried four integral driving studs. The rear wheel was still quickly detachable, but was of a slightly different layout. Removal of a rubber plug in the rear of the chaincase provided access to taper-seated domed nuts on the driving studs; the wheel spindle was withdrawn as before.

Rear brake operation from the foot pedal on the nearside (left) was achieved by a cross-over shaft arranged co-axially with the hollow spindle of the swinging-arm pivot, and thereafter by cable.

Optional Total Rear Chain Enclosure

BSA had also introduced an optional totally enclosed final drive chaincase for all its A and B group roadsters. This new assembly was manufactured from 22-gauge sheet-steel pressings, and was in four sections. A fixed forward section enclosing the gearbox final drive sprocket was bolted to the rear of the primary chaincase. Bolted to lugs on the swinging-arm fork were the upper and lower middle sections. The rear section, which completely enclosed the rear wheel sprocket, was bolted to the middle sections.

At the rear of the case, metal-to-metal tongue-and-groove joints were employed to mate the upper and lower sections. At the front of the case, the edges of the upper and lower sections were radiused and fitted flush along the arm of the swinging fork. An overlapping joint was used between the middle and forward sections of the case, and a small clearance was maintained between the joint faces to accommodate movement of the rear fork. To allow for chain adjustment (which was carried out in the conventional manner), the chaincase was slotted where the wheel spindle protruded. Chain tension could be checked, simply by the removal of a rubber inspection plug. The chaincase was listed in October 1955 at £3, including UK taxes.

Revised Engine Specification for the Shooting Star

Engine specification for the A series twins remained unaltered for the 1956 model year, with the exception of the Shooting Star. To raise volumetric efficiency and further improve the performance, siamezed inlet ports had been cast integrally with the light alloy cylinder head. This arrangement, said official BSA sources, was intended to provide a smoother gas flow, and superseded the Y-shape inlet manifold that had formerly been used. This also meant the carburettor was now bolted directly to the head.

Prices of the two five-hundred twins had been increased to £231 for the A7 and £243 for the more sporting Shooting Star.

Testing the 1956 A7

The Motor Cycle tested the latest A7 in its 24 May 1956 issue. The test's headline read: 'A Smart, Tractable Touring Mount Capable of High-speed Cruising with Marked Comfort for Two People'. The actual test began:

Many changes have been made in the specification of the BSA A7 during the 10 years which have elapsed since the model made its debut. The modifications have kept abreast of modern trends in

design but have not altered its basic character as an economical and flexible touring five-hundred with a well-blended engine performance.

A mean (two-way) maximum speed of 90mph (145km/h) was recorded, whilst the highest one-way speed was 92mph (148km/h). But the A7 was able to cruise at virtually any speed, plus 'Top gear was used not only when riding

ABOVE: *A 1956 BSA factory illustration showing a quickly detachable rear wheel with swinging-arm rear suspension. It was only necessary to unscrew the nut on the brake anchorage bar and the four nuts connecting the sprocket to the hub. The spindle could then be unscrewed and withdrawn, leaving sprocket and brake parts rigidly in position as shown.*

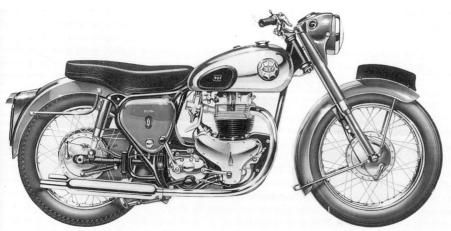

LEFT: *1956 Shooting Star, with Ariel hubs, the same as on the latest A7.*

at the legal maximum of 30mph [50km/h] in built-up areas, but also in the normal course of events when accelerating from as low a speed as 25mph [40km/h].' And 'Away from speed restrictions, the A7 was equally pleasant to ride whether it was burbling along at 30mph in top gear, humming at 45 to 50mph [72–80km/h] on a mere whiff of throttle or proceeding at a purposeful 70mph [110km/h]. If and when required, a cruising speed of 80mph [130km/h] could be sustained indefinitely for the engine, which was entirely untroubled by hard riding.'

Starting – as usual with the A7 series – was praised:

> Engine starting drill was not critical. Provided the carburettor was flooded lightly, the air lever closed and the throttle set a fraction open, one sharp thrust on the kickstarter would bring the engine to life from cold. No preliminaries were required for a first kick-start when the engine was warm. Hot or cold, the engine would idle slowly, reliably and unobtrusively when the throttle was closed.

What of the Ariel-type stoppers? *The Motor Cycle* tester's words on the subject were:

> The speed of the twin was well matched by the efficiency of its brakes, both of which were smooth and powerful. Applied independently, they could easily be made to evoke squeals of protest from the tyres. When used together the brakes would arrest the model remarkably quickly from any speed of which it was capable.

A comment was made regarding a potential problem in setting the headlamp to give maximum vision:

> It was necessary to remove the strip of rubber beading from the front edge of the headlamp cowl before the lamp could be swivelled upward far enough to obtain a beam setting suitable for out-of-town riding after dark. When correctly set, the beam permitted speeds of 60 to 70mph [100–110km/h] to be maintained with safety on unlit main roads.

The test machine was equipped with the optional fully enclosed chainguard, upon which the tester commented:

> Though no automatic lubrication is provided for the enclosed rear chain, it benefited greatly from protection. The messiness from oil which usually accumulates on and around the rear wheel was non-existent, while the chain retained its well-cared for appearance and required no adjustment during a test which would certainly have necessitated resetting of an exposed chain.

However, potential buyers of a machine with a fully enclosed rear chaincase should carry out a check of what condition the chain and sprockets are in before parting with their money! Quite simply, half a century later one never knows what one may find inside. It could be a fully serviceable chain and sprockets or just the reverse. The May 1956 test concluded: 'With its smart maroon and chromium-plated finish, its refined performance and ample speed, the BSA A7 is one of the most attractive of touring five-hundred twins.'

Revisiting the Shooting Star

The Motor Cycle had, as already mentioned, tested one of the first production Shooting Stars to be built, this test appearing in December 1954, so when the rival Green 'Un, *Motor Cycling*, published its own test in the 6 September 1956 issue, this made for an interesting comparison. And whereas the earlier test had been held in far from perfect weather conditions, this was not the case for the 1956 outing: 'Weather and road conditions current when the machine was undergoing maximum speed-testing, were ideal; the air was still and the road surface dry.' It was also mentioned that 'the recently released 100-octane grade petrol was used for the speed tests'. Even the performance figures gained were somewhat disappointing. Not only were they only marginally different from the 1954 test, but hardly different from *The Motor Cycle*'s May 1956 A7 test, with a maximum recorded speed of 93mph (150km/h).

Unlike many tests conducted at the time, this one was 'Over a period of several weeks, a current production Shooting Star was on loan to *Motor Cycling* for test purposes and the model was used for practically every conceivable type of work; the mileage covered exceeded 2,000 miles [3,220km] and the average consumption was 64mpg [4.4ltr/100km].' As the tester went on to say: 'Ownership of a high-performance model is often associated with heavy pecuniary demands for fuel but, bearing in mind the sparkling road performance of which this machine is capable, the fuel consumption figure mentioned gives a clear indication of the machine's ability to combine speed with acceptable running economy.'

Actually, it is interesting to compare the Shooting Star with BSA's other performance five-hundred – the single-cylinder Gold Star. The latter was considerably faster (a 1955 test by *Motor Cycling* recording 110mph/177km/h). However, the Gold Star was some 30 per cent more expensive and the engine far less flexible than its twin-cylinder brother. Also the riding position offered by the Shooting Star was much more comfortable for normal road use – the Gold Star as tested had clip-ons and rear sets.

Little Change for 1957

BSA decided to make little change for the 1957 model year, at least as regards its 500cc-class twins. But there was now the option of black instead of maroon on the standard A7 tourer. The year also saw the effects of inflation in Great Britain beginning to be felt. In the 2 May edition of *The Motor Cycle*, the editorial leader reported 'During the past three weeks price increases have been announced by many motorcycle and sidecar manufacturers.' And it went on:

> In comparison with September 1954, the price of general bar and steel strips had gone up by 11 per cent; electricity and gas by 12 per cent; rail charges on the delivery of motorcycles by 24 per cent.

Expressed another way, these increases mean that the factor cost of complete machines have risen by about 17 per cent. Yet the average basic price rise passed on to the public during the entire period was under four per cent. And this, above all, was the reason why there were so few changes by BSA for the 1957 season – in a bid to restrain price increases to the bare minimum.

In the same issue, 2 May 1957, the new BSA price list was announced; this showed that the UK price (including purchase tax of almost 25 per cent) of the A7 had risen to £256 1s 3d and the Shooting Star £264 2s 5d.

New Wheel Hubs for 1958

A major change for the 1958 model year was the introduction of new wheel hubs. These were now of cast iron with flanges formed to permit the use of straight-pull, chromium-plated spokes. The hub periphery, cover plate and shoe plate were enamelled black, but had polished rim bands to add a touch of brightness. And the front wheel now disposed of the brake torque arm; in its place, a slotted boss on the shoe plate engaged with a matching lug incorporated onto the fork leg.

For the A7 there were 7in (178mm) brakes at the front and rear (as shared with the B

The author with his 1959 A7, c.1962.

ABOVE: 1958 A7 with revised hubs (full-width, cast iron) and fork nacelle.

RIGHT: Details of new-for-1958 nacelle design.

BELOW RIGHT: 1958 497cc Shooting Star, with cast-iron brake hubs, alloy head and flush-mounted headlamp. The Shooting Star also had a more sporting front mudguard design than the standard A7 of that year. It now had a black instead of dark green frame.

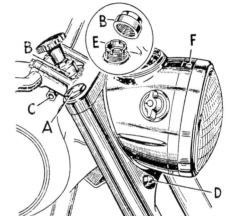

group touring singles), but on the Shooting Star (and A10 six-fifty) the front hub, though of similar design, housed an 8in (203mm) diameter assembly. From the author's own experience of owning an A7 thus equipped, this was a bad move as, weighing in at almost the same figure as the larger-engined A10 six-fifty, the smaller model was underbraked, especially when carrying a pillion passenger.

Other details that were introduced for 1958 are listed below:

- provision for sidecar attachment;
- new centre stand;
- improved silencer design;
- front fork nacelle;
- five-plate clutch with strengthened drum;
- compression ratio on Shooting Star raised from 7.25 to 8:1;
- new finish for the A7 of Princess Grey for the mudguards, toolbox, oil and petrol tanks;
- frame of Shooting Star now finished in black.

Consolidation for 1959

For 1959 the buzz word at BSA was 'consolidation', with the only really new product being the C15 Star two-fifty unit single, introduced a few months earlier. Otherwise, the factory policy was mainly one of consolidation and therefore (except for a couple of exceptions that do not concern this book) production was carried forward without major alteration and without a break in the production flow.

ACU (Auto Cycle Union) National Rally

David Frost tested an A7 for *Motor Cycle Mechanics* in the September 1959 issue. He began by saying:

> This BSA is probably the friendliest bike I have ever ridden. I practically lived on it for a week – covering 1,264 miles [2,034km]. Drove it up and down the A5. Drove it two-up 60 miles [97km] a day in London traffic. Drove it all over London. And for good measure I did the ACU National Rally on it – 600 miles [965km] virtually non-stop in 24 hours, then home again. And if a machine and rider can't get to know each other in that time they never will.

Actually, Frost's test report was very refreshing after reading the far more clinical affairs produced by the big-selling weeklies: he was quite happy not to pull any punches. For example, he made it quite clear what was good – and not so good – about the bike. Here are some samples:

> First I must make it quite clear that nobody is going to break any speed records on the A7, nor is it specially designed for hauling a sidecar – BSA make other machines for that sort of thing. This is a sports twin equally suitable for fast touring or riding to work. It will meander along in built-up areas without fuss in top gear, yet can be cruised on the open road in the upper 70s. That is the great beauty of this bike – flexibility.

The test report continued:

> This is a quiet bike. Even at speed there is little noise, and by rolling the grip back in the early hours of the morning I was able to burble through sleeping villages without even waking the dogs. How about vibration, the curse of the vertical twin? On the A7 I would prefer to call it a slight tremble – strongest at 50, it almost disappears at 60.

But in typically honest fashion, David Frost goes on to point out the bike's weaker points, ones which the author agrees with having owned just such a model/year as the one tested:

> Nothing is perfect – not even the A7. This is a heavy bike, and the first-class prop stand listed as an optional extra should be fitted as standard. The headlamp switch is a good arm's length away from the throttle, and the ammeter's invisible at night. The brakes were good – very good. But would it cost a lot more to fit the fabulous 8in front stopper from the Gold Flash?

The test ended with Frost summing up:

> Here is a sound, British-made machine – reliable and well built. It is as much at home on a run to the north of Scotland as it is on a shopping expedition down the High Street on a Saturday afternoon. A first-class all-rounder. Yes, it was a sad moment for me when I had to return this machine to BSA.

Incidentally, at the final control in the 1959 ACU Rally, David Frost not only gained a First Class Award, but the A7 'finished in perfect condition with no oil leaks'.

Detail Improvements for 1960

In publishing details of the 1960 BSA model year range, *The Motor Cycle* dated 3 September 1959 had this to say: 'The aim of the BSA factory is to provide machines exactly suited to the needs of various types of motorcyclist, be

'M.M.' MACHINE TEST REPORT No. ....5....

Machine ....B.S.A..... Model A.7. (GREY) c.c. 497

TEST Mileage ...1264... .Examiner... D. Frost

Supplied by ..B.S.A. MOTORCYCLES LTD.

Maximum Points 10 (compared with machines in same c.c. and price range)

Brakes (front)	8	Lights	9
Brakes (rear)	8	Engine accessibility	9
Brakes (both)	8	General performance	9
Steering at high speed	9	Overall finish	8
Steering at low speed	9	Electrical layout	8
Gearbox action	8	TOTAL	93

OVER WHOLE TEST

Fuel consumption ...74... m.p.g.

Acceleration 0-50 ...7.25... secs.

Top speed ...85... m.p.h.

Remarks ..MAX SPEED OBTAINED ON STRAIGHT LEVEL ROAD, NO WIND, RIDER CROUCHED SLIGHTLY FORWARD.

BRAKING GRAPH

M.P.H. / STOPPING DISTANCE IN FEET

The Test Sheet from David Frost's A7 test, published in September 1959.

he tourist, road burner, competitions rider or an enthusiast in need of economical personal transport.'

The improvements for 1960 applied principally to the larger machines – the 499cc B33 single and the A group 497 and 646cc twins. In addition, the range of colour schemes had been revised. This latter move was made so that production and store-keeping might be simplified – all frames and forks were black, but for the mudguards and fuel tanks there was an extended choice of what BSA described as 'bright finishes'.

The major change for 1960 was in the design of the A group primary chaincase. An aperture, closed by a screwed plug (both the plug and chaincase being in aluminium-alloy), was so placed that each of the clutch springs could now be adjusted in turn without removing the chaincase outer half. The adjustment

was further simplified by the provision of Simmonds self-locking nuts on the spring studs instead of the earlier nuts and lock nuts.

Previously, the chaincase oil level was checked by removing one of several screws, with a second screw serving as a drain plug. However, this system led to problems and the 1960 A group models featured a combined drain and level plug assembly screwed into the chaincase base. Integral with the assembly body, a standpipe projected upward to the normal oil level, but was so positioned that it could not be damaged by a slack primary chain. Removal of a plug in the assembly base opened the standpipe and hence the oil level was correct when no more would drain down the pipe. To drain the chaincase, the complete assembly was unscrewed.

The rear brake cam lever had been repositioned to provide increased initial pressure on the leading shoe. This modification had been implemented in an attempt to improve braking performance – and also to reduce pedal pressure.

For all the twins there was also a new front mudguard of the valanced type but without a registration number background, which had been a feature of the A7 and A10 touring models previously. The new 'guard incorporated a reinforced attachment to the fork legs and the forward stays had been dispensed with. The appearance of the rear mudguard had also been tidied up, this being achieved by the fitment of side stays which had forged ends resting against the valances. These were secured from inside the guard.

There was now, on the nearside (left) of the handlebar, inboard of the grip, a Wico Pacy Tri consul ring-type fitment incorporating the dip switch and the horn and engine cut-out buttons.

Seat height had been reduced by 1in (25mm) and BSA claimed that 'the latest seat has better airflow passages in the foam-rubber filling to provide greater resilience'.

A new finish for the A7 was Fuchsia Red. Prices on 3 September 1959 were A7 £249 1s 10d and Shooting Star £256 18s 8d (both including UK taxes). Then in early June 1960 the prices increased again, the A7 costing £255 2s 6d; the Shooting Star £262 1s 2d.

Testing the Latest Shooting Star

Also in June 1960, *The Motor Cycle* tested the latest version of the Shooting Star. There is no doubt that this particular example was blessed with a considerably superior performance to the earlier bikes tested by *Motor Cycling*, achieving a best one-way maximum speed of 98mph (158km/h). The mean (two-way) figures were equally impressive – 95mph (153km/h) in top and 92mph (148km/h) in third – although it should be pointed out that the latter figure had the proviso of valve float occurring. One particular quote from the test really summed up the 1960 machine: 'Steadily improved over a number of years, the BSA Shooting Star engine gives the model a fine blend of pep and good manners.'

The June 1960 test really was one BSA could be proud of – here is just a small section of the text:

> Its top speed and, more important, its acceleration and effortless fast cruising would do credit to a good six-fifty. Yet the Shooting Star is among the smoother vertical twins and can hold its own with the best for fuel consumption. The level of exhaust and mechanical noise is no higher than one would expect from a model of much more moderate performance, so the rider has no fear of giving offence to any reasonable bystander.

1960 Shooting Star, now fitted with A7 front 'guard and new teardrop tank badges.

Little Change

When the 1961 BSA range was announced in early September 1960, potential customers did not realize that the new A50 (five-hundred) and A65 (six-fifty) unit construction twins

were only months away from their launch in January 1962. As for the A7 and Shooting Star models, the only change for the 1961 model year concerned a silver-sheen finish that had been adopted for the wheel hubs and brake plates (in fact, this feature had been adopted for every other BSA that year with the exception

1961 A7 Specifications	
Engine	Air-cooled, ohv vertical twin, 360-degree crank, single camshaft at rear of crankcase, cast-iron cylinder head and barrel, bolt-on rocker box covers, aluminium vertically split crankcases
Bore	66mm
Stroke	72.6mm
Displacement	497cc
Compression ratio	6.6:1
Lubrication	Dry sump, with oil pump featuring worm drive; a pressure relief valve screwed into crankcase
Ignition	Magneto
Carburettor	Amal 375 Monobloc ^{15}⁄₁₆in (24mm)
Primary drive	Simplex chain
Final drive	Chain
Gearbox	Separate, four-speed, foot-change
Frame	All-steel, tubular construction, duplex
Front suspension	BSA telescopic, oil-damped forks
Rear suspension	Swinging arm, twin Girling shock absorbers
Front brake	7in (178mm)
Rear brake	7in (178mm)
Tyres	Front 3.25 × 19; rear 3.50 × 19

General Specifications

Wheelbase	56in (1,422mm)
Ground clearance	6in (152mm)
Seat height	30in (762mm)
Fuel tank capacity	4gal (18ltr)
Dry weight	425lb (193kg)
Maximum power	28bhp @ 5,800rpm
Top speed	88mph (142km/h)

1961 Shooting Star Specifications	
Engine	Air-cooled, ohv vertical twin, 360-degree crank, single camshaft at rear of crankcase, alloy cylinder head, cast-iron barrel, bolt-on rocker box covers, aluminium vertically split crankcases
Bore	66mm
Stroke	72.6mm
Displacement	497cc
Compression ratio	7.25:1
Lubrication	Dry sump, with oil pump featuring worm drive; a pressure relief valve screwed into crankcase
Ignition	Magneto
Carburettor	Amal 1in (25mm)
Primary drive	Simplex chain
Final drive	Chain
Gearbox	Separate, four-speed, foot-change
Frame	All-steel, tubular construction, duplex
Front suspension	BSA telescopic, oil-damped forks
Rear suspension	Swinging arm, twin Girling shock absorbers
Front brake	8in (203mm)
Rear brake	7in (178mm)
Tyres	Front 3.25 × 19; rear 3.50 × 19

General Specifications

Wheelbase	56in (1,422mm)
Ground clearance	6in (152mm)
Seat height	30in (762mm)
Fuel tank capacity	4gal (18ltr)
Dry weight	416lb (189kg)
Maximum power	32bhp @ 6,250rpm
Top speed	93mph (150km/h)

ABOVE: *1961 Shooting Star; new that year were silver hubs and light grey knee-grips. Production ended in spring 1962.*

LEFT: *Late Shooting Star (registered 1962) showing details such as front-mounted dynamo, alloy head, polished primary chaincase and duplex frame.*

of the D1 Bantam and 646cc Super Rocket twin).

End of the Line

And so with no more than some increases in prices, the A7 and its sporting sister, the Shooting Star, continued to be offered until the spring of 1962, when finally they made way for the new unit models. By then, the A7 cost £267 17s 7d and the Shooting Star £275 3s 3d (including UK taxes).

As Owen Wright points out in his book *BSA – The Complete Story*, 'Slowly and sadly, the glory was surely fading away.' Certainly this was true of the five-hundred A7 and Shooting Star. They were quite simply pensioned off – even though the A50 was far from a suitable replacement for a design that had done BSA so proud over some fifteen years of service all over the world.

5   Dirt Bikes

Although BSA only rarely built and raced anything that approached a specialized Grand Prix
racing motorcycle, it did nonetheless do
extremely well in most branches of off-road
sport, notably trials, scrambling (moto–cross)
and the International Six Days' Trial (ISDT).

This policy paid off, too, with the BSA factory dominating for many years, winning
British, European and World titles in the

process. Much of this success was garnered by
single-cylinder bikes; however, on occasion
twin-cylinder A7 and A10-based models were
campaigned. This not only added additional
interest – and sometimes considerable publicity for both the marque and the riders involved
– but also helped the engineering team with
vital technical data and experience under
harsh service conditions.

The BSA company was
successful during the 1920s
and 1930s with its single-
cylinder machines in events
such as the International Six
Days' Trial. Here L. Ridgway
is shown during the 1939
event, staged in Austria.

1938 International Six Days Trophy teamsters. Left to right: Fred Rist, R. Gillian, and J. T. Dolby – all on BSAs

Competitions Supremo

The man given the task of organizing and carrying through BSA's off-road sporting activities, both before and after the Second World War, was Bert Perrigo. Born in 1903, Albert (Bert) E. Perrigo was brought up in the very shadows of the giant Small Heath Birmingham industrial complex.

His father would have liked Bert to have joined him in Perrigo Senior's bakery business, but instead the youngster started work as a driver, ferrying former War Department vehicles for dealers during the immediate aftermath of the war in 1919. He later became a van driver with the Bordesley Engineering Company, a small concern that manufactured motorcycles under the Connaught brand name. Whilst at Bordesley's, Bert Perrigo was entered by the firm in the London to Edinburgh twenty-four-hour trial – winning what was to be the first of many 'golds' in such events.

Then came a short spell with Humphries & Dawes, makers of the OK Supreme motorcycle range. In 1926 he joined BSA as a trials rider (replacing George McLean who had left to join rivals Douglas in Bristol). By 1932 Bert had been appointed Competitions Manager – a position which, except for the war years, he held until 1952. During the late 1920s and early 1930s, whilst at BSA, he won hundreds of sporting events on a variety of Small Heath models.

Over the years he became increasingly involved with development work, which benefited from BSA's sporting activities. To provide Perrigo with an increased understanding of the motorcycle business in general, he was appointed BSA sales representative for the South West of England area in 1937. But his role as a salesman was to be short-lived, for he was almost immediately taken ill and subsequently spent some six months' recuperating in South Africa. This time also brought to an end his riding career.

February 1952 advertisement showing BSA's thirteen victories in the British Experts from 1929 through to 1951.

Bill Nicholson

Bill Nicholson was a key figure, together with Fred Rist, in the use of the twin-cylinder BSA for off-road sport, even though the former's use of such a machine (in one trials) was to be brief.

On mainland Britain, motorcycle sport took some time to get going again after the end of the Second World War. However, in Southern Ireland some form of competition had managed to continue throughout the war years – this proving to be a training ground for up-and-coming stars. One such rider was Bill Nicholson, who was employed at the Belfast Short and Harland aircraft plant in the north, manufacturing Bombay transporters and Hampden bombers for the Royal Air Force.

In January 1939, having never ridden a motorcycle before, a young Nicholson was persuaded by good friend Artie Bell (later to be a works Norton GP star) to purchase a brand new Triumph Tiger 80 single-cylinder three-fifty competition model. Within a fortnight he had learned to ride the machine and entered a trial. Not knowing what to do, other than keep both his feet on the pegs and keep going, he found he had 'immense fun' and, to his great surprise, won the event outright.

Although the Triumph was subsequently commandeered for the war effort in 1940, by the end of the conflict, Bill, who by then worked for Chambers of Belfast repairing military bikes, had amassed a collection of BSAs, including a B25, B29 and a 1939 M24 Gold Star.

Regular trips over the border kept his hand in, and in 1945 Bill won the first post-war Bangor Castle road race on the B29, beating local aces Artie Bell and Ernie Lyons, both mounted on 500s. The B29 was used in both grass and road racing, with nothing more than a change of tyres and footrest position, whilst the B25 was used solely for trials. In 1945 Bill won every trial in which he rode the B25, which featured a modified steering head angle and a set of homemade cams that provided both power and torque. In 1946 Bill Nicholson's employer – in collusion with BSA Competition Manager, Bert Perrigo – obtained a new B32 competition model to campaign in trials, but before it was 'good enough' for the Ulsterman, he had to fit his own cams, alter the fork angle and carry out numerous other changes.

The B32 was used in the English Colmore Cup Trial, where Bill gained runner-up spot behind winner Fred Rist. In truth, he should have won – except for the fact that he didn't know how to make an official protest. A few weeks later he won Ulster's Hurst Cup Trial by a wide margin – this time being watched closely by not only Bert Perrigo, but also BSA Sales Manager, George Savage.

And so, after the Hurst Cup Trial had finished, he was invited by Bert Perrigo to come over to the mainland for the Cotswold Scramble. Having never ridden in a scramble before, Bill was 'sceptical'. But he was assured that his performance in the Hurst Cup was up to scrambles standards, for this was a timed as well as an observed event. The B29 was decided upon for the Cotswold event, but prior to leaving Belfast, the bike was fitted with one of the McCandless swinging-arm rear ends.

At the venue this new rear suspension system was the cause of much mirth amongst the English riders, who placed their faith in the rigid-framed machines. However, there were to be a lot of red-faced people around when Bill Nicholson went on to win both the 350cc and Unlimited races that day.

For over eight years between 1946 and 1954, Bill Nicholson (centre) gave BSA over fifty major awards. Besides his usual Gold Star singles, he also campaigned an A7 twin-cylinder trials model during the first half of 1948.

To prove this was no fluke, Nicholson then used his McCandless-framed bike to take other victories, including a repeat double Cotswold victory the following year.

As a result of his original 1946 Cotswold victories, Bert Perrigo had recruited Bill to join the Competitions Department at the Small Heath works. One major problem this presented was that working for a factory like BSA meant that the bikes he rode were supposed to look like the standard BSA product. However, the resourceful Nicholson could usually find a way around this ruling. For example, the fitting of improved hydraulic damping to the suspension systems and internal engine modifications could always be hidden from view, although external changes often led to managerial rebukes. For example, he built an all-alloy-engined 350 road racer, which he considered was a better start for the new Gold Star than the B31 that the management was considering. Other ideas were also put forward but in virtually every case they were discarded by the design hierarchy with the comment: 'We are the designers, you are only the rider.'

But even though he had his problems communicating with other sections of BSA, Bert Perrigo did have the knack of getting the best from his riders, including Bill Nicholson. However, after Perrigo relinquished his position as Competitions boss in 1953, Nicholson for one began to have increasing problems. This was because he was not simply satisfied to be a rider, but was also deeply interested in the development side.

Finally, in 1954, Bill quit the BSA works squad, by which time, as he was later to admit, he had become so dispirited with the factory's management that he left to join the Jaguar car factory.

During his stay with the Birmingham works, Bill had some notable successes in trials, scrambling and even road racing. On the trials scene he had not only ridden the A7 prototype model (in 1948), but gained a sixth place on the 1947 Scottish (on a single), and subsequently three Special First Class medals. He fared better in the ISDT; after retiring with a broken clutch in the 1949 event, he went on to win a gold the following year. This medal is now part of the Mayoral chain for the city of Belfast.

On the scrambles circuit Bill was a force to be reckoned with and one of his successes was the 1947 Isle of Man Grand National, where he won by more than seven minutes!

In his book *BSA Competition History*, ex-BSA works rider Norman Vanhouse called him 'The Irish wizard', a fitting tribute to someone who in eight years at the Birmingham company achieved in excess of fifty premier awards in the top trade-supported trials.

In a final twist of the story, Bill Nicholson was invited back to the BSA factory in 1969, to take charge and reorganize the entire engineering side at Small Heath. This offer was rejected, for as Bill put it, 'By then it was too late.'

The 1950 BSA trials team of (left to right) Bill Nicholson, Harold Tozer and Jack Wilks (passenger). All were British Experts winners that year.

Post-war, Perrigo oversaw a golden period of BSA involvement in off-road sporting activities, in which the company enjoyed many important victories and gained several championship titles.

Entirely self-taught, Bert Perrigo was a man of many talents, including his capability as a rider, publicist, salesman, engineer and executive – all of which he performed at one time or another whilst at the BSA Group, in a career which continued almost unbroken until the demise of the company in the 1970s. As far as his role as Competitions Manager went, he held this post until October 1953, when he was succeeded by *Motor Cycling* journalist, Dennis Hardwicke.

Due both in part to his long service with the company and his considerable talents, Bert Perrigo was to earn the title 'Mr BSA', and as Owen Wright recalls 'As if to confound them all, his final work at BSA was spent liaising with Dr Gordon Blair at Queen's University, Belfast, working on a computer-oriented project dealing with exhaust systems for advanced two-stroke engines.' He was also one of the very few people who 'had the measure of Edward Turner', with his willingness to call a spade a spade.

Bert Perrigo died in 1985, at the age of eighty-two; but his efforts for the BSA cause live on.

An A7 Trials Prototype

First reports of a new BSA trials twin appeared at the beginning of February 1948. Based on the A7, BSA announced that the machine would be ridden by works rider Bill Nicholson in the Colmore Cup Trial later that month. BSA stated that the bike was 'still in the experimental stage'.

Considerable attention had been paid to reducing weight. A 'C' model two-fifty front hub had been fitted with its 5½in (140mm) diameter front brake. Specially lightened BSA telescopic front forks were employed, which, like those fitted to the production A7, were oil-damped. The fuel tank, with a capacity of 2gal (9ltr), very much resembled the type fitted to the B32 competition model. Siamezed exhaust header pipes were fitted, exiting into a single hi-level silencer on the nearside of the motorcycle. With a 2.75 × 21 front and 4.00 × 19 trials 'knobbly' tyres and revised gear ratios of 17, 12.7, 7.9 and 5.4:1, the A7 trials prototype certainly looked purposeful. And in fact the development team had succeeded in producing a machine that was actually lighter than the existing B34 five-hundred trials single. This quest for weight pruning was assisted by the use of aluminium for both the cylinder head and barrel, whereas of course the stock A7 roadster employed cast iron for both assemblies.

Initially testing had, it was said, gone well, Nicholson commenting that he was 'enthusiastic' about the newcomer.

A Successful Debut

First of the new season's trials, the 1948 Colmore event was run in what *The Motor Cycle* described as coinciding with the 'first blast of real winter'. The area of Shipston-on-Stour, Warwickshire, was snow covered and, said *The Motor Cycle* report, 'the centre of the keenest sub-zero winds and blizzards that Britain has experienced for many a year. The roads were as slippery as ice-bound rivers, and the hazards were nearly all so frozen as to be entirely changed in character from that associated with the names.'

A section of the report stated:

> Among the recognized stars, B.H.M. Viney (498cc AJS) dealt with the loose corner before the climb, the climb and the corner before the ledge higher up with his usual quiet competence. W. Nicholson on his snarling BSA twin 'wowsed' through, and C.N. Rogers on a spring-frame Royal Enfield (the prototype Bullet) struck a good compromise between the caution of Viney and the zestfulness of Nicholson.

There was great interest in the A7 trials prototype, with it being reported 'When W. Nicholson arrived on his new BSA trials twin he was immediately surrounded by the little knot of doughty spectators.' And 'On both Mill Lane 2 and 3 he was superbly confident and never in any danger of dropping marks.'

By the end of the event Bill Nicholson had only dropped two marks, making him fourth overall and winner of the Bayliss Cup, awarded for the best Sunbac club member. When one considers that virtually every top trials star was there, this was an impressive debut ride. Other competitors included: Phil Alves, Hugh Viney, Charlie Rogers, Fred Rist, Vic and Johnny Brittain and even future World Champion Geoff Duke, plus the full works teams from not only BSA, but Norton, AJS, Matchless, Royal Enfield, Triumph and Ariel.

A PR Exercise at Small Heath

A few days after the Colmore Cup, budding young motorcyclists taking part in the RAC-ACU training scheme with the Derby Technical College visited the BSA works at Small Heath. Here they were able to meet works trials' stars Fred Rist and Bill Nicholson, the latter with the new A7 trialster.

Additional publicity came by way of an editorial by 'Nitor' in his 'On the Four Winds' column in *The Motor Cycle*, dated 26 February 1948, when he commented 'A couple of new competition models caught my eye during the Colmore Trial last Saturday, and I lost no time in booking a short flip on both of them.' The first was the new 346cc Royal Enfield Bullet with a swinging-arm frame. And in 'Nitor's' words:

> The other model was Bill Nicholson's A7 twin BSA which he had prepared for competition work. He has got the weight down to somewhere in the region of 280lb [127kg]. It handles like a machine weighing considerably less and on the ice I felt easily confident even when taking liberties. The low-speed pulling is altogether remarkable. The twin could be throttled down till the firing was as slow as a tick-over of which most of us would be mighty proud, yet there was no transmission snatch; and it would pull away smoothly and smartly. At the other end of the scale, the combination of light weight,

low gearing and inherent liveliness of the engine made the acceleration quite breathtaking. With the limited wheel grip I could find last Saturday it was an easy matter to raise the front wheel by tweaking the throttle. Nicholson likes his twin very much I'm fairly sure that before the year is out there will be other stars using twins for trials.

Another Good Performance

Nicholson put in another good performance on the new twin at the Kickham Trial, held by the Wessex Centre on 6 March 1948. In contrast to the awful conditions experienced a couple of weeks earlier, *The Motor Cycle* said 'the weather last Saturday was magnificent'. Two laps of the 30-mile (48km) circuit had to be covered. On each lap there were eight observed sections separated into more than twenty sub-sections. *The Motor Cycle* report said 'Fastest solo rider seen among the early numbers was W. Nicholson (495cc BSA Twin), who was clean and confident.'

Once again, the combination of Nicholson and the A7 were to come away with silverware, this time in the shape of the Unlimited cc Trophy, having lost twenty-one marks. The best overall performance had been put in by Hugh Viney's 498cc AJS with nine marks conceded. Nicholson's score also meant he finished runner-up in the solo results.

An Irish Victory

On 13 March the Hurst Cup Trial was held on the Clandeboye Estate, near Bangor, Northern Ireland. In many ways a speed event, and organized by the Knock MCC, the Hurst was staged over six laps of a 7½ mile (12km) circuit, each circuit having twenty-two observed sections. Therefore each of the fifty riders entered had the prospect of concentrating on a feet-up performance at 132 sections during the trial. Every section was worth ten marks for a clean, seven for one dab, three for footing and nought for stopping or running alongside. The course was described by *The Motor Cycle* as 'a tough

1948 BSA advertisement showing the factory's trials success, including Bill Nicholson's excellent showing in the Kickham Memorial Trial – best 500 and member of the Team Prize winning team.

one and, in spite of dry weather, offered plenty of mud as it became cut up'. At the end, Nicholson was proclaimed the winner of the Hurst Cup with 1,025 marks gained, minus fourteen lost on time = 1,011 marks total. He was also part of the victorious Manufacturer's Team Award (Fred Rist, R.T. Hill and Nicholson). Interestingly, not only was Geoff Duke (Norton) a competitor that day, but also Artie Bell (Norton) and Ernie Lyons (AJS).

The Victory Trial

Next came the Victory Trial, which was organized by the Birmingham club and held on 20 March 1948. Here Nicholson and the A7, together with team-mates Fred Rist and Harold Tozer, won the Watsonian Cup (for the best trade team). *The Motor Cycle* report once more had reason to praise the twin's performance: 'Star descent among the early numbers was that of W. Nicholson (495cc BSA), who was clean.'

Even though he crashed in one section, Nicholson still came out of the trial with only twenty-nine marks lost, which when one considers that the winner with the best performance had been J. Blackwell (490cc Norton) with twenty-one marks lost, this was a magnificent performance. The famous Bemrose Trial, staged in an area round Buxton in Derbyshire on 3 April 1948, was run in wintry conditions. This was won by Triumph star Phil Alves (eight marks lost); Nicholson lost thirteen marks to gain a First Class Award.

For the next trial, the Cotswold Cups on 10 April, Nicholson rode a B34 single for the first time that year and promptly won, with the only unpenalized performance. And after another victory in the Open Travers Trial later that month on the single-cylinder machine, Nicholson decided to mothball the prototype twin-cylinder model.

ISDT

During the early 1950s, Great Britain dominated the ISDT Trophy contest. The 1950 event had seen the event won with BSA's Fred Rist as team captain, riding a 499cc B34 Gold Star single.

For 1951, the event was to be staged around Varese in northern Italy. Again Rist was nominated as captain, but this time he was riding a 646cc A10 Golden Flash. The full team was as follows.

- F.M. Rist   646cc   BSA (Captain)
- B.H.M. Viney   498cc   AJS
- P.H. Alves   649cc   Triumph
- C.M. Ray   498cc   Ariel
- W.J. Stocker   496cc   Royal Enfield.

This was the twenty-sixth International Six Days' Trial. The event began on Tuesday, 18 September 1951, when a total of 246 miles (396km) was covered. For most of the six days mileages were about the same, with a mixture of on and off road going, with some of the latter being extremely tough. The final day, Sunday, 23 September, saw speed tests held at the Monza autodrome near Milan. And it is worth recalling that besides the established dirt-bike stars were several of the world's leading road racers who had taken part that year, including sidecar champion Eric Oliver (who rode an Italian Mi-Val solo), plus Georg Meier and Walter Zeller (both BMW mounted). With no marks lost, the British team emerged victorious after six gruelling days to take home the coveted Trophy for the fifteenth time.

The victorious British Trophy winning team for the 1951 ISDT. Left to right: Hugh Viney (AJS), Phil Alves (Triumph), Charlie Ray (Ariel), Bill Stocker (Royal Enfield) and team captain Fred Rist (BSA Golden Flash).

Fred Rist – Top Twins Rider

Fred Rist was a brilliant all-rounder, competing in a wide variety of competitive events, including road racing, the ISDT and sand racing. He also rode both A7- and A10-based machinery, when most other BSA works riders of the early post-war years chose the Gold Star single.

The very first motorcycle that Fred Rist rode – at the age of seven – was an open-frame lady's two-stroke Royal Enfield, on his father's poultry farm near Stokesley in North Yorkshire. On reaching the legal age he graduated to a 350 Coventry Eagle. Having learned about engineering through an apprenticeship at Dorman Long & Co, he embarked on this vocation, but soon yearned for the outdoor life, and joined the regular Army in 1934. Posted to the Royal Tank Corps base at Bovington, he continued his motorcycle career on a 350 AJS and then a 350 Humber, meeting up with the legendary T.E. Lawrence (Lawrence of Arabia) just before the latter died.

Whilst serving at Farnborough Rist volunteered to train for motorcycle trials, and as a result was selected to represent the Army in the 1938 and 1939 ISDTs. With BSA Competitions Manager Bert Perrigo looking after the interests of the Army bikes and riders, Fred Rist was soon elevated to a works rider for many British events. And the Tank Corps team of Rist, Doyle and Wood soon dominated the trials scene with a whole host of important victories. Their success was such that it resulted in one civilian rider complaining that serving soldiers should not be paid prize money. Fred's activities were curtailed with the declaration of war, when he found himself posted to the Western Desert, and then on to Italy, where he was to meet his future wife, Elvena.

When Rist was released from his Army duties he became an active member of the newly formed BSA team in 1947 and notched up many competition successes on the trials scene. Riding alcohol-burning Gold Star singles in grass-track and hill-climb events, Fred soon became the man to beat. Being a devoted clubman, the BSA rider used to ride bikes to and from all his meetings, in preference to being transported by the works van, carrying a straight piece of pipe in his haversack to replace the road-going silencer. His three-fifty Gold Star was also used for road races, and actually won a race at Scarborough.

Fred also excelled in other types of event, particularly sand racing, which was probably due to his Army experiences in the Western Desert, where he rode a number of captured German and Italian bikes. His debut on the sand back home came at the Welsh Speed Championships at Pendine in 1948. With the Gold Star running on alcohol again, Rist achieved a clean sweep of wins, with victories in all his races, including the main 1,000cc event. Having got a taste for the sand he campaigned other BSA models, notably an awesome 140mph (225km/h) dope-burning Golden Flash.

Such was Fred Rist's international competition experience that he was selected to captain the British team for the 1951 ISDT, held in Italy; riding a works A10 six-fifty twin he gained a gold medal. The final ISDT in which this great sportsman participated was in 1952, when, together with Brian Martin and Norman Vanhouse, he again won a gold medal. As related elsewhere in this chapter, the trio also won the team award (riding for the Birmingham MCC) on their A7 Star Twins, and went on to complete a 3,000-mile (4,827km) European tour to gain the coveted Maudes Trophy for the BSA factory. After this spectacular achievement Fred Rist stepped down to concentrate on his own motorcycle business in the South Wales township of Neath, before finally retiring in Teignmouth.

Fred Rist died in 1995 and was described by his team-mate, Norman Vanhouse, 'as one of the greatest and most versatile riders of the post-war era'.

A Fantastic Test

In the 11 September 1952 issue of *The Motor Cycle* it was reported that 'Three 498cc BSA Star Twins were ridden away from the works at Small Heath, Birmingham, last week for the start of an ACU-observed test of reliability.' This test was scheduled to take the bikes and riders on a 4,500 mile (7,240km) trip. This was the Continental European journey which was to include competing in the ISDT (held that year in Austria). After taking part in the trial, the machines would have at least a further 1,300 miles (2,090km) to cover and, at the end of the exercise, were to be put through a maximum speed test.

The motorcycles were selected off the production line by ACU observer, John McNulty, from a batch of thirty-seven Star Twins. Prior to leaving, the bikes were allowed certain modifications, expressly so that they could compete in the ISDT. The full list was as follows:

- rear wheel sprocket (and bearing) changed from forty-five teeth (standard solo size) to sidecar size with forty-nine teeth;
- rear chain length increased to suit larger sprocket;
- speedometer head replaced to suit altered sprocket;
- saddle removed and standard BSA dual seat fitted;
- pillion footrests fitted (for speed test);
- clock fitted;
- ISDT-type number plates fitted;
- tank-top toolbag fitted;
- oil tank, gearbox and primary chaincase drained and refilled with Essolube 40 oil;
- petrol tank drained and refilled with Esso fuel;
- holes for ISDT sealing drilled in the cylinder head, cylinder barrel and crankcase.

Countries included in the route to be followed were Holland, Belgium, France, Switzerland, Austria, Germany, Denmark, Sweden and Norway. On 17 September 1952 the bikes were to be handed in for ISDT scrutineering and sealing at Bad Aussee.

The route to Bad Aussee was by way of Harwich, The Hague, Antwerp, Paris (where the oil was to be changed at approximately 500 miles/800km), Geneva, Zürich and Innsbruck. At the finish of the trial (providing of course they actually achieved this!) on 23 September, the machines would be handed to the supervision of the observer, and thereafter would travel via Stuttgart, Dusseldorf, Kiel, Copenhagen, Malmö and Gothenburg to Oslo. This test programme would finish in Oslo with the speed runs on 30 September. As for riders, BSA chose Fred Rist, Norman Vanhouse and Brian Martin.

The Trial

As for the trial itself, a background is provided by *The Motor Cycle* report, dated 25 September 1952:

Before the International Six Days' Trial began last Thursday, Bad Aussee, the headquarters town in Austria, was probably to most people no more than a name. Competitors and officials converging upon the town before the trial started found it a small, beautiful and hospitable spa, situated in what writers of travel brochures describe as 'a bijou setting'. Set 45 road miles [72km] east of Salzburg, Bad Aussee lies 1,700 metres [5,500ft] above sea level. To the north is the lake Altaussee, to the north-west another lake, Grundlsee, and to the south-east yet another, the largest of the three, Hallstattersee. On a fine day, the surrounding area exudes peace and tranquillity. Fir- and pine-clad slopes drop steeply from the mountain heights to the edges of the lakes. Slopes are so steep that the trees seem to tumble headlong into the cold, translucent waters which take their colour from the sky. Boulder-strewn gullies wriggle up into the heights until they fade from sight. Wooden houses with wide, overhanging eaves dot the fresh, rich green of the lower slopes. Even in September, snow patches cap the topmost peaks.

And this ISDT was a tough one, certainly for larger capacity machines. For example, the Germans, it was said, had decided to employ lightweights after experience on the course had shown the speed schedules to be impossible for a capable rider mounted on a 500cc BMW. Many even maintained that the routes would be so severe in parts that the British teams would never reach the final speed test intact!

Over 260 riders weighed in before the start, making it one of the largest entries in ISDT history up to that time. *The Motor Cycle* reported: 'Men with long ISDT experience present in Bad Aussee maintained that competition in the Trophy and Vase contests had never been keener.'

On the evening before the trial got under way, the sun went down 'in a blaze of golden scarlet and promised fine weather for the first day of the Trial'. However, it was not to be, and by the start the following morning 'rain sleeted down. It was a poor outlook for a 280-mile [450km] run mainly on rough tracks and roads.'

And in fact as *The Motor Cycle* reported there was 'very wet weather for five days of the Trial', over an 'arduous course' with 'heavy retirements'. However, by the fourth day it was commented 'performing impressively were members of the Birmingham club team – F.M. Rist, B.W. Martin and N.E. Vanhouse – riding their standard ACU-observed BSA twins. The team was the only one from Britain still intact,

manufacturers team included.' Whilst the fifth-day report said 'The BSAs of Rist, Vanhouse and Martin were still running well and in as prime condition as any machines in the Trial.'

The Motor Cycle described the final day thus:

> The closing stages of an International Six Days' Trial are always severe. In this instance, men and machines had taken near-brutal punishment for

---

The International Six Days' Trial

In December 1897 the Automobile Club of Great Britain and Ireland (ACGBI) was founded to look after the interests of the early motorist. No distinction was made at that time between four-, three- or two-wheel vehicles.

These early motorists were a sporting bunch and in 1900 the ACGBI ran the 'Great 1,000 Mile Trial'. Amongst its entrants were a pair of quadricycles, two motor tricycles and a tricycle with a trailer. A couple of French Werner motorcycles were also entered but didn't start. By 1903 the development of the motorcycle was such that ninety-three members of the motorcycle branch of the parent body set up the Auto Cycle Union. In the very first year of its existence, the ACU organized a 1,000 mile (1,600km) trial, which became an annual event as the ACU Six Days' Reliability Trial. The object of the event was to demonstrate the advantages of one machine over another. In 1913 it was decided to incorporate the FICM rules, and thus the first International Touring Trial began.

This event in 1913 is generally regarded as the first ISDT (International Six Days' Trial) and the ancestor to not only this famous event, but also of its ultimate successor, the International Six Days' Enduro (ISDE).

The organization of the 1913 event, held under ACU direction, was in the hands of the Westmorland and Cumberland County Motor Cycle Club. The only national teams were from Britain and France, the former providing the winning trio of W.G. Gibb, Billy Little and Charlie Collier (he of Matchless fame). The 1914 event would have been the first full International, but was cancelled due to the outbreak of war, so the next event did not take place until 1920. Based in France, Switzerland took the coveted Trophy – the same country going on to win again for the next two years.

The 1920s were a period of technical development and progress, and there was a parallel growth in the size and status of the ISDT. The 1929 event was uniquely staged as the International Six Days' Trial – Munich – Geneva and was generally regarded as the greatest motorcycle reliability trial ever held.

The 1930s was to see Great Britain, Germany and Italy as the dominating countries as regards the Trophy (team) contest. The 1939 event was marred by what was to become known as the Salzburg Incident. Back in March 1938, Hitler had marched into Austria, which then became a German province. This fact obviously confused much of the foreign press, which could not make up its collective mind in 1939 whether Salzburg, the headquarters of the ISDT that year, was in Austria or Germany. And so it came to pass that German and British riders were to sit side-by-side in the sun at Salzburg in late August 1939. The trial got under way and for the first few days everything went to plan, but by midweek rumours abounded about the political situation, to the extent that many foreign competitors, including the British, left for home before the final day. The German Trophy team won, but this did not matter, as war broke out a few short days later, and the results were declared void by the FIM in 1946.

The first post-war ISDT was held in Czechoslovakia in 1947. The host country won both the Trophy and Vase contests.

Then came a run of British successes, the last in 1953. During this period BSA twins and singles were not only to help win the national awards, but also to gain a large number of individual medals. Amongst these successes were none greater than the trio of BSA riders, Fred Rist, Brian Martin and Norman Vanhouse, who, riding essentially production Star Twins, not only won golds, but also the coveted Maudes Trophy.

But from the mid-1950s, due mainly to rule changes that tended to favour small lightweights, machines such as the BSA twins were to be found in the Six Days' less and less. Much of the 1960s belonged to the all-conquering

---

East Germans. Using their MZ two-strokes to full advantage they won no fewer than six Trophy contests in that decade. In a similar way, the 1970s was the era of the Czechs astride their purposeful Jawa machines. These, like the MZs, were two-stroke singles of various capacities.

The final ISDT was held in Brioude, central France, in 1980. From then on it became the International Six Days' Enduro, and instead of the road-based machinery of earlier days, the bikes had become virtually full-blown motocross racers with the bare minimum of equipment to make them legal on the highway. Gone were the great days when the world looked on as virtually every motorcycling nation battled for honours on domestically built bikes with which the general public was familiar – bikes, in fact, such as the A7 and A10 BSA twins.

The three B.S.A.s leave the factory—following them in the car is the A.C.U. observer, Mr. J. McNulty.

BSA advertisement for the successful teamsters.

The Maudes Trophy

The Maudes Trophy was for over fifty years the pinnacle of achievement to which manufacturers would aim. Its purpose was to be a much-valued award for an outstanding feat of reliability, economy and endurance, and it began in 1923 as something to offset the concentration upon speed events that had sprung up after the First World War. These involved not just road races such as the TT and Brooklands, but hill climbing, sand and grass track, plus the ever greater pursuit of speed by record-breaking attempts.

Unfortunately, although enthusiasts loved the glamour of speed, the general public was far less keen, often giving rise to negative publicity regarding motorcycling in general. This deeply concerned a good section of the motorcycle industry itself, who felt that something was needed to prove that motorcycles offered a serious form of transport rather than simply acting as a speed vehicle.

This led George Pettyt, the owner of Maudes Motor Mart, Exeter, to present the ACU with a distinctive and valuable silver vase. Originally entitled the Pettyt Cup, this was later renamed the Maudes Trophy. The original concept was that this should be awarded annually to the company 'whose observed and certified test was considered by the ACU to be the best that year, provided it reached an acceptable standard'. To begin with, manufacturers devised exceedingly challenging tests. These usually entailed selecting from stock (under the eye of ACU officials), or in some cases even building up motorcycles from spares on a dealers' shelves, the essence being to prove the quality and reliability of the British motorcycle industry.

Cover from the booklet produced to celebrate the Maudes Trophy victory in 1952.

The first winner of this coveted trophy was Norton. In fact, the company's boss, James Landsdown Norton (but known throughout the trade as 'Pa'), was a great supporter of the event. Following its victory in 1923, Norton went on to record more Maudes Trophy successes, in 1924 and 1925.

BSA's first Maudes Trophy victory came in early 1926, when a 350 Sports, with ohv single-cylinder engine, selected from random on the production line, was married up to a sidecar, then set on no fewer than sixty consecutive assents of the tortuous Welsh Bwlch-Y-Bala mountain pass. With an ACU observer in the chair, Harry Perrey achieved the task with only minor glitches. The company's Managing Director, Godfrey Herbert, was also there to witness the event – and even did an 'honorary' sixty-first climb to show BSA's confidence.

Then it was the turn of the Ariel marque, who won in 1927 and 1928. Next came Dunelt with victories in 1929 and 1930; Ariel took it back in 1931.

The Maudes was not awarded in 1932, but Triumph won in 1933 and Panther in 1934. Then came another break before Triumph was successful in 1937.

BSA's second success came in February 1938. From the official factory dealer list two machines were selected, an M23 Empire Star and an M21 sidecar outfit. These then travelled to Snowdonia, where they took part in twenty non-stop climbs of Bwlch-Y-Groes (considered to be probably the toughest of toughest climbs in Great Britain). Then they returned south to the Brooklands circuit, where the M21 outfit undertook 100 laps, averaging 16.12mph (74.2km/h), whilst the solo completed the 100 laps averaging 58.57mph (94.2km/h). Then it was back to Bwlch-Y-Groes for another twenty ascents. Finally, as a means of demonstrating the flexibility of the machines, both were driven through London during traffic hours from north to south and east to west, using only top gear and the clutch!

In 1939 Triumph won back the trophy, with Panther and BSA also making attempts.

After the Second World War, interest in the Trophy waned for several years until in 1952 BSA decided that it was time to reclaim it. As Ray Bacon described in his book *BSA Twins & Triples*, 'The BSA plan was simple, if audacious. It was to take three stock Star Twins and run them over nearly 5,000 miles (8,045km) of European roads under strict supervision. The catch was that they would include the International Six Days' Trial en route.' And as described in the main text of this book, Brian Martin, Fred Rist and Norman Vanhouse not only completed the test – but also sensationally won the ISDT team trophy.

Thereafter the Maudes Trophy lapsed until the mid-1960s, when a team of riders mounted on Japanese Honda machines won. This was followed during the 1970s by another team, this time riding a pair of the new BMW R75 seven-fifty flat twins, which circulated the Isle of Man TT circuit for seven days and nights to take the trophy. But the BMW effort was to be the last such attempt. In recent years the famous Maudes Trophy seems to have passed into the history books, rather than remaining as an ongoing exercise that the industry could continue to embrace.

five hectic days. Bodies and brains were tired, and most machines were the worse for wear. It was hoped that, at least, the weather might improve for the 77 miles [124 km] along the Anif Autobahn where the one-hour speed test was to be held. But when Tuesday dawned and competitors were easing tired bodies out of bed, the rain lashed down with as much fury as during the first three days and Monday. Roads glistened black under the ominous, grey skies. How anyone would average the scheduled speed for five-hundreds [62.8mph – 100km/h] in such conditions, seemed inconceivable.

At the end, the incredible fact was that all three BSA riders had completed the entire six days without losing a single mark, and in the process had each gained FIM Gold Medals!

Awarding the Maudes Trophy

At a meeting on Thursday, 9 October 1952, the trio were awarded the Maudes Trophy – or at least BSA was – by the ACU committee.

After the ISDT was over, the test continued through Germany, Denmark, Sweden and Norway, finally being concluded by speed runs at Oslo aerodrome over a distance of 400m (almost a quarter of a mile). Standing-start figures showed a mean speed of 49.99mph (80.43km/h) for the three machines respectively. Flying start speeds were 82.12mph (132.13km/h), 84.43mph (135.85km/h) and 80.27mph (129.15km/h). The best speed achieved from a standing start – one-way speed – was 51.44mph (82.77km/h); and the best flying-start speed – one way – was 85.23mph (137.14km/h).

Servicing Requirements

During the long run through Europe and Scandinavia, normal servicing requirements were attended to – for example, inspection of tyres and chains, lubrication and so on. In the ISDT the machines were ridden under the normal rules appertaining to the trial, which meant that components were marked and, therefore, could not be replaced. The only replacements required during the time the machines were under the jurisdiction of the ACU observer were, according to the official report, as follows:

- two headlamp bulbs replaced;
- three tail lamp bulbs replaced;
- two frayed rearlamp lighting leads replaced;
- one replacement primary chain filler cap replaced;
- two petrol tanks repaired by welding;
- loose horn lead refixed on one bike.

During the final speed test at Oslo, the main jets of two machines were found to be partially blocked – both were cleaned out and replaced.

Fuel and oil were supplied by Esso and all filling-up was from Esso service stations in both Britain and Continental Europe, except in Vienna where no Esso branded products were available. During the ISDT, Esso products were obtained from the official ISDT refuelling depots.

Standard BSA equipment and accessories were used. These included:

- Dunlop tyres and tubes;
- Renold chains;
- Ferodo brake and clutch linings;
- Amal carburettors;
- Smith's instruments;
- Tecalemit grease nipples;
- Champion sparking plugs;
- Lucas electrical equipment.

The official presentation of the Maudes Trophy was made on the eve of the London Earls Court Show on Friday, 14 November 1952 at the RAC headquarters in the city. Besides the three riders, those attending included BSA Sales Director, S.F. Digby, James Leek, the BSA Managing Director, and Professor A.M. Low on behalf of the RAC.

The whole exercise had been a magnificent achievement. Harry Louis, editor of *The Motor Cycle*, in his editorial of 16 October 1952 had this to say:

The Swedish team on their BSAs, winners of the 1955 Moto Cross Championship at Randers, Denmark. Later in the USA, a version of the Gold Star Scrambler was sold with the six-fifty A10 type twin-cylinder engine.

At a time when the pains of the changeover from a sellers' to a buyers' market are becoming acute, it is salutary that a manufacturer has had the courage to embark on a test under ACU observation. As reported on a later page, for the first time since 1939 a manufacturer has staged a test to qualify under the rules of the Maudes Trophy, and has proved successful. The fact that there was no competition from other manufacturers in no way detracts from the achievement. The test of three standard machines over almost 5,000 miles [8,045km], which included the arduous International Six Days' Trial in Austria, was clearly ambitious and deserves the highest recognition.

Scrambling and Sand Racing

Besides the A7 trials prototype and the successful Maudes Trophy-winning Star Twin trio, the BSA twin was also campaigned in scrambling and sand-racing events.

The arrival of the larger A10 Golden Flash six-fifty for the 1950 season meant that BSA had a more powerful big twin. Its most successful use came in the hands of Fred Rist, who not only rode one of the new models when he captained the British Trophy team in the 1951 ISDT, as already recorded, but also built a

dope-burning, 140mph (225km/h) A10-powered missile to compete in sand-racing events such as Pendine and St Andrews. This machine was probably the fastest sand racer of its era and Rist's antics on it were legendary to anyone who witnessed his achievements.

As for scrambling the A10, this was tried by Basil Hall (another of BSA's works stars who had joined the Birmingham marque in 1950) at international level in 1951, but he was forced to admit that it was 'too vicious' and after a few outings the A10 was discarded.

On Three Wheels

The A10 also was successful as a sidecar machine. British Sidecar Trials Champion, Harold Tozer (passengered by Jack Wilkes), crewed a beige-coloured Golden Flash outfit in the 1950 ISDT. Tozer and Wilkes went on to put in a brilliant performance, winning one of only three gold medals awarded that year to sidecar outfits in the event.

This, the twenty-fifth International Six Days' Trial, was staged around Llandrindod Wells in Radnorshire, Wales, and was run in what were described as 'extremely unsettled weather conditions'.

6 Golden Flash

Together with the Gold Star and Bantam, the Golden Flash is one of the truly classic BSA models of the Birmingham marque's great days in the boom years following the end of the Second World War in 1945 until the beginning of the 1960s, when the once great British

The plunger-frame Golden Flash at the time of its launch in late 1949. With 70 × 84mm bore and stroke dimensions, the engine displaced 646cc.

During the 1920s BSA offered the Model E (771cc) and Model F (986cc) side-valve V-twins. Largely intended for sidecar duties, these machines gave sterling service.

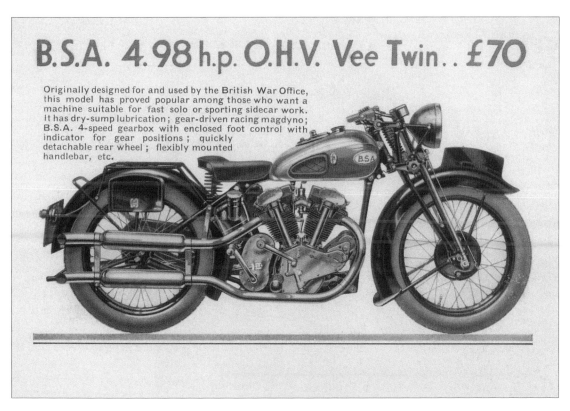

B.S.A. 4.98 h.p. O.H.V. Vee Twin.. £70

Originally designed for and used by the British War Office, this model has proved popular among those who want a machine suitable for fast solo or sporting sidecar work. It has dry-sump lubrication; gear-driven racing magdyno; B.S.A. 4-speed gearbox with enclosed foot control with indicator for gear positions; quickly detachable rear wheel; flexibly mounted handlebar, etc.

Originally designed for the British War Office, this 498cc (63 × 80mm) 45-degree V-twin was offered to civilian customers for the 1935 model year onwards. It was a particularly attractive machine for its day.

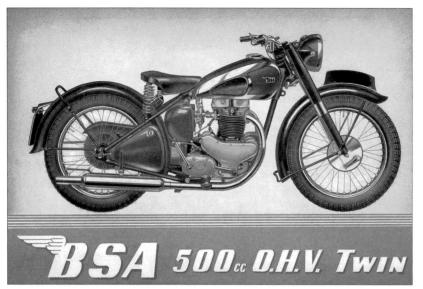

BSA 500cc O.H.V. TWIN

ABOVE LEFT: *The BSA vertical twin, in the shape of the brand-new A7, arrived in October 1946, costing £171 9s including UK purchase tax.*

ABOVE: *Rigid-framed A7, circa 1949. Customers could have also ordered (at extra cost) plunger rear suspension.*

THE MOTOR CYCLE

4⁴

Leader of the World's Leading Range of Motor Cycles

BSA

Model A7 500 c.c. VERTICAL TWIN
with many outstanding features.

The complete B.S.A. range from 125 c.c. to 500 c.c. caters for every motor cyclist. Write for new catalogue.

YOUR FIRST CALL — THE CENTRE OF THE SHOW AND THE CENTRE OF ATTRACTION

LEAVE IT TO YOUR BSA

November 1948 BSA advertisement for the Model A7 500cc Vertical Twin, with Earls Court in the background.

May 1950 'Measure You for a Motor Cycle?' advertisement showing that BSA could offer the potential customer a complete range of models, by now including 500 and 650cc twins.

The 1950 A10 Golden Flash, a new addition to the range that year and soon to become a top seller.

ABOVE: 'BSA Golden Flash' tank badge.

In the autumn of 1952 a trio of Star Twins won the coveted Maudes Trophy for an extended 5,000-mile trip across Europe – including taking part in the ISDT.

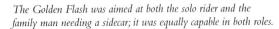

The Golden Flash was aimed at both the solo rider and the family man needing a sidecar; it was equally capable in both roles.

New for the 1953 model year, the five-hundred Shooting Star replaced the Star Twin as BSA's sports model in this class.

From the Bantam
to the Golden Flash

BSA

makes the Show

The centre of admiration
the B.S.A. Shooting Star
500 twin with new
swinging arm
suspension.

ABOVE: *The 1954 model year also saw the arrival of the A7 Shooting Star with the new swinging-arm frame.*

RIGHT: *A nicely restored 1960 Super Rocket with alloy cylinder head and after-market rear carrier.*

OVERLEAF:
BSA 'The Most Popular Motor Cycle in the World'. Absolutely true when this two-page advertisement appeared in the Show Issue of Motor Cycling dated 11 November 1954. The bike is the newly released swinging-arm framed A10 Golden Flash.

FIRST

from 125 c.c. BANTAM
to GOLDEN FLASH
650 c.c. Twin

BSA 650

BSA

THE MOST POPULAR MOTOR CYCLE
IN THE WORLD

Send coupon for the Catalogue showing full range from the 125 Bantam to the Golden Flash 650 Twin to :

B.S.A. Motor Cycles Ltd.,
48, Armoury Road, Birmingham, 11

NAME ....

ADDRESS..

FOREMOST

BSA 650 OHV TWIN MODEL A10 SUPER ROCKET

£280. 19s. 2d.
including £51. 19s. 2d.
purchase tax and surcharge

This view shows the robust construction of the flywheel assembly on the Golden Flash and Super Rocket models which has been specially developed to handle the enormous power output of these engines.

An exceptionally fast, safe standard road machine, the Super Rocket has a specially tuned and brake-tested engine, improved light alloy cylinder head with high compression pistons, reinforced crankshaft, sports camshaft, etc. It is undoubtedly the world's greatest motor cycle, and to get the feel of this powerful 650 engine when the twistgrip is turned is to know the thrill of road supremacy at its best.

"A full-blooded sports machine with a docility and economy which make it entirely suitable for everyday use"—that's what "Motor Cycling" says about the Super Rocket.

The re-designed drive provided for the rev-counter which is available on the Super Rocket is neater, more compact and less vulnerable than the previous design. It is taken from the front of the timing case and is directly coupled through a dog drive to the oil pump spindle which is adapted for this purpose. All Super Rocket engines are fitted with the special pump in readiness to receive the rev-counter drive.

A Super Rocket from the BSA range brochure published in October 1961.

The sensational Rocket Gold Star – a successful marriage of Gold Star cycle parts and a tuned 646cc Super Rocket engine – it arrived in spring 1962.

motorcycle industry began what was to turn out to be a terminal decline. But during its lifetime the A10 Golden Flash stood supreme as the ultimate 650cc-class touring motorcycle – equally suitable for fast intercontinental solo work or sidecar duties.

The A10 Arrives

The issue of *Motor Cycling* dated 6 October 1949 (together with *The Motor Cycle*) brought to the public's attention the arrival of a newcomer that would not only earn worldwide sales and prestige for its makers, but genuine love and affection from its enthusiastic owners:

> Of the 1950 BSA programme it can be truly said that it offers the most comprehensive and widely differing range of motorcycles that has emanated from one factory since the boom days of the 1920s. Although every machine in the catalogue is modernized right up to the minute – and several old favourites are available in new, alternative forms – it will undoubtedly be on the very latest addition to the range, the A10 Golden Flash vertical twin, that attention will principally be focused when Earls Court visitors arrive at the BSA stand.

Technical Details

Technically speaking, although the new six-fifty bore a strong resemblance to the by now firmly established 495cc A7, and many of the same parts were employed in its design, the engine had numerous important differences from A7 practice.

Bore and stroke dimensions of the new engine were 70 × 84mm, as opposed to the 62 × 82mm of the A7 at that time, giving a displacement of 646cc. The crankcases of the A10 and A7 were not interchangeable, even though it was possible to change the respective engines in the frame (either rigid or plunger). And it should be noted that internally the dimensions of the A10 crankcases (still of aluminium, two-piece, vertically split) were different, not only due to the increase in width between the centres of the cylinder bores, but also because the crankshaft was longer.

Like the existing A7, the crankshaft of the A10 was a one-piece design with a bolted-on central flywheel. It was a high-grade steel forging comprising the two mainshafts, two crank webs, the big-end journals, and the central flywheel flange. Half a dozen bolts connected the

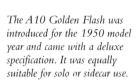

The A10 Golden Flash was introduced for the 1950 model year and came with a deluxe specification. It was equally suitable for solo or sidecar use.

forged-steel flywheel to the crankshaft flange. Bobweights for balancing were incorporated in the flywheel and crank webs. And again A7 practice was seen by way of crankshaft support, a ball-race bearing on the drive side and a plain bearing on the timing side. The journals of the plain bearing were, said BSA, 'induction-hardened, ground and polished'.

Light-Alloy Connecting Rods

The early A7 had one-piece steel connecting-rods (later replaced by steel split-type), but right from the start the A10 had light-alloy (RR56) con-rods with conventional split big-ends, the big-end bolts being of high-tensile nickel chrome steel. The 1.46in (37mm) big-end bearings were of indium-flashed lead bronze. The retaining bolts used castellated nuts and were split-pinned. Con-rods were of H-section and measured 6½in (165mm) between centres.

Although the timing gear design was on A7 lines, the camshafts (still positioned at the rear of the crankcase) were not interchangeable. The cams were wider than on the smaller-capacity engine, and car-type barrel tappets with chilled rubbing surfaces were employed. The outer timing cover was of similar, but not identical, design to that on the existing A7.

A New Cylinder Head Design

As with the A7, the one-piece cast-iron cylinder block had the pushrods running centrally at the rear, the pushrod tunnel being cast integrally. The cylinder head was of an entirely new design, with revised finning to provide additional cooling. It also had narrower angle valves (58 degrees) than the five-hundred, and a flatter, shallower combustion chamber, which BSA said was 'nearer to the ideal since the ratio of the combustion surface area should always

Although based on the existing A7, the A10 had many notable new features – these being adopted to a large extent in the later A7 series machines.

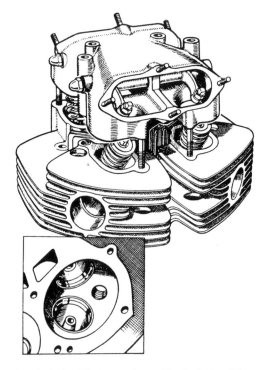

The cylinder head design was changed for the A10 and the Mark 2 A7. There were now elongated inspection covers on the rocker box.

be as high as possible'. In line with the low octane fuels available at the time, the compression ratio was 6.5:1. Besides the 'official' BSA statement there were in fact several real advantages in adopting the new valve angle for the A10. These included a flat combustion chamber, which in conjunction with a concave piston top improved the shape of the total combustion space and was a step towards the spherical ideal. The 6.5:1 compression ratio had been achieved without a dome-top piston and the attendant complications of valve pockets. Gas flow and porting were improved. It was also possible to employ shorter rocker arms and, owing to the reduced weight, springs with a lower seat pressure could be used – all leading to a reduction in valve noise.

In place of the A7's pair of rocker boxes, there was a single rocker box on the A10. Access for valve adjustment was via a pair of elongated polished alloy plates (one for the exhaust and one for the inlet). Each of these covers was retained by four ¼in (6.4mm) nuts. As with the A7, there were dual coil springs for each valve. Oil drainage of the rocker gear was via internal oilways in the cylinder head and cylinder barrel castings.

Rocker spindles were of the fixed type, drilled axially and radially for lubrication purposes. The rockers themselves are of case-hardened, unbushed steel, bearing directly on the rocker spindles. The new head had the induction manifold cast integrally with it, and a single Amal 276 1¹⁄₁₆in (27mm) carburettor was specified, having a downdraught of 7 degrees.

Although the basic lubrication system was unchanged in the timing case, the diameter of the timed breather was smaller and its path to the open air more tortuous as it travelled, by drillways, across the timing cover and through both crankcase halves to a pipe that ran from a point above the camshaft nearside (left) bearing housing down behind the crankcase casting, just forward of the final drive sprocket, before exiting to the left of the sump cover.

There was now a new, longer dynamo of increased capacity and at the same time the electrical system had been changed from negative to positive earth. The method of drive and the placement of the dynamo remained unchanged.

Also unchanged was the semi-unit construction of the BSA-made four-speed gearbox and its fixed-length primary chain. In fact, because of this all the A7 and A10 models that featured either rigid or plunger frames not only used the semi-unit gearbox, but also identical engine and clutch sprockets. The change in gearing between the 500 and 650cc engine was actually achieved by way of the final drive sprockets (gearbox and rear wheel). This was not to change until the new swinging-arm frame was introduced in late 1954. The early A10 models (in both rigid or plunger-frame guises) used essentially the same cycle parts as the A7 series of the same era.

A More Powerful Front Brake

Although tyre sizes remained the same at 3.25 × 19 and 3.50 × 19 front and rear respectively, to cope with the increase in performance a new front brake was fitted to the A10, measuring 8in × 1⅜in (203 × 35mm). The drum was manufactured as a Millenite casting (Millenite being a high-grade iron alloy that offered a high degree of rigidity and superior fatigue resistance, according to BSA sources). The shoes and brake shoe plate were of aluminium alloy, the latter being webbed internally and heavily ribbed externally.

At its launch date in early October 1949, the standard (rigid-framed) A10 cost £152 (for export) and £193 0s 10d (with UK taxes). A plunger-framed bike cost an additional £10 (£12 14s with UK tax).

A Debut at Earls Court

Although advance details of the A10 had been published in early October, it was not until the end of that month and the opening of the London Earls Court Show that the new BSA twin was actually put on display to the general public. *The Motor Cycle* show issue, dated

27 October 1949, said of the Golden Flash: 'It is being referred to as one of the smartest machines in the mighty hall. The finish is polychromatic beige and chromium. On the tank is an attractive motif with red BSA lettering and a zig-zag flash of lightning.' Another report on the show commented:

> You can see it complete, and also the engine in section – the new BSA 650cc overhead-valve Golden Flash (Stand 40). Externally, this model bears a strong resemblance to the already established 500cc twin model A7. Probably the quickest way to identify the two machines is to note the difference in the cylinder head and rocker box design. The larger engine has narrower-angle valves and shallower combustion chambers; a new finning arrangement gives improved cooling. Another difference is that the Golden Flash A10 has a single-piece rocker box.

Why 650cc?

In the 27 April 1950 issue of *The Motor Cycle*, George Wilson interviewed Herbert (Bert) Hopwood (BSA's then Chief Designer) and David Munro (Development Engineer) regarding the pre-production stages of the A10 Golden Flash.

Wilson's first question was 'Why 650?' And 'Why not go to 750 or 800c, or even 1000cc? Why, indeed, increase on 500cc? ...' As George Wilson went on to say: 'Their answers amounted to what I expected; the usual reason for a major change – public demand!'

In this case, the demand for a larger than 500cc engine came particularly from overseas buyers and sidecar men; and as for the type of machine, a mount with a bigger engine would, of course, be a very economical proposition from a production point of view, if it retained as many as possible of the 500cc A7's best features.

Fixing the Displacement

As for fixing the exact displacement of the power unit this, Messrs Hopwood and Munro admitted, 'was not easy'. Their main concern had been as to whether a parallel twin of over, say, 600cc 'could be satisfactorily balanced'. Experiments with singles had shown that an engine of just under 600cc had 'markedly better balance than a similar engine of slightly greater than 600cc capacity'. Hopwood said he had had experience with a 600cc vertical twin that he 'liked immensely'. He felt that 600cc was as high as he could go 'without prejudicing smoothness' and that 'an additional 50cc would be the absolute limit'.

So, with the decision reached, a stock A7 was 'bored out and used for 18 months'. Its first long outing took place when the bike was ridden from Birmingham to the Lancs Grand National Scramble in 1948. Thereafter it covered 'approximately 20,000 miles [32,180km]'. Mystery surrounds this prototype, in that Hopwood simply used the term 'bored out' to increase the displacement, whereas the A10 used bore and stroke dimensions of 70 × 84mm, the A7 from 1946 to late 1950 used 62 × 82mm and from then on 66 × 72.6mm. Or did the original 'bored-out' A7 have a capacity considerably less than 650cc? Hopwood continued:

> Doubts about possible poor balance snags were completely dispelled. There was excellent power right through the range. It was then decided that the design of a new engine could go ahead. Though retaining as many of the A7's features as practicable, the new engine would obviously incorporate whatever features were considered advisable in view of the increased power output.

Bert Hopwood says he laid down the original 'scheme' on paper, this task taking 'about three days'. His priorities were:

> a new and more efficiently cooled cylinder head, increased-section crankcases and crank cheeks, and larger-diameter main bearings. In order to keep the weight of the reciprocating masses down, light alloy connecting rods were decided upon. The centres of the cylinders had to be spread for additional air space and new tappets were designed.

Passing the 'Scheme' to the Sub-Designer

Next Hopwood revealed that the 'scheme' was passed to 'the sub-designer'. This was actually Herbert Perkins, who since Hopwood's arrival at BSA (in early 1949) had been 'demoted to Assistant Chief Designer'. Again, here one sees the possibility of events actually being slightly different to how Hopwood had explained them during *The Motor Cycle* interview with George Wilson that was published in April 1950. As *The Motor Cycle* reported in its 17 March 1949 issue, 'Mr H. Hopwood, the designer, until recently with Nortons, has joined the design staff at BSAs.' So was the real truth that Hopwood didn't do quite as much of the initial planning work as has been made out since? As the personalities at the centre of this particular controversy have now all passed on, the real truth is unlikely to come to the surface.

In his book *BSA – The Complete Story*, Owen Wright has this to say:

> The A10 was one of the great all-time feats of design and manufacture, carried out at a hectic pace. Seldom did any other machine go together

1951–2 plunger frame A10 Golden Flash, in standard guise except aftermarket screen, carrier and top box.

so easily and pass through the test and development section with so few snags. By August (1949), the prototype (pre-production) engines had been on the dynamometer (worked by the famous Jack Amott) and had shown 35bhp on the scale against

a crankshaft speed of 5,700rpm. A team of three riders working in interminable shifts ran up 12,800 miles (20,600km) in just three weeks.

Although much useful development work had been done on the dyno, actual testing to determine the reliability of the engine and cycle parts under ordinary working conditions – and thus examine the quietness of the engine and exhaust, to carburation, response to controls, vibration and cooling were of vital importance – was still to be carried out. This side of the operation was headed by Len Crisp. Although some of the problems had been tackled when the engine was on the test bench, it was the conditions experienced out on the road with the engine in the frame that were the final process in the whole development phase. As George Wilson put it: 'Gone, for instance, is the constant forced draught and the tendency for the engine to be run at constant speed and load – the static conditions of the test bed.'

But whatever else may be said of the A10's development history, what is without doubt is that the whole process passed more smoothly than most projects. Obviously, this was made easier by already having a template in the shape of the existing A7 five-hundred twin.

A Long Weekend

By early 1950 production of the new A10 was proceeding apace, with deliveries being made both at home and abroad. And so that man George Wilson of *The Motor Cycle* once again was able to write a six-page article (in the issues dated 17 and 24 August 1950) on the new BSA six-fifty twin. Entitled 'Long Week-End', it described the tale of a round-Britain trip with a Golden Flash (with plunger frame) and side-car – 2,212 miles (3,559km) covered between Thursday morning and Monday evening!

The trip began and ended at Feridax House, Frederick Street, Birmingham, due to the fact that accessory mogul Jim Ferriday's company had been instrumental not only in providing components such as the experimental dual

1950 A10 Golden Flash

Engine	Air-cooled, ohv vertical twin, 360-degree crank, single camshaft at rear of crankcase, cast-iron cylinder head and barrel, bolt-on rocker box covers, aluminium vertically split crankcases
Bore	70mm
Stroke	84mm
Displacement	646cc
Compression ratio	6.5:1
Lubrication	Dry sump, with oil pump featuring worm drive, a pressure relief valve screwed into the crankcase
Ignition	Magneto
Carburettor	Amal 276 1$\frac{1}{16}$in (27mm)
Primary drive	Duplex chain
Final drive	Chain
Gearbox	Bolt-up, four-speed, foot-change
Frame	All-steel construction, double front downtube
Front suspension	BSA telescopic, oil-damped forks
Rear suspension	Rigid or plunger
Front brake	8in (203mm) single-sided hub
Rear brake	7in (178mm) single-sided hub
Tyres	Front 3.25 × 19; rear 3.50 × 19

General Specifications

Wheelbase	55in (1,397mm)
Ground clearance	4.5in (114mm)
Seat height	30in (762mm)
Fuel tank capacity	4.25gal (19ltr)
Dry weight	Plunger 408lb (185kg); rigid 380lb (172kg)
Maximum power	35bhp @ 5,500rpm
Top speed	100mph (160km/h)

A BSA dealership yard in Glasgow during the early 1950s; the bikes include various singles plus several A7 and A10 models.

seat, but also a prototype of a new screen. Fer-riday had in fact accompanied Wilson on this epic journey, which took in England, Scotland and Wales.

In response to Wilson's personal request, BSA had provided a machine with 'manual ignition control, a special handlebar bend, pillion rest of the type supplied to oversea police forces'. A single-seat sidecar was fitted. Very early on in the journey two problems were encountered: picking up of the layshaft bushes (which recurred a few miles later, but then never came

back), and then a piston tightened up. Again, this was not experienced again – once the engine had been allowed to cool down. It should be pointed out that Wilson had been told that the engine and gearbox were fully run-in. But as he said after the second problem:

This time realization dawned! The engine-gear unit had obviously not been sufficiently run-in! So when the job had cooled off a shade, we set off again, keeping the speed in the region of 50–55mph [80–88km/h] on the straights, working up to that fairly quietly, and letting the engine turn over easily. With these tactics the miles sped by.

Other problems that were experienced during the journey were a split fuel tank, failed dynamo, two replacement rear tyres and a broken sidecar spring. However, it should be noted that except for the engine and gearbox the rest of the machine had already competed in the Monte Carlo rally (used then by Colin Edge).

As for the route, this, as already said, began in Birmingham and travelled south by south-west to Worcester, Gloucester, Bristol, Bridgwater and Taunton, followed by lunch in Plymouth and tea in Bournemouth. Then it was on to London. The next morning Wilson and Ferriday headed north up the A1 to Stevenage and Cambridgeshire. Then they cut inland to Sleaford, Lincoln, Goole and finally Hull, where they stopped for lunch. After this, they:

Plunger rear suspension from a 1950 A10. Although not up to swinging-arm standards it provided a greater degree of comfort than with rigid frame.

drove to Middlesbrough by way of Bridlington, Filey, Scarborough, Whitby and then across a moorland road – bleak, lonely, sinuous and undulating – to Middlesbrough (where the first rear tyre was replaced). Then it was on to Edinburgh for the night (via Roxburgh).

Edinburgh was left for next morning for the journey north to John O'Groats by nightfall.

But rather than simply go up the A9, the outfit travelled via Dundee, Aberdeen and Elgin to Inverness, then up the east coast road taking in Dingwall, Bonarbridge and Wick.

From John O'Groats they took the road west to Tongue, but then cut south to join their route of the previous day. From Inverness they journeyed south-west to Fort William and eventually Glasgow by evening.

From Glasgow they travelled south to Liverpool and into North Wales, taking the road to Colwyn Bay, Conway and Betws-y-Coed. But the road from Conway to Festiniog (some 50 miles/80km) was for Wilson 'the most tiring of the trip so far'. From Wales it was a case of returning home, Wilson saying, 'From here on, the road back to Birmingham was wide and fast and the BSA was given the gun. During the final 50 miles, in fact, I did my utmost to blow it up. I drove it flat out, on top, or in third as required.' He also went on to say how much 'cooler' it had run than on the first day. And that 'I am convinced that had we realized we were starting on a new engine, or had we started with the engine in the condition in which it was at the finish, the entire trip would have been accomplished without those early bothers. Vibration,' he continued, 'was considerably less noticeable after the third day.' In addition: 'The brakes provided the best stopping power I have ever experienced with a sidecar outfit.' Finally, George Wilson concluded, 'In the company of the Golden Flash and Ferriday [these were] among the most memorable few days I have ever spent. It made me decide definitely not to spend my holidays riding abroad, but to go back to Scotland.' Something with which the author can but concur!

1951 A10 in export guise with chrome-plated fuel tank – British models did not have this feature due to a nickel shortage. The dual seat was offered as a cost extra.

Changes for 1951

As is covered in Chapter 4, for the 1951 model year the A7 was revised in line with the A10. However, both models also benefitted from a new lubrication system, new pistons (featuring a 'flexible shirt', which was achieved by 'splits' extending upwards only as far as the centreline through the gudgeon-pin bosses – these 'splits' were at the front and rear of the piston). The new pistons were manufactured from silicon-alloy and retained the three-ring format used previously (two compression and a single scraper). Finally, as with the 1951 A7, the latest A10 featured sidecar lugs on both sides.

Prices as of 19 October 1950 were as follows:

- A10 (rigid frame) basic £152 (with UK taxes £193 0s 10d);

- with plunger frame basic £10 (with UK taxes £12 14s 0d).

Rear Springing as Standard

The announcement of the 1952 BSA range of models brought with it the news that all of the twin-cylinder models, including the A10, would be fitted with the company's plunger-type rear suspension; the rigid frame had therefore been dispensed with (some single-cylinder models continued to be offered in this vogue).

Other changes and modifications for the 1952 A10 were as follows:

- special oil seal on gearbox mainshaft;
- damping improved on telescopic front forks;

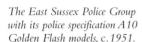

The East Sussex Police Group with its police specification A10 Golden Flash models, c.1951.

LEFT: *A special police version proved popular, both at home and in export markets.*

BELOW: *Golden Flash engine (as used on rigid- and plunger-frame models).*

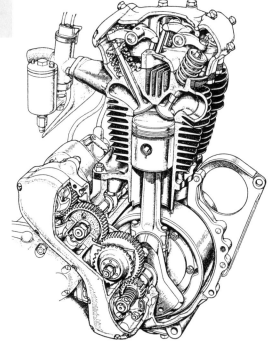

- modified centre stand – to allow for more clearance under the wheels;
- brake operation improved – by stiffening up the fulcrum pin and cam bearing;
- dual seat made available at a cost option (£2 16s 8d including UK taxes);
- modified engine breather – a circular shroud had been cast around the breather on the inside of the timing cover to act as a baffle;
- many 1952 model-year A10s were built without the chrome plating on the fuel tank, because of material shortages that year.

The basic prices, as of 1 November 1951, for the A10 (plunger frame) were: £175 (with UK taxes £223 12s 3d).

Testing in Solo and Sidecar Guises

An interesting testing of the latest A10 Golden Flash in both solo and sidecar guises was published in *The Motor Cycle* dated 27 December 1951.

In solo trim a maximum speed (mean – two-way) of 96mph (155km/h) was recorded, whilst with a BSA-made single-seat sidecar this figure was reduced to 70mph (110km/h). These figures (solo) were obtained at the MIRA Proving Ground near Nuneaton in Warwickshire. The absolute maximum one-way speed recorded (down-wind) with the air filter connected was 102.75mph (165km/h) and without the filter 104.5mph (168km/h).

At the end of the solo part of the test the bike was returned to the factory, where the sidecar was fitted. Alterations to the machine included changing the forty-two-toothed rear wheel sprocket for one with forty-nine teeth, and fitting heavier fork springs. At this time, too, the stock six/four throttle slide in the Amal 276 carburettor was replaced by a six/three (which had 1/16in/1.6mm less cut-away). This was in order to enrich the mixture at smallish throttle openings – as in solo guise this particular machine had proved difficult to start.

The best maximum cruising speed with the sidecar fitted 'appeared to be anything from 55 to 65mph (89 to 105km/h)', whereas at the lower end of the scale the outfit 'would trickle along in top gear without snatch at speeds of just over 20mph [32km/h]. The tester also commented upon:

The Golden Flash assembly line at Small Heath, early 1952. The machine shown here is undergoing inspection at the end of the line, prior to being wheeled down the ramp, filled with fuel and oil, and road-tested.

The riding position for sidecar work was excellent, and no change was required either in footrest position or angle of the grips from the settings used earlier in the test (solo). Some high-powered machines of the past have been criticized when fitted with sidecars because the brakes have not provided adequate stopping power. No such criticism could be levelled at the BSA however.

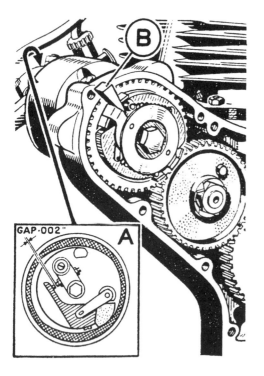

A New Headlamp Cowl for 1953

The 1953 BSA range was announced in late September 1952 and certainly as regards the larger singles and all the twin-cylinder A-series, including the Golden Flash, the most distinctive feature was a streamlined steel cowl, which covered the top of the headlamp and forks. This neatly encased the speedometer, switch and ammeter. At the same time, an amount of swivel adjustment was left at the headlamp mounting, contact between the lamp shell and the cowling being provided by a thick rubber gasket (BSA described it as a 'beading').

There was, again, on both the larger singles and the twin-cylinder range, a redesigned rear number plate, stop-tail lamp and small red circular reflector. This new assembly also neatly enclosed the wiring behind the number plate.

A feature on the twins was a newly designed tank mounting. This employed a horizontal through-bolt at both the front and rear. The arrangement incorporated two rubber bushes which were placed under compression. Two smaller modifications concerned a new prop stand which now featured lugs on the frame, rather than simply being clipped on as previously.

Changes to the A10 Golden Flash only were in short supply for 1953, with *The Motor Cycle* commenting: 'Outstanding among the three

ABOVE: Automatic advance – standard on A10 and A7 touring models.

RIGHT: The 1953 BSA range was announced in late September 1952, its most distinctive feature being a streamlined steel cowl, which covered the top of the headlamp and forks; the speedometer was now housed in the lamp shell.

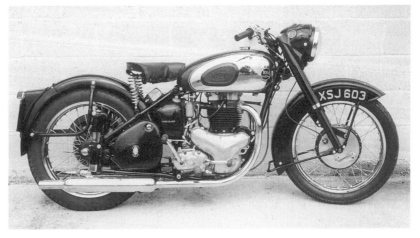

Ariel FH Huntmaster

When the Huntmaster (known as the Cyclone in North America) was launched in October 1953, no mention was made of its BSA connection. But in fact it was powered by a version of the existing 646cc A10 unit. And it should be pointed out that for the Ariel's entire life (production ended in the summer of 1959), only the iron cylinder head and barrel type with the narrow cylinder base flange was used. None of the alloy head versions (as found on the Road Rocket or Super Rocket) were produced; whilst only in 1958, the year prior to the Huntmaster's demise, was the thicker base flange (and therefore more robust and tunable engine) introduced. And all A10 engines, whether for BSA or Ariel, were manufactured in the former's Small Heath works.

As fellow author Steve Wilson says in his *British Motor Cycles Since 1950*, 'A BSA motor may have been the beginning of the erosion of marque identity'. This referred to Ariel's subsequent ever-increasing involvement with BSA components.

However, if the basic A10 powered the Ariel 650, the rest of its specification was very much down to the Selly Oak marque itself. For a start, the engine was outwardly modified (new outer covers, for example), whilst there was a Burman, rather than BSA gearbox – the same applying to the clutch and primary transmission. As for the cycle parts these were also Ariel components, including the company's excellent duplex frame with swinging arm and twin-shock rear suspension. Interestingly, BSA itself was to use the full-width alloy Ariel brake hubs for a couple of seasons during the mid-1950s on not only its A series twins, but also B series three-fifty and five-hundred singles.

ABOVE: The Ariel FH Huntmaster was launched in October 1953 (1956 model is shown) and employed the BSA-sourced A10 twin-cylinder engine.
BELOW LEFT: Last throw of the dice, the Ariel 650 Cyclone export version, still with A10 mechanics.
BELOW: Details of the 646cc Huntmaster engine – essentially an iron BSA A10 unit with modified outer casings.

twins (the others being the A7 and Star Twin five-hundreds), forming the A-group models is the world-famous 646cc Golden Flash. This remains essentially unaltered, but is enhanced by the all-chromium wheel rims and plated side panels on the tank.'

New Frame – Revised Engine and Gearbox

A major change for the A10 came for the 1954 season, with a brand new pivoted-fork (swinging-arm) frame (also new that year for other A and B series models). Buyers had a choice of either the existing plunger frame (recommended for sidecar use), or the new swinging-arm frame. Actually, that year there were four separate prices for one of BSA's six-fifty twins:

- with plunger springing and black finish £213 12s (including UK taxes);

- as above but with beige finish £217 4s (including UK taxes);
- with pivoted-fork spring and black finish £219 12s (including UK taxes);
- as above but with beige finish £223 4s (including UK taxes).

Where plunger-type rear springing was incorporated, the gearbox was built, as previously, in semi-unit bolted-up with the engine. However, pivoted-fork A models (including the A10) employed a separate gearbox, with the crankcases having been modified accordingly. The separate gearbox was adjustable to provide correct chain tension and there was a revised, longer primary chaincase.

Gear ratios on bikes equipped with pivoted-fork suspension were also slightly different from those standardized hitherto. The new ratios for the six-fifty were: 4.52, 5.47, 7.95 and 11.67:1.

A major change for the A10 (and A7) came for the 1954 season, with a brand-new pivoted-fork (swinging-arm) frame. Note the fatter rear shocks of the first year's production. Customers could still order a plunger frame, which was mainly retained for sidecar duties.

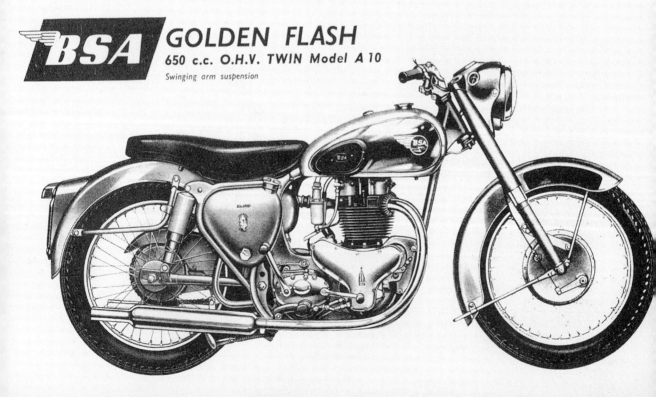

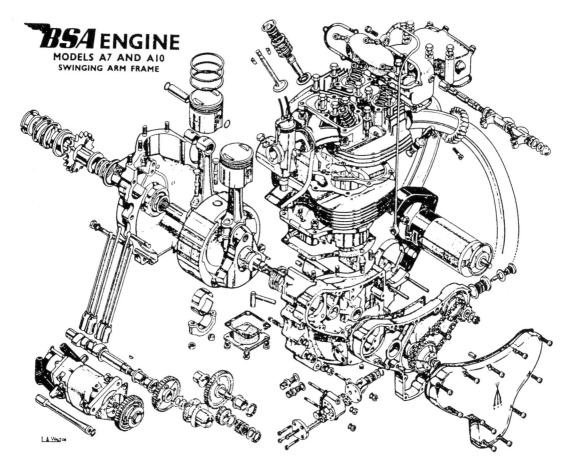

BSA ENGINE
MODELS A7 AND A10
SWINGING ARM FRAME

ABOVE: Official BSA drawing of the A10/A7 engine fitted to the swinging-arm frame models.

RIGHT: Another change notable on the swinging-arm frame models was the use of a simplex primary chain, whereas the rigid-plunger machines had duplex chains. Also shown here is the factory clutch extractor tool.

Another change, again to all the A series twins, was modified timing on the cast-iron cylinder barrels and heads. This had been extended to increase the cooling area and at the same time gave the top end of the ends of these engines what *The Motor Cycle* called 'a bolder appearance'.

On the machines with pivoted-fork rear springing, the BSA design team had provided a new matching oil tank and toolbox. These were bigger than before, but blended in well with the new frame; the basic shape remained until the last of the A7 and A10 models left the factory in the early 1960s.

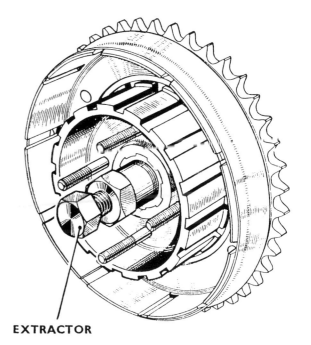

EXTRACTOR

The Frame Design

In designing the new frame, BSA engineers had in mind two priorities, function and style. Function meant that the machine had to handle in a superior fashion to the existing plunger-framed machine. And style meant it had to be acceptable in the looks department. To be honest, the BSA swinging-arm frame could be placed behind the Norton Featherbed and in front of the Triumph of the period. Actually, the basic chassis had been introduced a few months earlier on the BB series Gold Star singles. It featured twin front downtubes that were continued beneath the engine and then swept upward to form twin seat pillars; at the top, they were welded into the single tank rail. Twin rear subframe loops were welded to the seat-pillar tubes. From the underside of the tank rail to the lower end of the steering head ran a bracing tube, which, together with the upper ends of the downtubes, provided substantial triangulation of the steering head. The rear fork (swinging arm) pivoted on a pair of bonded-rubber and metal bushes. The hydraulically damped shock absorbers featured three-position adjustment for load. This task was achieved by way of a c-spanner, supplied with the machine's toolkit.

BSA still manufactured and sold sidecars at this time; for 1954 three types were listed, the 22/47 de Luxe Tourer, the 23/51 Family and the 22/48 Commercial box. The first two could be ordered at additional cost with the Golden Flash: beige finish.

Testing the Swinging-Arm Golden Flash

The Motor Cycle tested one of the new swinging-arm framed Golden Flash models in its 20 May 1954 issue. They noted that this new frame was 'solo only' and that 'Advantage has been taken of the moveable engine – and clutch-sprocket afforded by the separation of engine and gearbox to effect a slight reduction in overall gearing. The new ratios are a trifle better suited to the engine's performance characteristics.' It was

also explained that 'the footrests are further rearward relative to the seat'. And 'The effect is to provide a riding position which, for a person of medium stature, is more conducive to reducing fatigue at sustained high cruising speeds, while sacrificing nothing in comfort at town speeds.'

The highest one-way speed recorded was exactly 100mph (160km/h). This was achieved with a strong tail wind, and the rider wearing a two-piece suit and overboots.

A comment was made that 'the suspension units are sensitive to minor road irregularities and absorb major shocks in exemplary fashion'. For solo riding it was found that the 'softest of the three settings' of the Girling rear suspension units was best for an 11-stone rider. When a pillion passenger was added, 'the hardest setting gave excellent compensation for the added weight', whilst 'the intermediate position was suitable for a heavy solo rider' and 'at times [was] employed by a lighter rider to obviate fouling of the ground by the prop stand when the machine was well banked over to the left'.

Although all three stands (front, centre and side) were classed as 'accessible and efficient in use', it was also 'imperative to turn off the petrol taps when the machine was supported on the prop stand; otherwise, carburettor flooding owing to the relative dispositions of float chamber and mixing chamber would result.'

Both brakes were 'reasonably light to operate and extremely powerful' and 'Applied together, even from 100mph [160km/h], they pinned the machine down firmly and without the slightest hesitation.' However, 'At first, the front brake emitted a loud and annoying squeal whenever it was used.' The defect was cured by dismantling and cleaning the brake and, at the same time, chamfering the ends of the linings.

Although 'A shade heavy at low speeds, the steering was really first class and rock steady; it responded to the slightest banking of the machine. The steering damper was treated purely as an ornament.'

It was also noted that although 'a contributory factor to the engine's outstanding economy' (60mpg at 60mph), the carburation was a shade lean at small throttle openings. As a result, it was necessary to leave the air lever partially closed for about 1½ miles (2.4km) after starting off from cold if the engine was to respond without hesitation to snap throttle openings.

The official test figures gave the test machine's weight as '443lb [200kg] fully equipped, with full oil tank and 1gal [4.5ltr] of petrol'. The motorcycle was also fitted with the cost options of prop stand and pillion footrests.

Few Changes for 1955

There were few changes to the Golden Flash for the 1955 season, although it was now the only twin-cylinder model to continue with the choice of swinging-arm or plunger frame – the 500cc model having only the former as an option. And in truth the plunger set-up was only retained because the factory considered it more suitable for the task of hauling a sidecar around. Certainly as a solo mount, the swinging-arm frame was much superior in every way.

The actual changes to the A10 for the 1955 model were as follows:

- redesigned engine shock absorber;
- steering head lock;
- Amal Monobloc carburettor;
- one-piece rear mudguard repositioned (on swinging-arm frame model);
- new, one-piece valanced front mudguard.

The tractable and docile A10 was always a popular choice with the sidecar enthusiast; this is a 1955 machine, with single sided brakes (an 8in assembly at the front).

113

New, Higher Prices

In early April 1955, new higher prices for BSA motorcycles, including the A10, came into effect. This was due, said the company, to 'A substantial wage increase applicable to operatives in the engineering, and allied trades which became effective on 14 March.'

The Golden Flash's new pricing structure was as follows:

- A10 with plunger springing (black finish) £228 (including UK taxes);
- A10 as above, but with beige finish £231 12s (including UK taxes);
- A10 with pivoted-fork springing (black finish) £237 12s (including UK taxes);
- A10 as above, but with beige finish £241 4s (including UK taxes).

However, price rises or not, BSA motorcycle sales were booming both at home and in the export market as the 1950s unfolded. As Owen Wright so aptly described the times: 'Slowly, the 1950s were turned upside down, from ration coupons to the "never had it so good" era.' And, in fact, the middle of the decade was something of a high point for motorcycle sales, due to the general increased prosperity, but not yet dampened by the advent of the small car sales boom, which began just as the 1950s was coming to an end, headed by the new Mini.

Full-Width Alloy Hubs for 1956

When details of the company's 1956 programme were published in October 1955, the main innovations were full-width hubs and an optional, fully enclosed rear chaincase. It was very much a case of the two going together – and all the A-series swinging-arm twin frames had been given the new (Ariel-type) brakes. Actually, although these new stoppers looked good, they were rather less efficient in use, with many preferring the outgoing single-sided assemblies that had been the standard fitment for

The A10 Police Model, with swinging-arm suspension and new-for-1956 7in full-width alloy brake hubs.

many seasons. And there is no doubt that the new brakes' lack of bite were most felt on the Golden Flash, particularly if a sidecar was fitted – and some owners of the swinging-arm model were now beginning to fit a third wheel. Instead of an 8in (203mm) assembly at the front, both brake diameters were now 7in (178mm).

These full-width hubs featured centrally disposed brakes. In cast aluminium with integral spokes flanges, each hub was ribbed externally for brake cooling and webbed internally for rigidity. The hub also featured iron brake liners and steel bearing-support housings. The brake shoes and shoe plates were aluminium die castings. The brake lining's width was 1½in (38mm).

The hubs were not interchangeable, due to the fact that the rear assembly incorporated a quartet of integral driving studs. And although the rear also retained its QD (Quickly Detachable) ability, this latter feature was slightly changed from previous practice. Removal of a rubber plug in the rear of an optional chaincase provided access to taper-seated domed nuts on the aforementioned driving studs; the wheel spindle, however, was withdrawn as before.

Rear brake operation was, in the author's opinion, compromised, because of the need for a somewhat over-complex operation, which was achieved by a cross-over shaft arranged co-axially with a hollow passageway through the swinging-arm pivot, and thence by cable. In other words, the brake pivot arm was on the offside (right) of the motorcycle, whereas the foot brake pedal operated by the rider was on the nearside (left). This gave the rear brake a rather spongy feel.

The optional rear chaincase is fully described in Chapter 4, but briefly this gave full enclosure of the final drive chain and was manufactured from 22-gauge sheet-steel pressing in four sections. Although purchase costs of the plunger-framed A10 (with the old-type brakes) remained the same, those of the swinging-arm model had risen:

- with pivoted-fork-springing, black finish £240 12s (including UK taxes);
- and as above, but with beige finish £244 4s (including UK taxes);
- the rear chaincase cost an additional £3 (again including UK taxes).

Dual seats and pillion footrests were standard-ized on the swinging-arm machines, although a single rider's saddle could be specified if

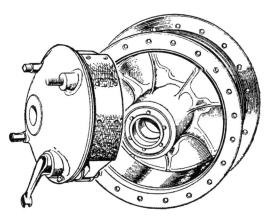

Ariel-type hubs used in 1956 and 1957. These featured internal and external webs.

1956 A10 Golden Flash	
Engine	Air-cooled, ohv vertical twin, 360-degree crank, single camshaft at rear of crankcase, cast-iron cylinder head and barrel, bolt-on rocker covers, aluminium vertically split crankcases
Bore	70mm
Stroke	84mm
Displacement	646cc
Compression ratio	6.5:1
Lubrication	Dry sump, with oil pump featuring worm drive, a pressure relief valve screwed into the crankcase
Ignition	Magneto
Carburettor	Amal 376 Monobloc 1 1/16 in (27mm)[1]
Primary drive	Duplex chain (rigid); Simplex chain (swinging arm)
Final drive	Chain
Gearbox	Separate, four-speed, foot-change[2]
Frame	All-steel construction, double front downtube
Front suspension	BSA telescopic, oil-damped forks
Rear suspension	Swinging arm or plunger
Front brake	7in (178mm) full-width alloy hub[3]
Rear brake	7in (178mm) full-width alloy hub[3]
Tyres	Front 3.25 × 19; rear 3.50 × 19

General Specifications

Wheelbase	Plunger 55in (1,397mm); swinging arm 56in (1,422mm)
Ground clearance	Plunger 4.5in (114mm); swinging arm 6in (152mm)
Seat height	30in (762mm)
Fuel tank capacity	4gal (18ltr)
Dry weight	408lb (185kg)
Maximum power	35bhp @ 5,500rpm
Top speed	100mph (160km/h)

Plunger frame models: [1] Amal 276 carb; [2] bolt-up gearbox; [3] single-sided hubs, 8in (203mm) front.

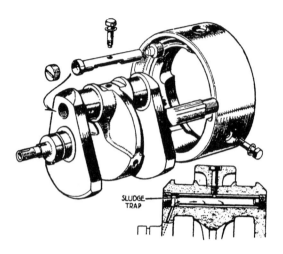

The three-bolt crankshaft with sludge trap and held by two plugs, which was used on 650cc models only.

preferred at no additional cost. BSA also now listed an additional sidecar – the 22/54 saloon, priced at £76 8s (including UK taxes).

In June 1956 BSA announced that it was introducing the new sporting brother of the Golden Flash, the Road Rocket, to the home market, the roadburner having been introduced some two years earlier, primarily for the North American distributors. This high-

performance machine is described in Chapter 7.

As for the Golden Flash itself, this was to remain virtually unchanged until the autumn of 1957. The same applied to prices, at least until April of that year, when, due to inflation, increases were introduced.

Major Changes for 1958

If the previous months had been quiet on the development front, the same could not be said when the 1958 models were launched in mid-November 1957.

All A group twins were now equipped with new full-width hubs in cast iron with flanges formed to permit the use of straight-pull, chromium-plated spokes. The headlight unit, ammeter, switch and speedometer were now housed in a nacelle that embraced the upper part of the telescopic forks. Another change (only on the 646cc A10 series engine) was a reinforced crankshaft of new design with modified big-end and timing-side bearings.

BSA had also seen fit to discontinue several models, including the plunger-framed A10. And the company had responded by attaching sidecar rear and underseat connections on the

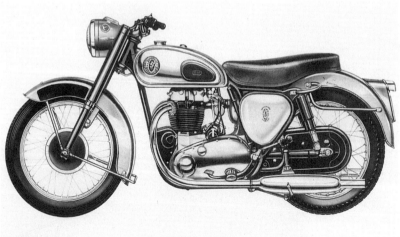

The A10 as sold in 1958 and 1959. It now came with full-width cast-iron hubs, and headlamp nacelle. A rear chaincase was an optional extra.

BSA 650 c.c. O.H.V. TWIN model A10 GOLDEN FLASH

frames of pivoted-fork A (and B) series machines.

In the 13 November issue of *Motor Cycle News*, the headline in a specially produced BSA Supplement read: 'A BSA To Suit Every Taste: Models from 125 to 650cc – numerous practical improvements for 1958.'

The New Hubs Described

The following excludes the Gold Star and 650 Rocket Scrambler. On the 650 A10 (and also the Road Rocket and Shooting Star five-hundred), the front brake diameter was 8in (203mm). All, including the standard A7 used a 7in (178mm) rear unit. The official reason for the new brakes, said BSA, was to 'improve efficiency and at the same time enable straight spokes to be employed'. Due to its construction, though of cast iron, it was, claimed BSA 'no heavier than the iron-lined light alloy Ariel component it replaced'. Also because there was no joint between the braking surface and the finned central part of the hub, heat dissipation was improved and the danger of distortion minimized.

As previously, the brake plate was of cast alloy, but fulcrum point adjusters were no longer fitted. There were finger adjusters on the controls. On the side opposite the shoes, the hub was covered by a light metal pressing.

Because the spindle employed in the new pattern hub was not of the knock-out type, it had been necessary to modify the front fork ends, which were now of the split clamp type, with the caps held by a pair of $\frac{5}{16}$in (8mm) studs and nuts. There was still a knock-out spindle on the rear wheel.

The headlamp cowl used previously had not proved popular with owners, restricting as it did the amount of adjustment for the headlamp unit. *Motor Cycle News* described the new cowl as 'one of the sleekest items of its type yet produced by any manufacturer', and going on to say: 'So neat and unobtrusive is the new cowl that at first glance it looks merely like a conventional headlamp merged into a pressing shrouding the upper fork tubes.

In fact, though, lamp body and tube shroud are all in one piece.'

With the speedometer, ammeter and lighting-cum-ignition switch incorporated into the top, the electric horn was positioned underneath.

The underneath of the lamp was completely enclosed, in order to prevent damp reaching the wiring or reflector; there was, however, provision for altering the angle of the reflector/glass unit, which was a conventional 7in (178mm) Lucas item.

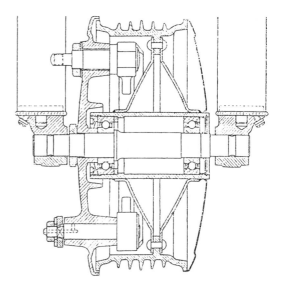

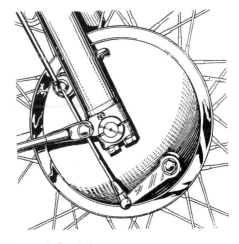

1958-onwards front hub details.

A New Roll-On Centre Stand

Another new feature was the 'roll-on' centre stand – which made this task easier. The new stand had 'egg-shaped' feet and a protruding foot-operating lever, which enabled it to be brought into action without the need for, as *Motor Cycle News* put it, 'groping even when waders are worn'.

Common to all the 1958 model year twins was a modification to the clutch drum. This saw a steel band going round the outside of the drum to prevent any tendency to 'spreading' when the plate tongues wore.

Compression ratios on the twins had been increased on all models except the A7, so as to take advantage of the higher octane fuel that had become available. On the Golden Flash, this had risen from 6.5:1 to 7.25:1. BSA claimed that the new ratio brought about improvement to both the power output and fuel consumption figures. There was also a new design of silencer.

A New Crankshaft

Although outwardly identical to its predecessor, the latest version of the 650cc engine in all its three forms (Gold Flash, new high-performance Super Rocket and the Road Rocket Scrambler) now had a new crankshaft.

This new crankshaft was a one-piece manganese molybdenum forging (En.16B) and the flywheel (still detachable as in the past) was now held in position by three set screws at right angles to the longitudinal axis of the crankshaft, instead of by bolts lying parallel to the axis of the shaft as previously.

The object behind the adoption of the new shaft, said BSA sources, was to improve both power output and length of bearing life. The new shaft, BSA said, was 'stiffer so that frictional loss on deflection at high speed and at high rpm is minimized, and this in turn brings about an increase in bearing life'. And, as a further aid to increased bearing life, the big-end shells on the trio of six-fifties were now of micro-babbitt metal, whilst the timing side bearing was of lead-bronze instead of, as previously, white metal.

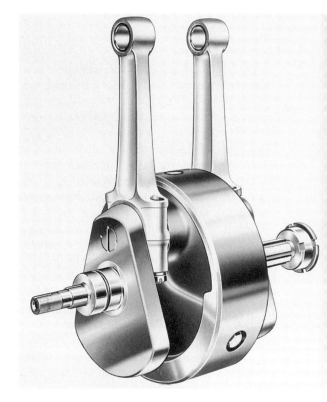

A post-1957 crankshaft with flywheel retained by a trio of radial bolts.

Revised Crank Lubrication

The twin-crank throw was hollow and contained a tubular sludge trap that was positioned end-wise and was prevented from rotating by an extension on one of the flywheel set-screws. One end of the sludge trap was of smaller diameter than the bore in which it was located. The ends of the crank-throw bore were closed by screwed plugs after insertion of the sludge trap. Oil was fed under pressure into the large-diameter end of the trap, emerging through a radial hole into the annulus between the trap and crank-throw bore, and thereafter to radial oilways leading to the big-end bearings. Sludge was retained with the trap by centrifugal force. The end of the trap remote from the oil entry was closed by a spigot on the plug, blocking that end of the crank-throw bore.

1958 Road Tests

During 1958 *Motor Cycling* published two separate road tests. The first, in the 2 January issue, was in solo guise; the other, dated 17 April, was with a sidecar. Interestingly, in both cases the same machine was used, registration number VOK 204, finished in beige, with a matching beige dual-seat covering. The first 'solo' test began with the words: 'A thoroughly good motorcycle – that in fewest words is the best snap description of the current A10 Golden Flash.'

This was the first time that *Motor Cycling* had tested an A10 with the new Monobloc carburettor, and although the tester admitted 'there is no marked difference in all-over speeds, standardization of this Amal instrument for the Golden Flash has coincided with an effort on the part of the manufacturers to tune down mixture settings with a view to obtaining a better economy figure'.

The test bike was fitted with a 3½ cutaway slide which was used with a 0.1065 needle jet in the third position; 25 pilot jet and 240 main jet provided what *Motor Cycling* described as 'carburation qualities which were satisfactory – if slightly weak at the cutaway stage'.

In fact, carburation and braking were gremlins, which, initially at least, affected the test:

In December weather, which provided several degrees of morning frost, first-kick starts were regularly achieved but there was weak mixture spit-back persisting for three or four miles running distance until, in fact, the engine had become thoroughly warm. That, plus the fact that initially the front brake grabbed slightly and had to be seen to at the works before high speeds were attempted, constituted the only debit items to which a development engineer might advantageously give further attention.

As the *Motor Cycling* tester said:

The now almost traditionally British vertical twin motorcycle with an 80–85mph (130–137km/h)

cruising speed, reasonable economy and high reliability is definitely epitomized in the current 'Golden Flash'. In riding the model, one's thoughts automatically turn to an autobahn in summer, and a fine, fast run, say, from Cologne to Salzburg in a single day, rather than to the limiting facilities provided by our own A5 highway around Christmas time.

The centre stand also came in for praise: 'The new tread-down stand is an absolute boon.' *Motor Cycling* recorded a maximum speed of 97mph (156km/h).

Fitting a Third Wheel

Choice of a sidecar to fill 'Part 2' of *Motor Cycling*'s 1958 test 'fell upon the Watsonian Avon, a single-seater of established design which has retained its popularity in this era of increasing demand for the larger family models'.

Of the A10's frame, the tester commented:

At all except the swan-neck location, sidecar lugs and pick-up points are now an integral part of the machine's fabricated and welded frame. Riding the outfit with the Avon attached in this way, one is aware of its excellent rigidity; from the outset, there is a sense of handling a unified vehicle, rather than an assembled combination.

The test speed figures were obtained with a 9-stone (57kg) passenger in the sidecar and an Avon-type screen/handlebar fairing (actually made in this instance by Screen & Plastics) fitted to the machine:

- second   58mph (93km/h);
- third   67mph (108km/h);
- fourth (top)   72mph (116km/h).

However, anything above 70mph (110km/h) was a real struggle, with the extra 2mph (3.2km/h) only achieved with great effort. When obtaining the acceleration figures, second and third gears really had to be 'wound on' to establish graphed acceleration. Compared with the machine in solo guise, fuel consumption was down by a third.

Adding a Third Wheel

Once the motorcycle had become firmly established the next question was: how could it carry additional passengers? The obvious answer was to add a third wheel and the earliest examples of what was to be termed the 'sidecar' arrived just after the turn of the twentieth century and by 1903 a couple of firms were already offering them for sale. Most sidecar bodies at this time were of wicker construction to cut down on weight.

Following the First World War there was an urgent need to provide motorized transport for the family – and conventional four-wheel cars were still only a dream for the vast majority. So this meant that not only were there many specialized sidecar manufacturers, but also several early motorcycle makers entered the field. This latter group included Matchless, Royal Enfield, Douglas, Sunbeam, Raleigh, Ariel, Chater-Lea, Triumph – and BSA.

By the mid-1930s there were half a million motorcycles on British roads, of which no fewer than a quarter had a sidecar fitted. By the outbreak of the Second World War in 1939 there were three sidecar combinations to every ten solos. The third wheel had arrived.

But the sidecar's real heyday was that of the immediate post-war period of the late 1940s and throughout the 1950s. With the ending of the conflict came a massive influx of personal transport for both commuting and touring. With increased demand many new specialized sidecar firms sprang up to join the established names such as Swallow, Watsonian, Blacknell, Garrard, Panther and BSA. As for the latter, the A10 Golden Flash was, in many ways, an ideal sidecar tug. And BSA had created the model not only for the lucrative export market, but also for sidecar duties on the home market.

The mid-1950s brought the use of a new material, fibreglass. One of the first sidecars to enter production using this material was the Watsonian Bambini, a single seater for lightweights and scooters. However, the Golden Flash was usually found attached to either a double-adult or single-seat sports sidecar.

With the advent of the 1960s, sidecar sales began the slump from which they never fully recovered. There were two main reasons: ever faster, more sporting motorcycles (many with frames unsuitable for a third wheel) and the advent of the small, affordable car to which even the most economy-minded family could aspire. By the 1970s, the sidecar combination had all but disappeared, a position which has remained since that time.

The heyday of the sidecar was from the late 1940s until the end of the 1950s – before the arrival of the small affordable car. This photograph shows the Watsonian stand at Earls Court. The nearest chair is hitched to an A10 Golden Flash, c. mid-1950s.

Consolidation

'BSA Consolidation', read *The Motor Cycle* headline when the Small Heath company's 1959 range plans were published in the magazine's 2 October 1958 issue, which went on to say: 'Factory policy for 1959 is mainly one of consolidation and therefore, with two exceptions, the present range is carried forward without major alteration and without a break in the production flow.'

Motor Cycle News, dated 15 October 1958, ran its own story on the BSA position in a similar vein:

> Apart from the recently announced BSA 250 Star (C15) described in MCN at the beginning of September, the Birmingham Small Arms company of Small Heath are to continue production of existing models with only minor standardizations. One is the adoption of a stiffer camshaft on the 650cc twins. High lift cams are also standard on all twin-cylinder models, providing more urge – if not marked increased in top-end speed – for the touring 497cc A7 and 646cc A10 Golden Flash.

Motor Cycle News also added, 'The cams are the same as fitted to the high-performance alloy head sports versions: the Shooting Star 500 and the Super Rocket 650.' Pricewise, the Golden Flash now cost £261 19s 6d, including British purchase tax.

Road Impressions by Harry Louis

The Motor Cycle's editor, Harry Louis, began by saying:

> No model produced in Great Britain has retained its identity, prestige and following better than has the BSA Golden Flash. When introduced almost 10 years ago it was heralded as a powerful luxury

1959 A10 and Watsonian single-seat sports sidecar.

mount to provide that balanced combination of effortless high-speed performance and docility sought by discriminating riders who use their machine for all-round road work. It was an immediate success and has remained in the forefront ever since.

Louis then went on to explain that although there were faster, more sporting machines in both the BSA and other ranges, 'on the give-and-take going of British roads, the Flash is capable of averages that are unlikely to be bettered by the versions with the slightly higher maximum speeds. Yet the machine has advantages of a lower level of mechanical and exhaust noise and better mudguarding.' It also 'is difficult to imagine a more suitable mount for long-distance trips. The overall top-gear ratio of 4.53 to 1 means rather less than 4,500rpm at 75mph (120km/h).'

At speeds in the seventies, Harry Louis said 'the engine purrs like a contented cat, and the noise level is so low and the roadholding and steering so good that high averages without conscious effort become commonplace'.

Performance-wise:

As compared with the engine of a few years ago, the 1959 unit has a higher compression ratio (7.25 to 1) and the Super Rocket camshaft gives more valve overlap (although earlier closing of the inlet valve). The most noticeable effect is that fuel consumption is considerably lower than before. On long runs involving hard driving, 60mpg [4.5ltr/100km] can be bettered and a fast touring speed of well over 70mpg [4.0ltr/100km] is usual.

Precise checks carried out during Harry Louis's riding on measured quantities of fuel at exactly sustained speeds were as follows:

- 70mph (110km/h) – 62mpg (4.6ltr/100km);
- 60mph (100km/h) – 69mpg (4.1ltr/100km);
- 30mph (50km/h) – 97mpg (2.9ltr/100km).

The test period extended over 2,000 miles (3,220km) and during this virtually every conceivable type of road surface was encountered 'and on no occasion could the steering be awarded less than full marks'.

And, as the author can testify from personal experience, 'Although it is indisputably a heavy machine, the Golden Flash belies its weight immediately it is on the move.' Harry Louis added: 'It has inherently good balance and can be ridden feet up at less than walking pace.' Both brakes were, in Louis's opinion, 'spongy and the rear brake lacked bite'. However, in contrast he found the front brake 'was extremely powerful and pleasurably light in operation'. Adjustment of the front brake cable was required 'at approximately 500-mile [800km] intervals'.

Although Louis praised the 'take up of the drive' and 'in its lightness the clutch was faultless', he noted that to 'give noiseless engagement of bottom gear on the first start of the day' it was necessary to free the plates off by pulling in the lever and depressing the kick-starter (a trait, to be fair, of many British machines of the period). He also found that a slight tendency to stickiness of the plates 'made it difficult to locate neutral when the machine was stationary while the engine was idling'.

As for gear changing, Louis said 'For completely clean changes a slowish movement of the pedal was desirable, particularly when engaging third from second. However, experience with BSA gearboxes suggests that a lengthy mileage – up to 5,000 [8,045km] – is often necessary before the gearbox is free enough for the best results.'

Harry Louis also commented at length upon the machine's appearance:

For 1959 the familiar all-beige finish was relieved by black enamel for the frame, engine plates, fork, shock-absorber covers, hubs and (if fitted) rear chaincase. The result is, unquestionably, a more attractive ensemble which reduces the apparent bulk of the machine and is probably more durable. An all-black finish is offered as an alternative. Wheel rims, exhaust system, tank panels, handlebar and controls, the headlamp rim and other detail parts are chromium plated and the aluminium primary chaincase cover, timing cover and gearbox cover are highly polished.

Louis concluded with the following: 'No machine can aspire to match everyone's ideal. Each has its points of appeal, and the Golden Flash offers most of those sought by real enthusiasts and earns its place in the affections of knowledgeable, hard riders by genuine merit.'

Detail Changes for 1960

A few weeks after Harry Louis's views of the Golden Flash were published came the launch of the 1960 BSA range for the 1960 model year, published in the motorcycling press at the beginning of September 1959. And it was very much a case of detail rather than major changes. The ones affecting the A10 are listed below:

- a combined drain and level plug for the primary chaincase;
- revised primary chaincase (with screw inspection plug);

- clutch adjustment simplified by provision of Simmonds self-locking nuts on the spring studs in place of previous nuts and lock nuts;
- new front mudguard, still valanced, but without the previous registration number-plate backgrounds;
- rear mudguard with side stays featuring forged ends resting against the valances; secured from the inside of the guard;
- Wipo Pacy Triconsul ring-type dip switch, horn and engine cut-out buttons;
- seat height reduced by 1in (25mm);
- larger bore carburettor; still Amal Monobloc, but increased from 1$\frac{1}{16}$in (27mm) to 1$\frac{1}{8}$in (28.5mm);
- increased inlet-tract diameter to suit;
- beige and black finishes supplemented by alternative Sapphire Blue;
- price (including UK taxes): £253 6s 3d.

On 9 June 1960 many prices of BSA motorcycles were increased, including the Golden Flash, which rose to £259 6s 11d.

1960 A10 with tear-drop tank badges, cast-iron hubs and new 'guards.

A Successful 1960

At a press conference in the summer of 1960, BSA's general sales manager W.L. (Bill) Rawson had this to say: 'We've had a very successful 1960. We're getting no service problems and no difficulties, and we feel it would be fickle to make alterations for the sake of making them.'

When the BSA plans were made known to the public shortly afterwards at the beginning of September, the centre of attraction was the new 343cc B40 unit single. Developed from the existing C15 two-fifty, the newcomer was not only intended to fill a gap left by the departure of the B31 heavyweight single, but more importantly it emphasized a trend which BSA were to pursue in the future on both its five-hundred and six-fifty class machines – that of full unit construction and lighter, more compact machines.

But What of the Future?

Although sales appeared buoyant, in fact in the all-important British home market the entire domestic motorcycle industry was on the verge of entering a period when sales would be far harder to come by. At this time the BSA group (*see* Chapter 10) was in a far healthier position than most of its rivals. But whereas mistakes made only a few years before would have been more than recovered by other better-selling models, mistakes in the 1960s – as history shows – proved costly millstones.

There is no doubt that by the time the 1961 model range was being announced, the BSA design team was already busy at work with the development of the new unit construction twins (the A50 and A65), which would surface on New Year's Day 1962.

When BSA celebrated its centenary on 7 June 1961 the Golden Flash was there to celebrate the event – as one of the best loved 'Beezas' of all time. But unfortunately love alone was not enough and so the following year this great motorcycle was replaced on the

1960 A10 Golden Flash	
Engine	Air-cooled, ohv vertical twin, 360-degree crank, single camshaft at rear of crankcase, cast-iron cylinder head and barrel, bolt-on rocker covers, aluminium vertically split crankcases
Bore	70mm
Stroke	84mm
Displacement	646cc
Compression ratio	7.25:1
Lubrication	Dry sump, with oil pump featuring worm drive, a pressure relief valve screwed into the crankcase
Ignition	Magneto
Carburettor	Amal 389 Monobloc 1⅛in (28.5mm)
Primary drive	Simplex chain
Final drive	Chain
Gearbox	Separate, four-speed, foot-change
Frame	All-steel construction, double front downtube; integral sidecar lugs
Front suspension	Swinging arm, with twin Girling shock absorbers
Front brake	8in (203mm) full-width cast-iron hub
Rear brake	7in (178mm) full-width cast-iron hub
Tyres	Front 3.25 × 19; rear 3.50 × 19

General Specifications

Wheelbase	56in (1,422mm)
Ground clearance	6in (152mm)
Seat height	30in (762mm)
Fuel tank capacity	4gal (18ltr)
Dry weight	430lb (195kg)
Maximum power	34bhp @ 5,150rpm
Top speed	101mph (163km/h)

Small Heath factory's production lines. A sad day for all concerned, even though the final pre-unit twin, the Rocket Gold Star (*see* Chapter 11), was about to start its short but eventful life.

Even so, BSA seemed incapable of making a clean split with the past, as not only did it build the RGS (Rocket Gold Star) until the spring of 1963, but also a small number of what was coded the A10GF. This latter model was actually a Golden Flash, but with alternator electrics and coil ignition, due to the fact that Lucas had axed production of its magneto and dynamo assemblies, and all the remaining stock was needed for the Rocket Gold Star. Today, the A10GF is the rarest of all the A7 and A10 series machines and is quite sought after, holding as it does the position of 'last of the line'.

A50/A65 Unit Twins

On 1 January 1962 BSA launched its new unit construction models, the A50 and A65. This is how the company described the newcomers in its advertising campaign at the time:

> From a long line of famous ancestors come these two new twin-cylinder models. With beautifully styled one-piece engine-gearbox unit and one-piece aluminium alloy cylinder head and rocker box, they have been endowed with lines which are graceful, elegant and exciting. Both 500 and 650

July 1961 advertisement promoting the BSA 650 (and 500) twins for sidecar work as 'reliable and economical' and having 'lusty performance'.

ideal transport for the family

BSA

For reliable and economical travel the B.S.A. 650 and 500 twins with sidecar make the ideal combination. The lusty performance of these popular twins with any sidecar is making them increasingly popular every day.

Remember you get the benefit of 50% insurance reduction with a sidecar outfit.

650 TWIN GOLDEN FLASH
500 TWIN A7 or A7 SHOOTING STAR } with SIDECAR

1961 A10 with silver sheen brake drums and improved engine performance.

BSA 650 GOLDEN FLASH

The Japanese Connection

Established in 1924, the Meguro Company began business manufacturing component parts for the automobile and motorcycle industry.

Meguro joined the ranks of the world's motorcycle producers in 1937, when it began building the 498cc ohv Z-97 single. This long-stroke design closely followed existing British practices. Then, together with Asahi, Cabton and Rikuo, Meguro built bikes for the Japanese armed forces during the Second World War.

After the conflict, Meguro continued its policy of offering British-influenced models, with a range of ohv single and vertical twins from 250 to 650cc. These included the 650cc model during the late 1950s, the engine of which was very similar to the one used on the Ariel Huntmaster (itself derived from the BSA A10 design).

Meguro had close links with Kawasaki Heavy Industries, which during the 1950s was not building complete motorcycles, but instead supplying engines to other Japanese producers, including Meguro. Then, in late 1960, Meguro became officially linked to Kawasaki, this bond being reinforced during 1961, when Meguro and Kawasaki were merged. This also saw Kawasaki Auto Sales formed separately from Kawasaki Aircraft. From 1962 Meguro motorcycles were marketed via Kawasaki in both the home and export markets.

The Meguro name was retained until 1964, by which time it was deemed advantageous to change over to Kawasaki. In September that year a new sales office was opened in Los Angeles. One of the first models sent to the States was a Kawasaki-badged two-fifty – based on the existing Meguro S8. This featured an ohv unit construction engine, but interestingly employed 66 × 72.6mm bore and stroke dimensions – identical to the A7 Mark 2. Next in March 1965 came the K2 twin. This was a near copy of the 497cc A7 and had been previously sold during the late 1950s as the Meguro K1, sharing the same bore and stroke dimensions. The K1 and K2 were particularly popular with the Japanese police services.

In October 1965 the Kawasaki BSA connection was increased when the W1 was introduced. This was essentially a bored-out version of the existing 497cc engine, giving a displacement of 624cc, the cylinder bore having been enlarged to 74mm. With a compression ratio of 8.7:1, it produced a claimed 50bhp at 6,500rpm.

Although the Kawasaki (Meguro) engine was very similar internally to the A7 Mk 2 and A10, there were differences. The Japanese unit employed one-piece connecting rods and needle-bearing big-ends. This meant that instead of the British one-piece crankshaft, the Kawasaki W1 had a three-piece, pressed-up crank.

The first series machines employed a single 31mm carburettor, but later examples featured twin 28mm instruments. Unlike the BSA, the dynamo was mounted at the front of the crankcases and the chain was tensioned by a slipper and lubricated by the engine oil – so it did not have a separate compartment as found on the British engine.

The gearbox (still a four-speeder) was British in design and like the A10 (and A7 Mk 2) was mounted separately from the engine, and so pivoted to provide primary chain adjustment.

The W1 soon became a good seller on the Japanese market, this being helped by the fact that at the time it was the largest-engined motorcycle built in the country.

In 1966 Kawasaki Motorcycles was formed and the American Kawasaki Motorcycle Corporation set up in Chicago to supply parts. But if the Japanese thought that they were onto a winner in the States they were soon to be disappointed; quite simply, the 624cc W1 'A10 Replica' didn't stand a hope, being viewed by American, if not Japanese, customers as a copy of a BSA.

But this didn't prevent Kawasaki from developing the theme further with the W1SS (Street Scrambler) in 1967, followed later that year by the W2. Finally came the W3, which ran from 1972 until 1975. But in truth, at least in the export markets Kawasaki in the late 1960s and early 1970s meant two- and three-cylinder two-strokes. Then came the Z1 dohc four and Kawasaki was on its way.

All the Kawasaki W series ohv twins employed the same 624cc (74 × 72.6mm) engine size – and Japanese cycle parts. The latter didn't owe much, if anything, to the BSA marque. The final W3 version (sold as the 650-RS) was only marketed in Japan. And so the Japanese BSA actually remained available for a full twelve years after the last A10 had left the Small Heath works back in 1963.

LEFT: *1966 Kawasaki W1SS – the BSA heritage is clearly seen in this view of the engine and primary chaincase.*

RIGHT: *Meguro built BSA-derived twins, which were based on the engine from the A7 and A10 models. This machine pre-dates the Kawasaki takeover of Meguro in 1963.*

The new A50 five-hundred and A65 six-fifty twins were launched in January 1962 to replace the A7 and A10 respectively.

power units are packed with biting performance kid-gloved at will into superbly quiet and docile masterpieces, and equipped with braking power to match. These new machines unquestionably represent the finest value-for-money twins in the world.

Fine-sounding words indeed, but unfortunately for BSA, the newcomers didn't quite match up to the advertising hype. Maybe the prices of £264 7s 10d for the A50 and £268 13s 9d for the larger A65 were competitive, but unfortunately in virtually every other sphere the A50/A65 models were inferior to the A7/A10 models they replaced.

Failings of the unit twins included vibration from the shorter-stroke engines, main-bearing failures, clutch slip, a triplex primary chain that could wear out far too quickly and in later, tuned form, was more generally fragile the higher the standard engine was stretched. However, modern-day owners are able to eliminate some of these problems with modifications introduced over recent years by after-market specialists like SRM.

A shorter wheelbase (mainly due to a switch from 19in to 18in wheels) made for a more compact motorcycle than the old pre-unit models, and decreased weight was a benefit of the unit bikes. However, in the author's eyes at least, styling was not anywhere near as good.

In fact, when introduced at the beginning of 1962 the A50 and A65 looked like enlarged C15 two-fifty singles! And from a personal view I never paid my own money out for either a unit BSA twin- or single-cylinder bike, whereas I did with pre-unit machinery, including an A7 twin and B33 single – plus my brother Rick's 350 and 500 Gold Star racers, but that's another story.

The older designs had *character*, whereas the original unit twins simply looked too clinical, almost like domestic household products than motorcycles. This situation was partly solved by the introduction of the sporting models, notably the Cyclone and Lightning in Clubman trim. But to be honest, even a 650 Lightning Clubman does not match a Rocket Gold Star in the looks department.

Throughout the 1960s the A50 and A65 series couldn't match their Triumph cousins, the TR6 and T120. And of course then came the 1970s and not only the infamous oil-in-the-frame models, but ultimately the collapse of the entire BSA group.

As history records, the introduction of the unit twins didn't do much to help the BSA cause. The pre-unit models were, and still are, highly regarded (even though they were not without fault), whereas the machines that replaced them failed to inspire the same level of enthusiasm. End of story.

7 Road Rocket and Super Rocket

The 646cc Golden Flash was one of the truly great motorcycles built by the giant BSA marque. Conceived, like its smaller 500cc A7 brother, in the early post-war years, the Golden Flash was born into a world just recovering from the greatest conflict in human history, and when, certainly on the home market, there was still much austerity – including food and fuel rationing. So the Golden Flash was conceived chiefly as a touring-cum-commuter bike. However, for its day it was also one of the fastest and smoothest of all British vertical twins.

Demand from Abroad

Great Britain might well have been suffering post-war, but abroad, particularly in the USA, everything was much brighter and more economically healthy. And so BSA began to be

The tuning of the Super Flash engine added some 10mph additional performance over the stock A10 Golden Flash.

The high performance – and rare – Super Flash model. Offered for only a few months in 1952/53, this was the forerunner of the Road Rocket, Super Rocket and RGS.

1953 Super Flash Specifications	
Engine	Air-cooled, ohv vertical twin, 360-degree crank; single camshaft at rear of crankcase, cast-iron cylinder head and barrel, bolt-on rocker box covers, aluminium vertically split crankcases
Bore	70mm
Stroke	84mm
Displacement	646cc
Compression ratio	8:1
Lubrication	Dry sump, with oil pump featuring worm drive, a pressure relief valve screwed into the crankcase
Ignition	Magneto
Carburettor	Amal TT 1 1/16in (27mm)
Primary drive	Triplex chain
Final drive	Chain
Gearbox	Bolt-up, four-speed
Frame	All-steel construction, double front downtube
Front suspension	BSA telescopic, oil-damped forks
Rear suspension	Plunger
Front brake	8in (203mm)
Rear brake	7in (178mm)
Tyres	Front 3.25 × 19; rear 3.50 × 19

General Specifications

Wheelbase	55in (1,397mm)
Ground clearance	4.5in (114mm)
Seat height	30in (762mm)
Fuel tank capacity	4.25gal (19ltr)
Dry weight	404lb (183kg)
Maximum power	42bhp
Top speed	109mph (175km/h)

end of 1952 BSA produced what was to be known as the A10 SF (Super Flash).

Essentially, this employed the A10's optional plunger frame and other running gear such as the 8in (203mm) front and 7in (178mm) rear, single-sided single leading shoe brakes, BSA telescopic forks, separate headlamp (for the 1953 season the standard A10 featured a cowl), plus a tuned (42bhp) engine with a hotter camshaft and high-compression pistons, an Amal TT carburettor (but still with iron head), lightweight sports mudguard with valancing, different handlebars and a dual seat. There were also Nimonic 80 exhaust valves and a toughened crankshaft (BSA referred to it as high-duty). In addition, there was a matching rev counter and speedometer (both mounted up above the headlamp); the former was driven from the camshaft, the drive gearbox being mounted on the timing cover. The SF was certainly an attractive bike, thanks to a bright silver-red finish for the fuel tank (chrome front panels).

Certainly, the Super Flash had a good performance, its engine and brakes proving more than adequate. However, the plunger frame, when subjected to the full speed potential of what was 100mph+ (160km/h+), was found wanting in the roadholding and handling departments. So the call went out to BSA to come up with a frame that would effectively control the power output.

The Road Rocket Arrives

These requests resulted in the A10 RR (Road Rocket). Again, at first it was an export-only model, but, unlike its forerunner, the RR was eventually sold on the British home market.

As with the Super Flash, much of the basic design was shared with the Golden Flash touring model, the main design features of which have already been recounted in Chapter 6. However, there were significant differences in engine tune, carburation, general specification and finish.

The first Road Rocket machines, built exclusively for the American market, were delivered

asked, soon after the Golden Flash's entry for the 1950 model year, how about a sports version?

The Birmingham company had already responded by offering a more sporting example of its A7, the Star Twin, the latter having arrived for the 1949 season, some two years after the A7 had been launched. And so at the during early 1954 and for a period of a few months were offered alongside the existing Super Flash. A major difference between the two machines was the frame – a plunger on the SF and a brand new pivoted rear fork (swinging-arm) type on the RR. Another was the use of an aluminium cylinder head instead of cast iron.

Other notable changes included a special camshaft, higher compression ratio (8:1 – same as the SF), Amal TT9 1¹⁄₁₆in (27mm) carburettor and revised gearing. The carburettor settings were as follows: number 6 slide, 340 main jet, a .109 needle jet and number 4 position needle. The float chamber was mounted at 15 degrees. And, as with the Golden Flash, the introduction of the swinging-arm frame meant that the semi-unit construction of the Super Flash, with its plunger frame, had been replaced by a separate gearbox, which, as with the other swinging-arm framed twins, meant a revised primary chain chaincase. The actual crankcases were also modified to meet the needs of the separate gearbox and of course there was the addition of engine plates. It is also worth consulting Chapter 4, as the Road Rocket was in many ways a larger-engined version of the newly introduced Shooting Star five-hundred.

Like the Super Flash, the Road Rocket stood out from the crowd, thanks to its bright red paintwork for the fuel tank (still with chrome panels) – and, in a change from the SF, it had chrome-plated abbreviated mudguards. An alternative silver-chrome finish for the tank was an option.

Manual Ignition Control

Another feature of the Road Rocket (and shared by the Shooting Star) was the manual ignition control for the magneto.

Unlike the other twins at the time (except the Super Flash), the Road Rocket was not equipped with the headlamp cowl housing the speedometer, ammeter and switch. Instead, the switch and ammeter were incorporated in the headlamp shell, whilst the speedometer (and optional rev counter) was mounted on the fork upper yoke.

As with the swinging-arm A10 Golden Flash, the 5½ pint (3ltr) oil tank fitted neatly into the offside (right) subframe loop and was balanced by a toolbox of matching shape on the other side of the machine. Again the suspension, including the hydraulically damped telescopic front forks, was shared with the Golden Flash – as were the brakes, which featured the excellent 8in (203mm) single-sided front hub, with a 7in (178mm) at the rear. The rear wheel springing was taken care of by a pair of Girling three-position adjustable shock absorbers. A single-point attachment was employed for the 4gal (18ltr) petrol tank. Gear ratios were 4.53, 5.48, 7.96 and 11.68 to 1.

Prices and Specification

It was not until some eighteen months later that British enthusiasts were at last given the news, in June 1956, that the dollar-earning Road Rocket would be offered for sale on the home market. Although *The Motor Cycle* published prices and brief details of the specification, it was not until mid-September of 1956 that more details were released, with BSA's 1957 model range details.

However, rivals *Motor Cycling* scored something of a coup when it got to test one of the very first UK-registered machines in its 19 July 1956 issue. Headed 'Impressions of a Potent Small Heath Product just off the Export-only List', the tester began by saying: 'Designed as a road-going solo with just that little extra in the way of speed and specification luxury likely to make it a dollar earner, BSA's Road Rocket well fulfilled its original purpose in the export field and made a mid-season début on the home market a few weeks ago.'

BSA official figures of 40bhp and 105mph (169km/h) were dubbed 'conservative' by *Motor Cycling*, and in fact when speed-tested the test bike recorded 109mph (175km/h). This speed figure was recorded at 6,200rpm, while BSA's own output of 40bhp was given at 6,000rpm. But it was out on the road where things really counted with *Motor Cycling*: 'This

BSA model, designated the A10 RR, could be cruised without signs of fatigue at speeds between 95–100mph [153–160km/h] – given suitable road conditions, of course.' The article went on to explain:

> It is the kind of motorcycle which a foreign-touring enthusiast would find delightful to own. It would be invaluable as a means of rapid, yet rock-steady, transport on journeys over the straight and relatively traffic-free routes nationals or autobahn of Europe. Nearer home, the chief appeal of the Road Rocket lies, not so much in its top-speed capabilities, which, alas, cannot always be fully used, but in acceleration qualities.

Even though it had a pukka racing carburettor, there were 'no signs of "flat spots" in the carburation'. Although tickover and slow running were 'a little erratic', this, in all truth, was to be expected from a sporting model with not only a specialized carb, but also a relatively high compression ratio. But the tester found that 'by discreet use of the manual ignition control, the tendency towards uneven firing at low rpm could be minimized'. But once on the move the control could 'be advanced fully' and, unless pinking was provoked by intentional 'ham handedness', the power build-up could be used efficiently right up to maximum speed.

Not only was the performance potential praised, but also steering and 'general ease of handling'; the dual seat was 'correctly angled to give comfort in conditions produced by hard acceleration and braking'; and the 'Fittings, generally, were of good quality and substantial.'

But there were criticisms. The machine tested by *Motor Cycling* featured the Ariel-type 7in (178mm) full-width, aluminium hub brakes front and rear. And 'Operation of the back "stopper" produced a spongy reaction which did not improve as the test proceeded.' Similar comments regarding these brakes can also be found in Chapters 3 and 6.

Another complaint was 'Although listed as an extra, the Smith's rev counter fitted to the test machine was regarded as an almost essential

complement to the speedometer, particularly in view of the engine's willingness to soar up above the manufacturer's recommended maximum.'

And 'A centre stand was fitted but seldom used because of the existence of a much more easily operated prop-stand. This, wrongly in the opinion of the tester, came under the heading of an extra.' Besides the rev counter and prop-stand, another cost extra fitted to the test machine was a chrome-plated grab rail at the rear of the dual seat. A rear chaincase was yet another option available at additional cost.

Prices as at 20 September 1956 were:

- 646cc A10 RR Road Rocket: basic £217 10s (with UK taxes £269 14s);
- rear chaincase: basic £2 10s (with UK taxes £3 2s);
- rev counter: basic £6 12s 6d (with UK taxes £8 4s 4d);
- chromium-plated grab rail: basic 15s (with UK taxes 18s 8d);
- prop-stand: basic 15s (with UK taxes 18s 8d).

The Motor Cycle finally published a road test of the A10 RR in its 14 March 1957 issue. Quite a bit of this review echoed comments already

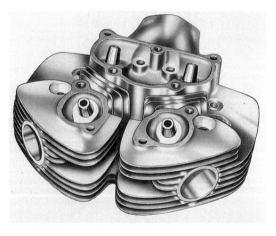

The 1956 Road Rocket cylinder head was made of light alloy and incorporated a siamezed induction tract. There were cast-in phosphor bronze inserts for cylinder bolts and rocker box, whilst cast-in austenitic steel inserts were employed for the valve seats.

1956 Road Rocket Specifications

Engine	Air-cooled, ohv vertical twin, 360-degree crank, single camshaft at rear of crankcase, alloy cylinder head and cast-iron barrel, bolt-on rocker covers, aluminium vertically split crankcases
Bore	70mm
Stroke	84mm
Displacement	646cc
Compression ratio	8:1
Lubrication	Dry sump, with oil pump featuring worm drive, a pressure relief valve screwed into crankcase
Ignition	Magneto, with manual advance and retard
Carburettor	Amal TT9 1⅟₁₆in (27mm)
Primary drive	Simplex chain
Final drive	Chain
Gearbox	Separate, four-speed
Frame	All-steel construction, double front downtube
Front suspension	BSA telescopic, oil-damped forks
Rear suspension	Swinging arm, with twin Girling shock absorbers
Front brake	7in (178mm) full-width alloy hub
Rear brake	7in (178mm) full-width alloy hub
Tyres	Front 3.25 × 19; rear 3.50 × 19

General Specifications

Wheelbase	56in (1,422mm)
Ground clearance	6in (50mm)
Seat height	30in (762mm)
Fuel tank capacity	4gal (18ltr)
Dry weight	418lb (190kg)
Maximum power	40bhp @ 6,000rpm
Top speed	110mph (177km/h)

and 'the comparatively long reach to the clutch and front brake levers, the slight heaviness of the clutch and gear change, and the high seat level [32in (813mm)], coupled with the model's weight'.

But the performance, handling and the 'tractability of a touring mount' still meant that the Road Rocket was well thought of in the final analysis.

In line with other BSA models, the Road Rocket price was increased to £281 9s 8d (including UK taxes) at the beginning of May 1957.

Launch of the Super Rocket

When the 1958 BSA model range was announced in mid–November 1957, not only were there several changes to the 646cc A Series twins, but a new model, the Super Rocket, had replaced the Road Rocket. The

'BSA Super Rocket' logo, on tank top.

made by *Motor Cycling*, although the highest speed recorded was 105mph (169km/h). But *The Motor Cycle*'s report did find a couple more things to complain about. One was the difficulty of finding neutral when stationary

The 1958 BSA Super Rocket was very clearly based around the Road Rocket. This is a British-spec bike with painted mudguards.

changes which also entailed the A10 Golden Flash are detailed in Chapter 6, but, even so, the new sportster was notably different from the outgoing model.

All models in the group now had a five-plate clutch with a strengthened drum. There were also new brakes with cast-iron drums. On both the A10 Golden Flash and the Super Rocket the front was an 8in (203mm) unit, with a 7in (178mm) rear; both, as before, were of the full-width variety. A tidying up process at the front had seen the torque arm dispensed

Matching speedo and rev counter. When the headlamp cowling was introduced this became an option (at extra cost).

with. Instead, there was now a slotted boss on the brake plate engaged with a lug incorporated into the offside (right) fork leg. Other changes to the cycle parts (shared with other models in the BSA range) included a front fork/headlamp nacelle, a new centre stand, provision for sidecar attachment on the duplex frame and improved Burgess-type silencers.

Engine Revision

Most notable were the changes made to the engine. The Super Rocket's compression ratio had been raised by fitting new 8.5:1 pistons (previously 8:1). Further, the cylinder head design had been changed in respect of the angle and sweep of the inlet and exhaust ports. In addition, the carburettor had been changed from the Road Rocket's TT9 to one of the new Amal Monobloc 376 carburettors. The size at 1¹⁄₁₆in (27mm) remained unchanged, but the jetting was considerably different with a 3½ slide, 250 main jet, 25 pilot jet, .106 needle jet and number 4 needle position. BSA claimed

an overall increase of 3bhp. The TT carburettor could still be specified, but at additional cost.

Internal modification to the 646cc power unit of both the Super Rocket and the latest Golden Flash included the fitment of a new crankshaft, which BSA said 'had a heavier load capacity', and a more substantial big-end bearing shell and timing side main bearing. The basis of the crankshaft was a forging in En.16B steel with a circular middle web. The flywheel was located on the middle web by means of three radial set-screws.

The twin-crank throw was of hollow construction and incorporated a tubular sludge trap positioned end-wise. This was prevented from rotating by way of an extension on one of the flywheel set-screws. One end of the sludge trap was of smaller diameter than the bore in which it was located. The ends of the crank-throw bore were closed by screwed plugs after insertion of the sludge trap. Oil was fed under pressure into the large-diameter end of the trap

The Super Rocket arrived for the 1958 model year. This example has a two-into-one exhaust, but is otherwise largely stock. As a rev counter has been fitted, the headlamp nacelle introduced that year has been replaced by the set-up shown.

and emerged the other end via a radial hole into a 'tube' between trap and crank-throw bore, thereafter going to radial oilways leading to the big-end bearings. Sludge was retained within the trap by centrifugal force. The end of the trap remote from the oil-entry and was sealed by a spigot on the plug blocking that end of the crank-throw bore. The sludge trap could be cleaned out during an engine overhaul and all the impurities removed.

A steel-backed, lead-bronze bush replaced the white metal timing-side main bearing that was formerly fitted. Replacement big-end bearing shells were faced with micro-babbit metal.

Fitting a Rev Counter

For the domestic British market the Super Rocket came with the new headlamp nacelle – unless the customer ordered the optional rev counter. If this was the case, the speedometer and rev counter were mounted on a bracket attached to the fork upper yoke (as per the Road Rocket) and a conventional headlamp was supplied.

The Super Rocket still had chromium-plated mudguards and the bright red fuel tank for export. But, unlike the Road Rocket, for the home market the guards were red; or again only for the UK, customers could specify silver as an alternative colour for the mudguards and tank.

Changes for the Early 1960s

Several detail changes were introduced for the six-fifty twins for the 1960 model year.

Applicable both to the Super Rocket and Golden Flash were changes designed to provide both improved fuel consumption and greater performance. Larger bore Amal Monobloc carburettors were specified, with a corresponding increase in inlet-tract diameter. For the Golden Flash the new choke size was 1⅛in (28.6mm), whereas on the Super Rocket this was now of 1⁵⁄₃₂in (29mm) bore. The new carburettor was a 389 with a 420 main jet, number 3 slide, 25 pilot

1958 Super Rocket Specifications	
Engine	Air-cooled, ohv vertical twin, 360-degree crank, single camshaft at rear of crankcase, alloy cylinder head and cast-iron barrel, bolt-on rocker covers
Bore	70mm
Stroke	84mm
Displacement	646cc
Compression ratio	8.2:1
Lubrication	Dry sump, with oil pump featuring worm drive, a pressure relief valve screwed into crankcase
Ignition	Magneto
Carburettor	Amal 376 Monobloc 1¹⁄₁₆in (27mm)
Primary drive	Simplex chain
Final drive	Chain
Gearbox	Separate, four-speed gearbox, foot-change
Frame	All-steel construction, double front downtube
Front suspension	BSA telescopic, oil-damped forks
Rear suspension	Swinging arm, with twin Girling shock absorbers
Front brake	8in (203mm)
Rear brake	7in (178mm)
Tyres	Front 3.25 × 19; rear 3.50 × 19

General Specifications

Wheelbase	56in (1,422mm)
Ground clearance	6in (152mm)
Seat height	30in (762mm)
Fuel tank capacity	4gal (18ltr)
Dry weight	418lb (190kg)
Maximum power	43bhp @ 6,250rpm
Top speed	109mph (175km/h)

jet, number 2 position needle and .106 needle jet. As with other settings contained in this chapter, these are for UK market machines; those for export markets were often different, even for the same model and year.

For the Super Rocket only there was a new, and what *The Motor Cycle* referred to as a

A 1960 Super Rocket, again with a rev counter and thus separate headlamp brackets (chromed).

'particularly neat method', for obtaining a rev-counter drive. The drive was provided by the oil pump mainshaft, the forward end of which was slotted to receive the torqued end section of the rev counter cable, which passed through an aperture in the forward face of the timing chest. The cable was driven at one-third engine speed (previously this was at half engine speed) and the Smith's-made rev-counter head gearing had been adjusted accordingly. Where a rev counter was not fitted the timing chest aperture was fitted with a small blanking plate.

There was a number of other changes shared with other A-group twins, but also in some cases the B group singles:

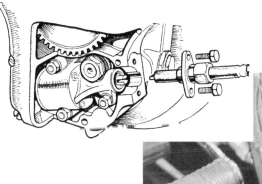

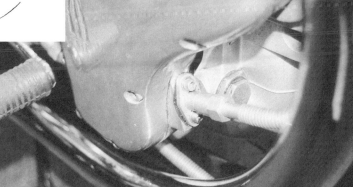

ABOVE AND RIGHT: The rev counter drive from the oil pump adopted by the Super Rocket for the 1960 model year and later models.

1960 Super Rocket with tear-drop tank badge.

- improved rear braking, achieved by repositioning the cam lever to face downwards instead of upwards;
- a modified primary chaincase – clutch adjustment screwed plug and chaincase oil level plug now acted as a combined drain and level plug assembly;
- clutch adjustment simplified by provision of self-locking nuts on the spring studs (replacing previous nuts and lock nuts);
- a new front mudguard of the valanced type;
- the rear mudguard tidied up by fitting stags with forged ends secured inside the guard;
- Wipo Pacy, tri-consul ring-type switch on the left-hand side of the handlebar, incorporating dip, horn and cut-out buttons;
- seat height reduced by 1in (25mm).

The Motor Cycle, in announcing the 1962 BSA programme in its 31 August 1961 issue, noted 'Nothing revolutionary, but a comprehensive programme of steady development – that's BSA for 1962.'

In most respects the twins were unaltered (except for the imminent arrival of the brand

1961 Super Rocket, in standard trim except for a later 2LS front brake from a 1969-on unit model. The latter is a popular and effective way of improving braking power.

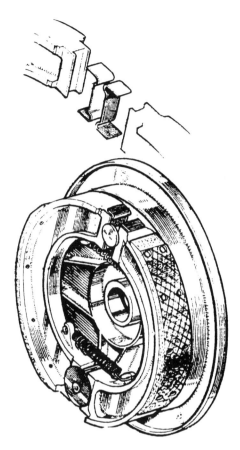

The floating front brake plate adopted for the 1961 model year Super Rocket.

any difference whatsoever, but internally the new silencer, BSA claimed, 'affords a lower noise level yet permits a slight increase in power at both the lower and upper ends of the output curve'. Very much a case of having your cake and eating it, as the saying goes!

1962 Super Rocket Specifications	
Engine	Air-cooled, ohv vertical twin, 360 degree crank, single camshaft at rear of crankcase, alloy cylinder head and cast-iron barrel, bolt-on rocker covers
Bore	70mm
Stroke	84mm
Displacement	646cc
Compression ratio	9:1
Lubrication	Dry sump, with oil pump featuring worm drive, a pressure relief valve screwed into crankcase
Ignition	Magneto
Carburettor	Amal 389 Monobloc 1$\frac{5}{32}$in (29mm)
Primary drive	Simplex chain
Final drive	Chain
Gearbox	Separate, four-speed gearbox, foot-change
Frame	All-steel construction, double front downtube
Front suspension	BSA telescopic, oil-damped forks
Rear suspension	Swinging arm, with twin Girling shock absorbers
Front brake	8in (203mm)
Rear brake	7in (178mm)
Tyres	Front 3.25 × 19; rear 3.50 × 19

General Specifications

Wheelbase	56in (1,422mm)
Ground clearance	6in (152mm)
Seat height	29in (737mm)
Fuel tank capacity	4gal (18ltr)
Dry weight	418lb (190kg)
Maximum power	46bhp @ 6,250rpm
Top speed	111mph (179km/h)

new unit models in January 1962). However, there were new features that applied to the Super Rocket only.

Principal of these was the adoption of floating brake shoes. Essentially, the new shoes operated in the following manner: the ends of the shoes remote from the operating cam were made flat, so that they could slide on the fulcrum pin in addition to pivoting upon it. The floating action of the shoes introduced a self-servo effect, but to prevent an over-fierce bite, the leading edge of each friction surface was chamfered back by 1¼in (32mm).

There was also a new type of silencer, which BSA said had '25 per cent greater capacity than before'. Externally one was hard pressed to see

For 1962 the Super Rocket was available with either separate exhaust header pipes (in which case, two of the new silencers were employed) or with a new siamezed exhaust system, with a single silencer. The latter was very much in vogue at the time – but it did have practical advantages too, including access to the final drive chain and improved access if one was fitting a sidecar.

Finally, BSA had, it said, increased the flexibility of the model by lowering the bottom-gear ratio – and second and third in proportion – whilst retaining the existing top gear ratio of 4.53:1. Price of the Super Rocket on 31 August 1961 was £280 19s 2d (including UK taxes).

The BSA range brochure issued in October 1961 described the Super Rocket thus:

> An exceptionally fast, safe, standard road machine, the Super Rocket has a specially tuned and brake-tested engine, improved light alloy cylinder head with high compression pistons, reinforced crankshaft, sports camshaft, etc. It is undoubtedly the world's greatest motor cycle, and to get the feel of this powerful 650 engine when the twist-grip is turned is to know the thrill of road supremacy at its best.

Surviving into 1963

Together with the Rocket Gold Star (*see* Chapter 11) the Super Rocket outlived all the other pre-unit BSA twins, as when the 1963 range was announced at the beginning of September 1962 the other models had been axed (A7, A10 and Shooting Star). And it was now possible to specify chromium-plated mudguards for the Super Rocket for an additional £4 15s 2d, the price of the machine itself having risen to a tax-inclusive price of £303.

A full list of optional extras was as follows:

- air cleaner;
- ball and control lever;
- chrome-plated mudguards;
- rear chaincase;
- handrail;
- prop stand;
- rev counter;
- safety bars, front.

The last Super Rockets were built in the spring of 1963 and, with its more sporting brother, the Rocket Gold Star, finally brought production of the A7/A10 series of overhead-valve vertical twins to an end, after almost seventeen years of manufacture.

8 Stateside

During the immediate post-war period the British motorcycle industry was at full stretch, working to recover from the war. The bulk of that production – around 90 per cent – was exported, with by far the biggest chunk going to the USA, itself recovering from participation in the conflict. However, having been involved for a shorter period (December 1941 to August 1945) and due to the fact that its mainland had not suffered from aerial bombing, the States had not been hit as hard as Great Britain. Thus it had more money to spend on leisure and sporting activities once normality returned. The BSA works obliged the returning GIs' thirst for two-wheeled transport.

American Motorcycle Culture

During the early part of the twentieth century, the majority of rural America still relied on the horse and cart for daily transportation needs, with the car and motorcycle being confined largely to the richer people of the big cities of the eastern seaboard. The few motorcycles then in use were seen as a rich man's plaything. Prior to the war, the Americans had little interest in two-wheeled transport, preferring to travel by automobile.

The reasons for this situation lay in the nature of the country, which still had vast tracts of wilderness with poor communication routes. When the petrol engine was mass-produced, Henry Ford's cheap and reliable Model T car flooded the market, effectively pushing out the over-priced domestically produced motorcycle. By 1925 there were only 134,679 motorcycles registered in the USA, compared with 628,955 in Great Britain and 287,000 in Germany. By 1935, the American figure had dropped even lower to a mere 95,643 machines.

The British Take Notice

This low degree of American motorcycle ownership came to the attention of Major Watling, at that time director of the British Cycle and Motorcycle Manufacturers and Trade Union, whilst on a visit there in 1928 to look into business opportunities. What he found was an attitude problem generated by the car-driving population, who perceived motorcyclists to be social misfits whom they labelled 'grease balls'. The Stateside motorcyclist, unlike his European counterpart at this time, was exclusively a die-hard enthusiast for sports and touring, and did not engage in daily commuting on his machine, this task being performed by the car. When the Great Depression hit, and money became scarce, then and only then was the motorcycle again looked upon as a viable way of cutting transport costs.

British manufacturers took note of this situation and began to export, making sales despite the adverse economic climate. Sales boomed, and just before the outbreak of war in Europe during 1939, a peak was reached with some 1,000 British machines being imported in 1937. Sales in Canada peaked the same year, with a total of 572 imports. The Stateside buyers liked the British bikes and were spurred on by the well-documented sporting successes achieved by the British factories on the eastern side of the Atlantic. Successes in trials and road races showed that the British product was more economical and easier to handle than its US competitors, and this greatly contributed to the pre-war popularity. After the war the British companies again capitalized on this enthusiasm for British bikes, and between 1949 and 1951 British motorcycles comprised 40 per cent of all US sales.

Americans Develop their Own Style of Racing

Between the two world wars, the Americans developed their own style of racing, which differed considerably from the Europeans, using higher and wider handlebars that were more suited to the unpaved tracks that sprang up all over the country. This type of event suited the home-produced machinery, which held the monopoly until the immediate post-Second World War era, when British bikes became easier to import. With the upsurge of world-wide trading and the export-oriented determination of British motorcycle manufacturers, the import of bikes to the States took off, to satisfy the cravings of the dollar-rich American public. In contrast to the rest of the world, the Americans came out of the war in better shape than they had entered it. They did not suffer ground fighting or aerial bombardment; instead, they greatly expanded their industrial capacity to meet the war effort. After the conflict, unemployment was low and overtime high, and the workforce had fat bank accounts with which to finance leisure activities.

The major British producers all contributed to fill this need, with the likes of Matchless, Norton, Triumph and BSA contributing heavily to the export drive. With the American distributors actively encouraging the racing of British machinery, the starting grids became very international in their line-up, and all forms of racing on both dirt and tarmac took on a transatlantic flavour.

Daytona Beach

The Americans loved all forms of motorized sport, and one of the premier post-war events, whether it be two or four wheels in the States, was without doubt the Daytona Beach races. Held annually in the Florida resort of the same name, the Daytona Beach race comprised a 50-mile (80km) amateur race on the Saturday, followed by a 200-mile (320km) race for experts on the Sunday. The first 200-miler took place in 1937, when Ed Kretz took the honours on his Indian V-twin, averaging 74.1mph (119.2km/h). The British victory in the prestigious event came in 1941, when Canadian-born Billy Mathews brought his overhead camshaft Norton single home ahead of the field. Wartime activities curtailed any further beach racing until 1947, when a Harley-Davidson ridden by Johnny Spiegelhoff once again took top honours at 77.14mph (124.1km/h).

In 1948 the venue moved to a less congested part of the beach, and employed a 2-mile (3.2km) length of tarmac coast road, connected at either end by a pair of sweeping loops onto the beach, giving a total lap distance of 4.2 miles (6.75km), instead of the original 3.2-mile (5.1km) lap. The tarmac road section was narrow, strewn with blown sand and contained humps that tested not only the courage of the riders, but also the handling of the mostly rigid-framed machines, which regularly reached speeds up to 130mph (210km/h). The simple layout of this hugely supported venue meant that the hand-change, side-valve machines favoured by many local riders were not disadvantaged on their home ground.

Until the late 1940s this event was dominated by the home-produced side-valve Harley-Davidson and Indian models, which were allowed to race alongside 500cc ohv British machinery. From 1949 to 1952, Norton dominated the 200-miler with modified plunger-framed Manx racers. This led to a rule change to prevent overhead camshaft specialized racing bikes from holding an unfair advantage over production road-based machines. The new

SHATTERS TWO U.S.A. SPEED RECORDS AT *BONNEVILLE

*BONNEVILLE is a bed of hard, flat salt about 15 miles long by 8 wide. It is situated about 100 miles from Salt Lake, Utah, the city made famous by the Mormons. As the picture shows, in bright sunshine the surface of the salt sparkles like snow.

1. Class 'C' in the United States is restricted to standard machines which must appear in a current maker's catalogue. Compression ratio may not be higher than 8 : 1 and only pump petrol may be used.

2. Class 'A' in the United States is the 'open' class. There is no limit on compression ratio and 'dope' fuels are allowed.

Rider Gene Thiessen astride the B.S.A. Star Twin immediately before the record-breaking run. Beside the model is Gene Rhynne, the Chief Engine Tuner.

1 MILE STRAIGHTAWAY

(1) CLASS 'C'
BSA 500 cc STAR TWIN
MODEL A7
123·69 m.p.h

(2) CLASS 'A'
BSA 650 cc GOLDEN FLASH
MODEL A10
143·54 m.p.h

October 1951 advertising after Gene Thiessen had just broken American speed records in Class C (Star Twin) and Class A (Golden Flash) at Bonneville Salt Flats, Utah.

ruling outlawed all overhead cam models and was seen by many as a manipulation in favour of the Harley-Davidson side-valve layout, but the BSA factory hierarchy saw it as a challenge, one which could yield further advertising and increased sales.

Record Breaking at Rosamond

In July 1951, Gene Thiessen, riding a specially prepared A10 Golden Flash, broke several American national records on the Rosamond Salt Lakes. Running on pump fuel, Thiessen recorded a speed of 130.90mph (210.62km/h), raising this to 137.30mph (220.92km/h) when using alcohol. At the same venue Thiessen also clocked 123.69mph (198.89km/h) with a five-hundred Star Twin running on petrol. Considering that the stock roadster models were stretched to achieve 90mph (145km/h) and 100mph (160km/h) in their respective engine sizes, Thiessen's speeds were impressive. Later that year Thiessen raised the speeds still further; the A10 clocking 143.54mph (231km/h).

The BSA Distribution Networks

The BSA distribution networks in the USA also realized the importance of racing, and the increase in sales that track successes generated. Hap Alzina was the representative who covered the west coast from Oakland, California, with Alfred Child looking after the east coast, from his establishment, Rich Child Cycle Co. of Nutley, New Jersey. It was the latter gentleman who suggested a factory engineer come to the States to run a four-week service school for local BSA dealerships. The man chosen for this task was Roland Pike, a former racer and employee of the newly opened development shop back at the Birmingham factory. Roland was detailed by Bert Hopwood to carry out this task in November 1952, a duty he readily accepted. The Englishman soon got into the swing of things, talking to dealers from as far afield as Texas in the south and New England in the north. During this first visit, Roland Pike was invited back for the following year's Daytona Beach races to be held in February 1953. Alf Child had also approached the BSA board and put forward the argument that a lot could be learnt about American short track racing requirements from this prestigious event. The board agreed and Roland Pike returned for a second time.

Alloy Head Star Twins

The 1953 Daytona 200 race saw the BSA team wheel out iron-barrel, alloy cylinder head Star Twins. These were supposed to develop 43bhp, and used the heavy plunger rear suspension system. The prototype built by the engine development shop at the factory did put out 43bhp, but the bikes sent to Daytona, built by the production shop and tested by Cyril Halliburn, did not reach these figures. The race also included three of the previous season's twins, one of which had been hand-built by Jack Amott – this proving faster than the 1953 models!

Many of the BSA twins fell by the wayside, but Warren Sherwood nursed his bike home to gain a fifth place. The upshot of this fiasco was that one of the twins (which had crashed out) was transported back to Small Heath and retested on the dyno. The retest showed that the engine was producing only 39bhp.

The 1953 event was won by Paul Goldsmith on one of the new generation Harley-Davidson KR750s; he also set a new lap record of 94.45mph (151.9km/h). This gave an added incentive to the Small Heath development team to put up a better show the following year.

An all-out effort was then made to develop a batch of bikes to contest the 1954 Beach race, which turned out to be a mixture of twins and Gold Star singles. The latter bikes were included at the insistence of Roland Pike, who pointed out that Daytona Beach was not a flat-out circuit, for it contained two quite slow 180-degree bends that needed lots of torque to accelerate away from. The twin-cylinder Daytona machine employed a much-modified A7/Star Twin motor, which by then was developing 46bhp, whereas the single had a BB Gold Star engine, both up to Isle of Man specification.

Lightweight, Rigid Frames

The frames for these machines, built in enough numbers to conform to AMA's production requirements, were of a special construction, being super-lightweight, all welded and with a rigid rear end. From a design penned by Bill Nicholson for one-day trials events, these were built to comply with the American preference for lightweight machinery that could be pressed into use on the many one-mile and half-mile oval tracks that abounded in the States. The frames were of duplex cradle construction and

AMA

The AMA (American Motorcycle Association) is the most powerful organizing body in motorcycle sport outside the FIM (Fédération Internationale Motorcycliste), and certainly the biggest and busiest national federation in the two-wheel world with its activities spanning a wide spectrum from Youth Division off-road riding to professional road racing. It is also necessary to understand how and why the AMA emerged and its rule book, in order to understand why BSA (and Triumph) achieved the successes in various speed events in the USA, when in Europe they were outperformed by pukka GP bikes.

The AMA was formed in 1923 to take over responsibility for promoting and organizing the sport in the USA in place of the virtually extinct Federation of American Motorcyclists (FAM). The FAM had been torn asunder by internal disagreement over a debate about professional versus amateur status, with no-one able to make a firm decision.

Enter the AMA. One of its first moves was to phase out the use of exotic works bikes in favour of the 'Class C' professional racing. Class C was intended to produce closer racing with its production-based formula. Not only did AMA officials see this as a way of keeping down rider's costs, but also of encouraging brand loyalty – the spectator being able to associate the machine he rode on the street with the motorcycles being campaigned on the race circuit.

The basic AMA Class C ruling was that one started with a stock bike and modified it for racing purposes. A minimum of 100 machines of a particular type must have been manufactured, it couldn't have more than two cylinders, and a 750cc side-valve was regarded as the equivalent of a 500cc ohv model. The weakness, as manufacturers such as Harley-Davidson, Triumph and BSA were to prove, was that the rider (or more often the factory!) with the money and determination to win will always find a way around the rules.

Class C was also intended to create the AMA racer as an extremely competent all-round motorcyclist. He had to be, riding in virtually everything from road racing to enduros. This system's weakness was that no one rider was allowed to develop to be ultimate in a single discipline. And, in the author's opinion, this held back American riders until the AMA finally teamed up with the FIM in the early 1970s.

The basic venue for American competition was the ½ mile (0.8 km) or 1 mile (1.6km) oval, with the wealth of fairground horse tracks encouraging the development of flat-tracking as the major Stateside motorcycle sport. The venues spread across the whole of the USA and produced close and fiercely contested racing. In addition, TT steeplechasing added another dimension to the flat-track theme by introducing at least one major jump, as well as left- and right-hand corners into the course layout.

The competition had a uniquely American flavour, and was quite unlike anything seen in Europe, where road racing was considered the premier two-wheel sport. The nearest thing to European-style racing was the annual Laconia, New Hampshire, meeting, which was staged over closed public roads. But long before Laconia's 1938 inception, the AMA hierarchy displayed a marked reluctance to join with other nations competing under the umbrella of the FIM. In fact, it was not until the early 1970s that the AMA became affiliated to the international body, and then only after much political intrigue and infighting amongst the various AMA senior officials who were either for or against the idea.

There is no doubt that from the immediate post-Second World War period to the 1960s, the AMA seemed more interested in maintaining the status quo and keeping foreign influence at bay, rather than promoting the sport and broadening its appeal. This explains why machines such as the Manx Norton and Matchless G50 were banned during the 1950s and 1960s respectively by the AMA – and why the thundering 750 side-valve Harley-Davidson continued to be raced many years after it was obsolete elsewhere in the world. And it is true that without the AMA rules the British 500cc pushrod twins from the likes of BSA and Triumph would not have enjoyed the success that they did in Stateside competition.

used a swinging-arm type BSA gearbox and a majority of standard Gold Star running gear, such as wheels, forks and fuel tank. The oil tanks were of special construction, being sited low and to the right in the rigid rear and frame tubes. The standard 8in (203mm) single-sided SLS front brake was used, but the operating lever on the brake plate was reversed in an effort to make the brake work more efficiently. To conform to their racing image, both the twins and singles were fitted with Feridax single racing seats.

Victory at Last

And so came the 1954 Daytona 200 race, and with it victory at last for the BSA marque, Bobby Hill of Columbus, Ohio, gaining first place (and a $2,000 dollar purse) on his works twin-cylinder model, averaging 94.24mph (151.6km/h). A similarly mounted Dick Klamforth finished runner-up, half a mile behind the winner. Klamforth was in fact riding the team's spare bike and the only one fitted with a sprung frame. In fact, the top five finishers were all BSA-mounted, but only the third-place bike, ridden by Tommy McDermott from Glens Falls, New York, was mounted on a Gold Star single. Fourth and fifth positions were taken by Al Gunter and Kenny Eggers, both riding rigid-framed Star Twins.

The weather that year was uncommonly cold for the sunshine state, and this probably helped the British machines, but nevertheless the result was very gratifying for the BSA factory.

A Clean Sweep

The first five places – a clean sweep – carried a lot of advertising value, and both BSA and Dunlop capitalized on this. To average 94mph (151km/h) for 2hr 7min 22sec proved that the winning BSA machine had both stamina and speed, and was well up to the job of beating arch rivals from the Triumph and Harley-Davidson factories, as well as the other 111 riders who had entered the race. In fact, the only distributor-sponsored BSA machine that failed to finish was the Gold Star single of Cliff Caswell, but even this was not due to mechanical problems – Caswell simply fell off. In all, no fewer than eighteen riders were mounted on BSA machines.

Daytona 200 BSA Results 1949–62

Year	Pos	Rider	Year	Pos	Rider	Year	Pos	Rider
1949	6th	Tommy McDermott		16th	Gene Thiessen		11th	John Muckentthaler
1950	3rd	Tommy McDermott		20th	Walter Grimm		16th	Lowell Moore
	12th	H.C. Simon	1955	7th	Dick Mann		20th	Jack Morrison
	16th	Warren Sherwood		9th	Al Gunter	1960	17th	Bobby Sirkegian
	19th	Gene Thiessen		14th	Norman Lyon		20th	Neil Keen
1951	7th	Jim Garber	1956	2nd	Dick Klamforth	1961	4th	Warren Sherwood
	11th	Warren Sherwood		3rd	George Everett		8th	Garnet Koehler
	13th	Don Rossi		4th	Tommy McDermott		11th	Warren DeLong
	18th	Don Nicolaides		5th	Gene Thiessen		16th	Joe Messaros
1952	5th	Al Gunter		14th	Warren Sherwood		17th	Elmer Morra
	9th	Gene Thiessen		16th	Pete Knight		18th	Edward Clifford
	10th	Kenny Eggers		17th	Bob Smith	1962	6th	Jody Nicholas
	11th	Jim Garber		19th	Don Rees		7th	Dick Klamforth
	16th	Warren Sherwood	1957	2nd	Al Gunter		8th	Garnet Koehler
	20th	Billy Mathews		3rd	Gene Thiessen		15th	Edward Clifford Jr
1953	5th	Warren Sherwood		5th	Tommy McDermott		19th	Warren Sherwood
	8th	John Haskell		8th	Rolland Hedgecock			
	9th	Gene Thiessen		9th	Glen Jordan			
	13th	Trevor Deeley		10th	Bobby Stilwell			
	18th	Pete Knight		11th	Warren Sherwood			The above results were gained by a
	20th	Jim Garber		12th	Warren Wolfe Jr			mixture of various twin-cylinder
1954	1st	Bobby Hill		13th	Neil Keen			BSAs (all 500cc) and Gold Star sin-
	2nd	Dick Klamforth	1958	9th	Warren Sherwood			gles. The famous top five positions
	3rd	Tommy McDermott		12th	Babe DeMay			in 1954 were gained by specially
	4th	Al Gunter		16th	Ronnie Gould			prepared Shooting Star twins (first,
	5th	Kenny Eggers	1959	7th	Neil Keen			second, fourth and fifth), with a Gold
	8th	Warren Sherwood		9th	Rolland Hedgecock			Star finishing third.

One of the 1954 Shooting Star racers, with rigid frame and siamezed exhaust.

Roland Pike (centre with motorcycle) and one of the Daytona five hundred twins. Note the low-slung oil tank.

BSA **wins!**

FIRST FIVE
POSITIONS IN
1954
200 MILE
Championship

AT DAYTONA, FLORIDA, MARCH 7th

"BSA" 1st
Bobby Hill on BSA "Shooting Star"
Time—*2 hours 7 minutes 22 seconds

"BSA" 2nd.
Dick Klamfoth on BSA "Shooting Star"
Time—*2 hours 7 minutes 42 seconds

"BSA" 3rd.
Tommy McDermott on BSA "Gold Star"
Time—*2 hours 7 minutes 50 seconds

"BSA" 4th.
Albert Gunter on BSA "Shooting Star"

"BSA" 5th.
Ken Eggers on BSA "Shooting Star"

*Subject to official confirmation

The finest record ever established at Daytona by any motorcycle manufacturer!

Ride a Winner - Make your next Motorcycle a 1954 **BSA**

DEALER INQUIRIES INVITED

In The East **RICH CHILD CYCLE CO.,** 639 Passaic Ave., Nutley 10, N. J.   In The West **HAP ALZINA,** 3074 Broadway, Oakland, Calif.

As this April 1954 Cycle World *advertisement shows, BSA took the first five places in the Daytona 200 that year; with twins coming home first, second, fourth and fifth.*

The 1955 Bikes

The following year, 1955, BSA hoped to repeat this performance, again using a mixture of twins and singles, but it was not to be. The latest bikes retained the cycle parts of the previous year's entries, but were now equipped with massive air filters to fight the swirling Daytona sand that got everywhere. However, this was not a full factory-backed effort and it showed, with only three BSAs finishing in the top twenty: Dick Mann seventh, Al Gunter ninth and Norman Lyon fourteenth.

Although the 1954 200-miler can be seen as the beginning of factory-supported BSA involvement at Daytona, it should be pointed out that many private entries had contested the event in previous years, although many of these rode the Gold Star single rather than the A7 series twins.

The 100-Mile Amateur Race

Even though in the experts' 200-miler BSA entries were largely made up of the Gold Star single from the mid-1960s, in 1956 Jack Schlaman came close to victory in the 100-Mile Amateur Race, but ultimately came home second on his BSA Star Twin; this again proving how competitive the twin was Stateside.

BSA GOLD STAR TWIN

MODEL A10 GOLD STAR TWIN 650 c.c. (40 cubic inches)

The 650 Rocket Gold Star was marketed as the Gold Star Twin in the States.

BRAND NEW, CUSTOM-BUILT 650!
WITH ALL THE SPECIAL FEATURES MOST WANTED BY SPORT RIDERS

HERE IS the Super-Sports models thousands of riders want—custom built, super-powered by the famous Rocket Big-Valve engine, specially tuned for top power output. Genuine racing equipment is *built in at the factory*—no expensive speed kits to buy!

Special Racing Features

Needle roller racing gearbox, 190 mm. racing front brake, ball-end levers (control cables adjust at handlebars), rod-operated racing rear brake, Gold Star tank and badges, quick-fill vented tank cap, alloy racing wheel rims, racing quick-detachable rear wheel, new road-track mufflers, open rear chain with chrome guard, many other special items.

This sensational new model is designed to give you the best in performance and road holding, powerful braking, genuine road-racing power and speed!

Finish: Metallic red-over gold, chrome, polished alloy.

SPECIAL RACING EQUIPMENT

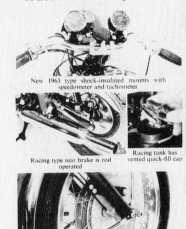

New 1963 type shock-insulated mounts with speedometer and tachometer

Racing type rear brake is rod operated

Racing tank has vented quick-fill cap

POWER! Famous Big-Valve high compression cylinder head and "357" full-race camshaft give *full power* to Gold Star Twin, Super Rocket, Spitfire.

Powerful 190 mm. racing front brake, racing alloy wheel rims

Managerial Changes

By the mid-1950s the American market had established itself as by far BSA's largest customer, with two main distributors: Hap Alzina ruled the West Coast distributorship, while Theodor 'Ted' Hodgson had become President of the BSA Eastern base, having succeeded Alfred 'Rich' Child, the founder of the BSA American business operation, in 1955. He held this position until his retirement some thirteen years later in 1968.

Again, Edward Turner rears his head in the story of BSA in the USA. When he became BSA Automotive Group director during the late 1950s Turner had it 'written into his contract'

(Steve Wilson) that he was to spend six months of each year in the USA. Unfortunately, this mainly assisted Triumph sales, rather than BSA. Bert Hopwood commented of Turner that he 'never got through on visits to BSA dealers, for whom he didn't feel responsible'.

Actually, after Edward Turner retired in 1973, Harry Sturgeon (*see* Chapter 10) made considerable progress in increasing BSA sales stateside. In fact, sales figures in dollars earned by combined BSA/Triumph sales in 1965–66 were superior to any single British car firm exported to North America. But as Steve Wilson commented: 'BSA-Triumph also began planning to take over their own stateside distribution from

BSA ENGINEERING

Every BSA motorcycle incorporates the long experience of a famous engineering firm with over 100 years in precision manufacturing. Depend on BSA for excellence of design, up-to-date features, *all that's best in motorcycling!*

POWER TO GO!

Thrill to instant, crisp response when you twist the throttle of your new BSA! Featured in many BSA high-powered models are sports or racing cams, high compression pistons, oversize valves, and many other equipment items tested and proven in years of racing experience. BSA motorcycles are *performance-engineered* for your greatest thrill in motor sports!

(Super Rocket engine illustrated at right)

POWER TO STOP!

BSA brakes are especially designed and built for the model to which they are fitted. BSA uses the knowledge gained in many seasons of racing experience in designing the brakes fitted to your road model. Many BSA competition models have genuine racing type brakes for the severe conditions to which they are subject. All BSA models are equipped with powerful brakes which make for sure, quick stops.

(Super Rocket brake illustrated at right)

See full specifications on all models pages 10-11

GOLD STAR SPITFIRE SCRAMBLER
MODEL A10 SPITFIRE
650 c.c. (40 cubic inches)
Most powerful BSA competition model!

Spitfire is finished in bright metallic red, chrome, polished alloy. (Full chrome fenders, chrome tank panels *outstanding appearance!*)

SPITFIRE has a full-race camshaft, straight-through exhaust system for maximum horsepower output, and new for 1963, Catalina type frame, and brakes. Rear brake rod operated.

The Spitfire Scrambler, an American-only model; it was essentially a Gold Star Scrambler, with a tuned 646cc A10-series engine.

BSA Incorporated at Nutley, New Jersey, in the East and from Hap Alzina, the man who over two decades had done so much for British motorcycles on the West Coast.' The Group already owned the Triumph Corporation of Baltimore, Bill Johnson's West Coast operation and BSA Incorporated. And so they swallowed up Hap Alzina, who retired in 1968, to form BSA Incorporated USA; one big corporate giant.

On paper this might have looked and sounded good. Unfortunately, the truth was something quite different. For a start, many of the original experienced management and staff from the previous smaller, privately owned distributors were axed. For example, expatriate Dennis McCormack, who had been head of the Triumph Baltimore operation since its beginning in 1951, was, as Steve Wilson says, 'passed over', with the presidency of the new corporation going to Peter Thornton. The headquarters for BSA Incorporated USA was an expensive set of buildings in Verona, New Jersey, with some 1,200 dealers nationwide. But by this time Honda had 2,000 – and many of these were former BSA-Triumph dealers!

Compounding this, the changeover and the fact that back at Small Heath things were going from bad to worse (*see* Chapter 10)

BSA Motorcycles for 1963

Destination *Fun!*

NEW MODELS
NEW FEATURES

THE NEW GOLD STAR TWIN
—Plus 14 other sparkling models

The Americans loved both the Rocket Gold Star and single-cylinder Gold Star models. They even threatened to stop imports if these models could not be delivered!

meant that the short American selling season was missed. Many of the bikes that eventually arrived too late in the States had to be subsequently returned to the UK and sold at discount on the home market.

Even the arrival of the BSA-Triumph triples couldn't change things around much, except on the race circuits on both sides of the Atlantic, where the Rocket 3 and Trident seven-fifties largely ruled the roost in 1970 and 1971. However, in the very same period sales and profits were plummeting and in June 1971 Peter Thornton resigned as BSA Inc. USA President. Dennis McCormack returned to handle the Stateside operation until Felix Kalinski took over in April 1972. All in all, the situation was grim.

The Final Straw

The final straw was when American banks that had been involved in underwriting the USA operation had pulled the plug on Thornton – hence his exit from the scene. America was suffering its own problems – this being shown by Richard Nixon devaluing the dollar, causing a recession. Several of BSA's American dealers now went bankrupt, causing the American arm and its British backers yet more problems.

McCormack tried to turn things around, but it was too late. All the hard work that individuals had done and the things they had achieved in the showroom and in sport during the immediate post-war period of 1945–60 had in a few years been totally destroyed in America and of course back in Great Britain. What a sad ending.

9 Road Racing

When originally drawing out what was to emerge in 1946 as the A7 vertical twin (and later, in 1949, the A10 Golden Flash), the last thing on the design team's mind was the possibility of road racing. As Roy Bacon said in the 1980 book *BSA Twins & Triples*: 'The BSA twin-cylinder machines were not originally intended to be sports models but to provide reliable transport with all the rather boring attributes such vehicles have. So, as well as reliability, the accent was on economy, ease of maintenance, spares and service back-up and other utilitarian values.' Not only this, but the phenomenal successes gained by the Gold Star singles meant that in practice anyone wishing to go racing during the immediate post-war period (1945 to early 1960s) was not likely to have considered the humble BSA pushrod twins.

But in practice the twins were raced and, perhaps even more amazingly, the A7-engine-based machine of sidecar ace Chris Vincent was to give BSA its only TT victory in 1962, just as the production of the pre-unit models was coming to an end.

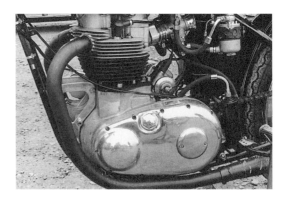

ABOVE: *VMCC racer showing alloy head, remote float carbs, exhaust, chaincase and magneto. Note the vacant space at the front of the engine where the dynamo would have sat on the roadster.*

LEFT: *Special A7-based racer prepared for VMCC events. The specification included Shooting Star alloy head, twin carbs, rev counter, twin megaphone exhaust, rigid frame and modified 8in front brake.*

Probably the very first appearance by a BSA twin came in the Isle of Man during June 1947, the event being the Clubman's TT. This was also the very first 'Clubman', the race being run on Wednesday, 11 June. It was a combined fixture with classes for 250, 350 and 500cc, the latter two running over four laps of the 37.73-mile (60km) circuit, thus making 150.92 miles (243km) in total.

Essentially the Clubman's race was for standard production roadsters of which at least twenty-five examples had already been sold to the public. Certain modifications could be carried out, mainly to improve safety (racing tyres, handlebars, footrests and air scoops for the brakes and the like). Straight-through exhausts were also allowed, but not full racing megaphones.

A pair of BSA A7 twins had been entered: J.E. Stevens of the Oswestry club and N. Kirby (Accrington) in an entry which comprised thirty-three bikes in the Senior (500cc) category. But there was to be no BSA glory this time, as first Kirby (broken fuel union) retired

on lap 1, then Stevens (who had been up with the leaders in fourth position, was forced out at Glen Helen with carburettor problems. The race was eventually won by Norton-mounted Denis Parkinson.

Next in the 1948 Clubman's, two more twins were entered, but again both retired. But in 1949 there were four entries and John Wright came home in eleventh spot. It was John Wright who came the nearest to success on the twins in the Clubman's series.

Milano–Taranto

Even though the A7 didn't leave its mark on the Clubman's TT, this was certainly not the case in the famous Italian road classic, the Milano-Taranto, when Leopoldo Tartarini (later to become the owner of the Italjet marque) won the sidecar class of this prestigious event. Partnered by Sergio Calza, the pairing completed the 876-mile (1,410km) open road course in 17hr 3min 3sec – this being almost an hour in front of the next finisher.

Mechanic Marsh Corcoran (left) helping John Wright to prepare his Star Twin for the 1952 Senior Clubman's TT.

T.T. COURSE—KEY TO DESCRIPTION

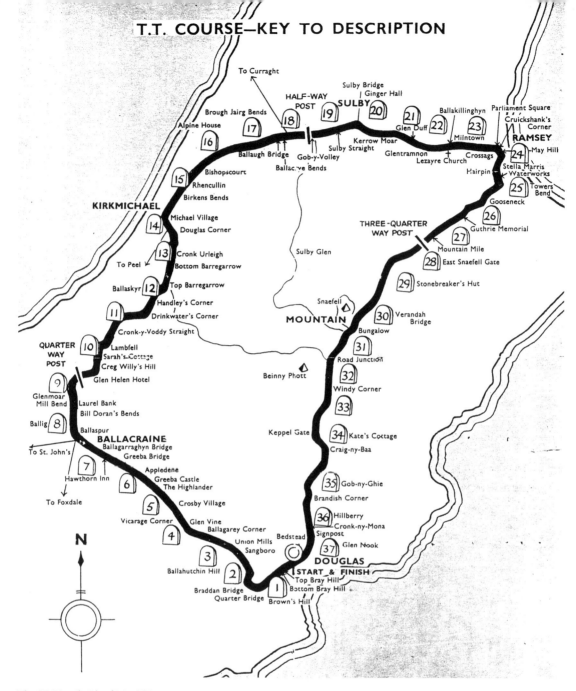

The 37.73-mile Isle of Man TT course.

Charlie Salt

Probably the best solo racing effort by a twin in Britain was that of Charlie Salt, who during the early 1950s put up a number of consistent rides with an A7 twin-based racer, including the Isle of Man TT. Salt, who worked in the BSA experimental department, was later killed on the final circuit of the eight-lap Golden Jubilee Senior TT in 1957, when riding a DBD 34 Gold Star single.

In his A7 days, Salt was closely connected with the Birmingham engineer Ernie Earles. The latter owned the Elms Metal factory in

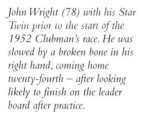

John Wright (78) with his Star Twin prior to the start of the 1952 Clubman's race. He was slowed by a broken bone in his right hand, coming home twenty-fourth – after looking likely to finish on the leader board after practice.

West Heath, not far from the BSA plant. And as both Salt and Earles were keen supporters of the TT, their partnership blossomed. However, it should be pointed out that a number of other riders – on other makes of machine – also rode for Ernie Earles, and in fact he was also closely involved with other manufacturers, notably MV Agusta and BMW. As for Charlie Salt, his first TT was in 1949 when he finished twenty-eighth on a Norton in the Junior race, then retired on another Norton in the Senior.

Salt's first year with the Earles-BSA was 1951. This was essentially a specially prepared and brake-tested A7 series engine mounted in

an Earles-made frame. Consisting of magnesium-alloy tubing and full-welded construction, the Earles frame was costly to build, but a real work of art. A surviving A7-Earles racer allegedly used by Charlie Salt is on display at Sammy Miller's museum in Hampshire.

Besides the frame itself, which featured swinging-arm rear suspension with twin hydraulically damped shock absorbers, the machine also boasted Earles' own design of front fork. Actually, the Earles fork was quite a breakthrough during the early to mid-1950s and ended up being adopted by several manufacturers, notably German, including BMW and DKW.

The Ernie Earles aluminium-framed Star Twin racer of the type Charlie Salt raced in the Isle of Man TT during 1951, 1952 and 1953. He finished eighteenth in 1952 and sixteenth in 1953.

In the 1951 Senior TT, Charlie Salt's race came to an end on lap 4 with a retirement. But in 1952 and still with the Earles-BSA A7, he had a trouble-free ride, finishing eighteenth at an average speed of 84.46mph (135.9km/h). Incidentally, Cecil Sandford (who went on to win the world championship with M.V. Agusta and F.B. Mondial) also rode an Earles-BSA A7 and had been in front of Salt (lapping in 26min 10sec) when he retired on the fourth lap.

In 1953, Charlie Salt again rode the Earles-BSA in the Senior TT and did even better, coming home in sixteenth position with an average speed of 83.51mph (134.37km/h) and a fastest lap in 26min 16sec. Together with Eric Houseley and Peter Davey, he shared in the winning club team prize for his local Derby Pathfinder MCC.

From 1954 onwards, Charlie Salt used the Gold Star single-cylinder engine for both his Junior and Senior rides in the TT. His full BSA TT 'scoreboard' is listed below:

- 1951   Senior   retired
- 1952   Senior   18th
- 1953   Junior   retired
- 1953   Senior   16th
- 1954   Junior   retired
- 1954   Senior   22nd
- 1955   Junior   17th
- 1955   Senior   retired
- 1956   Junior   32nd
- 1956   Senior   retired
- 1957   Junior   31st.

Then came the fateful 1957 Senior in which he was to lose his life.

Roland Pike

Roland Pike was a particularly gifted rider/ engineer who during the late 1940s was virtually unbeatable on the British short circuits with his home-tuned Pike-Rudge machinery. Then in 1951 he rode a two-year-old BSA Gold Star to twenty-first in the Senior TT, averaging 80.65mph (129.77km/h). This prompted the

idea of building a pair of racers using Gold Star engines in lightweight welded frames of Pike's own design. The engines were duly ordered via his local dealer, Halletts of Canterbury, Kent, and this brought about his initial contact with Bert Hopwood, then BSA's design chief.

Hopwood was well aware of Pike's reputation as a development engineer, rider and fellow racer, and BSA employee Charlie Salt arranged an interview with Bert Hopwood late in 1951. This resulted in Pike being offered the job of heading up the Development Shop. Replacing the long serving and well-respected Jack Amott, Pike was deeply involved with the MCI two-fifty single cylinder racing project and Gold Star development – plus working on the twins.

During the closed season of 1951–52 he built the first two Pike-BSA racers. These were powered by a 350 Gold Star and a 500 A7 Star Twin, the latter featuring an aluminium top end. The frames employed a large diameter oval and tapered single front downtubes and Girling rear shocks, the 350 using a five-speed Albion gearbox.

During the 1952 TT, both machines retired on lap 3 of their respective races. As both were experimental, their main purpose, certainly as

Roland Pike screaming his Pike BSA A7 twin racer down Bray Hill, during the 1952 Senior TT.

The BSA twins, both in pre-unit and unit guises, chalked up many successes in sidecar racing during the 1950s and 1960s; this is a scene from the South London Crystal Palace circuit.

regards BSA, was development rather than winning races. And although Pike himself decided to replace the twin-cylinder engine of the 500 with a Gold Star unit, there is no doubt that the lessons learned with the Pike-A7 Star Twin were of considerable use when building the successful Daytona racers that swept the board at the American classic in spring 1954. Pike, of course, was deeply involved in this latter exercise and built up valuable links for BSA in the States during his visits across the Atlantic (*see* Chapter 8). Pike also acknowledged the work on the twins that was carried out by Arthur Butler and Bert Hole.

Thruxton

Thruxton airfield in rural Hampshire was the scene of countless endurance racing battles during the 1950s and 1960s. And, although a BSA twin never won the event, they were usually to be found in the entry list, usually in larger 646cc A10 series form.

The inaugural event was staged one fine summer's day in June 1955 over a 2.76-mile (4.4km) circuit arranged at the airfield venue. The rules for this first event stated that two riders would be allowed for each machine and the winning team was to be the pairing that had piled up the most laps by the ninth hour. The original concept was to run a 12 or 24hr race, part of which would be in darkness. However, it was eventually decided that for this first event, at any rate, nine hours would be sufficient.

As things turned out, for the majority of the competitors, nine hours was quite long enough. Surprisingly, the real problem that surfaced was tyre-related, rather than rider fatigue or mechanical failure. This was due to the abrasive nature of the Thruxton tarmac. Front tyres seemed to suffer more than rear ones. This was to cause near panic, as very few teams had come prepared with spare rubber, let alone spare wheels and tyres. Remember this was fifty years ago, long before the advent of ultra-sticky tyres which only last a few miles! Countless SOS calls were relayed over the public address system. As a result, many spectators provided tyres from their own bikes, whilst mechanics were dispatched to the local town of Andover in a desperate search.

Even though there was a host of large-capacity machines from the likes of Triumph, Royal Enfield, Norton and a couple of BSA six-fifty twins, it was a 499cc Gold Star that eventually won. This was piloted by Eddie Dow and Eddie Crooks, and a 348cc Gold Star finished runner-up. In fact, the first machine larger than 500cc to finish was a 649cc Triumph, in sixth.

The considerable publicity generated by the 1955 event ensured a much higher standard of entry the following year, with several well-known short-circuit stars amongst the sixty teams. But again a Gold Star won, ridden by Ken James and Ivor Lloyd – but this time a three-fifty. A 646cc A10 Golden Flash was runner-up in the 750cc class, ridden by Jim Dakin and R. Eskins.

If anyone had placed bets that a Gold Star couldn't win a third time around, they would have lost. Rex Avery and Fred Webber took their Gold Star to victory in 1957, making it three wins in a row for the BSA single.

In 1958 the event became the Thruxton 500 Mile Race, and with it came new levels of interest from manufacturers, press and public alike. Not only this, but for the first time a multi-cylinder bike took the chequered flag, in the shape of a Triumph Tiger 110 ridden by Dan Shorey and a young Mike Hailwood. For the first time, none of the top six finishers overall was mounted on a Gold Star and all were twins; however, the only BSA twin, a 646cc Road Rocket ridden by J. Hatcher and J. Allington, finished outside the top six. The BSA pairing actually came home eighteenth overall and eleventh in their class. They completed 187 laps, compared to the 220 of winners Shorey and

Hailwood. Forty-three teams finished, in what had been by far the most competitive Thruxton endurance race up to that time.

The 1959 500-miler saw a BMW take victory. Early pacesetters Bob McIntyre and Eric Hinton's bid on Syd Lawton's 692cc Royal Enfield came to an end after McIntyre crashed following a broken primary chain. As for the BSA twin, sidecar star Chris Vincent, partnered by Norman Storr, brought a Road Rocket home in a very creditable seventh position.

In the 1960 and 1961 races only a single BSA twin was entered (646cc Super Rocket each time) and both machines retired with split oil tanks. Then came the 1962 event – the year that the new Rocket Gold Star had entered production. This saw the biggest BSA twins entry list up to that time:

- M.J. Spalding/D.J. Dixon;
- E.F. Wooder/R.P. Dawson;
- I.R. Goddard/R. Chandler;
- D. Powell/D. Williams.

All were mounted on the Rocket Gold Star. And even though the Spalding/Dixon bike was an official Syd Lawton entry, it was the pairing of Powell/Williams who achieved the most success, finished sixth in class and eighth overall, completing 212 laps at an average speed of 71.17mph (114.5km/h). By way of comparison, the winners, Phil Read and Brian Setchell, rode a Syd Lawton-entered Norton 650 SS, completed 228 laps and averaged 76.45mph (123km/h).

In June 1963 several BSA Rocket Gold Stars took part in the Thruxton 500-miler. Best-placed machine was Ron Langston/Dave Williams – sixth in the 1000cc class, completing 221 laps. Other finishers were Gordon Smith/Tom Sheaff, 185 laps. Don Face/Eric Denyer (crash) completed ninety-two laps before retiring.

From then on, the unit construction BSA twins carried on at Thruxton; during the mid-1960s the race was run at Castle Combe and Brands Hatch.

A high-speed trial at Silverstone, c. mid 1950s, showing Vincent, Matchless, Triumph and BSA big twins hard at it.

Silverstone 1,000

The BMCRC (British Motor Cycle Racing Club) staged a rival to the increasingly popular Thruxton 500-miler at Silverstone on Saturday, 20 May 1961. Named the 1,000 Kilometres, it attracted a huge entry and was won by Bruce Daniels/Peter Darvill (BMW R69S). BSA twins were represented by Ernie Wooder and John Holder, whose 646cc Super Rocket finished ninth, completing 188 laps at an average speed of 73.93mph (118.95km/h), compared to the winning BMW's 215 laps/84.73mph (136.33km/h).

A year later in May 1962 Wooder, now partnered by Robin Dawson and riding one of the new Rocket Gold Star models, put in a blistering performance in a rain-soaked race at Silverstone to finish a brilliant fourth overall. Full result below:

- 1st P. Read/B. Setchell Norton 650SS 215 laps/75.89mph (122.1km/h)
- 2nd E. Minihan/C. Conn Triumph Bonneville 213 laps/74.9mph (120.5km/h)
- 3rd B. Denehy/J. Stracey Triumph Bonneville 213 laps/74.86mph (120.5km/h)

- 4th E. Wooder/R. Dawson BSA Rocket Gold Star
- 5th D. Greenfield/F. Swift Norton 88SS
- 6th P. Darvill/N. Price BMW R69S.

The final year, when the Bemsee 1,000 Kilometres was staged, came in 1963. But by then not one single BSA 650 was entered. In fact, the meeting had been transferred to Oulton Park, with fewer than thirty entries – which signalled the end for the event.

Chris Vincent

Born in Birmingham in 1935, C.V. (Chris) Vincent joined the BSA factory straight from school. Chris made his racing début in 1954 on the grass with a JAP speedway-engined machine. But working at BSA he decided he knew more about 'Beeza' engines and that it would be to his advantage to use one for racing. This was to be the beginning of a partnership that would rise to the very top in the sport of sidecar racing.

In 1956 Chris won the British Grasstrack Sidecar Championship title. And in 1959 he decided to go road racing. Then in 1960 came the highlight of his season, the Sidecar TT. This

Chris Vincent, passengered by Eric Bliss, rounding Gerard's Bend, Mallory Park, during September 1961 with their six-fifty Super Rocket-engined outfit. The following year, 1962, the pair won the sidecar TT on their A7 machine.

was his first visit to the Isle of Man. And after impressive practice lap times, in the race itself he was mixing it with the BMWs and set the fastest lap by a British machine with a time of 27min 52.4sec – 81mph (130km/h). But then he struck engine trouble and was forced to retire.

Although he had joined BSA from school, he had a spell with rivals Norton during the mid-1950s and in fact it had been Norton's World Sidecar Champion, Cyril Smith, who had first got Chris thinking about sidecar racing. But later he rejoined BSA and the experimental department, where much of his work involved high-speed testing for the Birmingham company.

In 1961 Chris Vincent really began making a name for himself. Using a low-slung 'kneeler' outfit he had a brilliant year, winning and breaking lap records almost everywhere he went with his A7- and A10-engined machinery. For example, at the international meeting at Oulton Park at the beginning of April 1961, Chris was a mere couple of machine lengths behind the race winner, World Champion Helmut Fath (BMW), and the BSA man set the fastest lap of 78.51mph (126.3km/h).

The 3 May 1961 issue of *Motor Cycle News* carried the following headline: 'Invincible Chris Vincent'. This came in response to his record-breaking performance over the 2.65-mile Brands Hatch GP circuit, where he won both sidecar races and set new lap records.

During the 1960s in the British short circuit sidecar racing classes, half the entries would be BSA mounted, with names such as Chris Vincent, Peter Brown, Mick Boddice and Roy Hanks – all of whom worked at the BSA factory.

However, in the Sidecar TT he was forced to retire early on in the race after suffering problems in practice.

But it was 1962 when Chris Vincent really made history. *The Motor Cycle* dated 7 June that year really sums things up: 'Best of British Luck! Chris Vincent thumps Continental Aces in Sensational Sidecar TT.' Everyone had expected what *The Motor Cycle* referred to as 'the customary BMW benefit', but actually Chris had taken his A7-powered kneeler outfit to a sensational, history-making victory. He covered three laps of the 37.73 mile (60.7km) Mountain Circuit in 1hr 21min 16.4sec, an average speed of 83.57mph (134.5km/h). The race report ended: 'The crowds around the final miles gasped in astonishment, then recovered their senses to wave and cheer on the BSA wizard. It was incredible but it was happening. A British rider on a British machine was leading the Sidecar TT – for the first time, on the Mountain course, since 1924.'

Although officially BSA as a company was not directly involved at that stage with Chris Vincent's racing, it did see the value of the publicity he had gained the marque with his TT success. And so a delighted management celebrated the victory by quickly organizing a dinner in his honour at a Douglas hotel during TT week (the Sidecar Race having been the first in the programme). As Norman Vanhouse says in his 1986 book *BSA Competition History*, 'Working within the BSA factory Vincent did have the advantage of a degree of official support, though this varied enormously among those in a position to help – from the wholehearted co-operation and support of Len Crisp, one-time sidecar expert and then foreman of the experimental department – to the downright hostility of others.'

Chris Vincent's record in the British Sidecar Championships was impressive and, from his first title in 1961, he dominated the series for a decade – even though in 1962 he lost the crown to Bill Boddice (Norton) by a slim margin. Thereafter it was virtually his own, winning in 1963, 1964, 1965, 1969, 1970 and 1971. And the gap in the middle? Well, this was when Owen Greenwood 'cheated' by using a 1071cc Mini-engined car. But eventually the FIM stepped in and banned such vehicles in post-1969 events.

Initially, Chris employed 497cc A7 and 646cc A10 engines, and in fact continued to do so until the beginning of 1964, when at last he bowed to taking on board the A50/A65 engines that BSA had introduced two years before.

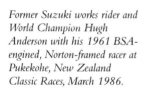

Former Suzuki works rider and World Champion Hugh Anderson with his 1961 BSA-engined, Norton-framed racer at Pukekohe, New Zealand Classic Races, March 1986.

10 The BSA Group

The early history of BSA is related in Chapter 1. However, it is really the post–Second World War era with which this later chapter is concerned. It is vital for the reader to appreciate just how large and important BSA was in the British motorcycle industry during the 1940s and 1950s – and why ultimately it was to fail in the late 1960s and early 1970s.

In very basic terms, the BSA Group evolved over a number of years, with 1910 being a vital year for the automotive side, not only because of the first production of BSA motorcycles, but also the acquisition of the Daimler car firm. This latter move was also to bring with it the arrival of James Leek, who was to be an instrumental figure in the success of BSA motorcycles until his retirement through ill health in 1956.

Then in 1919 BSA Cycles was formed (looking after both cycles and motorcycles) and the first V-twin (Model A) was manufactured. In 1928 the Redditch factory (previously used for motorcycle production) closed and all production transferred to Small Heath, Birmingham. In 1939 James Leek was instrumental in convincing the BSA board to switch to military production, months before war actually began. This policy was not only to see the company manufacture a vast range of military equipment, but also 126,000 M20 motorcycles.

The Acquisitions

The war years were, thanks in no small part to James Leek's foresight, extremely profitable. This enabled the company to make a number

LEFT: For over a century the piled arms BSA trademark stood for industrial strength, in a whole range of industries.
RIGHT: The Daimler car company had been taken over by BSA in 1910. The Regency Mk II was the latest Daimler in 1954. It was built in 3½ and 4½ litre engine sizes.

World-famous Motor Cycles

BSA ARIEL *SUNBEAM* TRIUMPH

World famous motorcycles from BSA, Ariel, Sunbeam and Triumph – all from the same group.

of acquisitions, namely Sunbeam (1940), Ariel (1944) and New Hudson (1945). The end of the war in 1945 brought a new challenge – to continue making profits in peacetime, rather than being able to grab military contracts from government departments.

But the end of the conflict did not stop BSA acquiring more companies. Without doubt, the most important was the purchase of Triumph in 1951. This, like Ariel, was from Jack Sangster (to gain fuller appreciation of the Sangster family's role in the British motorcycle industry the

reader is advised to consult *Ariel – The Complete Story* by the same author and also published by The Crowood Press). At the same time, Sangster joined the BSA board. Other key players in BSA's management at the time were Sir Bernard Docker (Chairman), James Leek (General Manager), Bert Hopwood (Chief Designer from early 1949), Herbert Perkins (Assistant Chief Designer) and David Munro (Engineer), plus Bert Perrigo (Development and Competitions departments). Although he was criticized by some observers, there is no

BSA, Sunbeam and New Hudson bicycles.

B.S.A., SUNBEAM AND NEW HUDSON BICYCLES

doubt that under the chairmanship of Sir Bernard Docker, BSA did steer a neutral path and made healthy profits year on year. In fact, it was to be the Dockers' lavish and expensive lifestyle, part funded by BSA, which really caused his ultimate downfall. He had married Norah Callingham in February 1949. 'Naughty Norah', as she was infamously known, had had two previous husbands and spent money like it was going out of fashion. For example, not only was there an era of wild parties at the Dockers' country estate in Hampshire, but also the famous gold-plated 'Docker' Daimler.

Record Sales and Sporting Success

The early 1950s were, as Owen Wright so correctly summed up, BSA's golden years: 'Everything, it seemed, turned to gold: Golden Flash, Gold Star and gold medals galore.' The company's advertising stated 'BSA The Most

Popular Motor Cycle in the World', which at the time was true – certainly if one added Ariel, Triumph, Sunbeam and New Hudson sales to the list. The BSA Group's biggest rivals during this era were AMC (Associated Motor Cycles) of Woolwich, south-east London, which by 1953 comprised AJS, Matchless, Norton, Francis Barnett and James. However, even this combination could not match the Birmingham-based organization. And of course if one includes BSA's other interests there was no one bigger.

The Mid-1950s

When the Directors' Report and Statement of Accounts was submitted to shareholders at the firm's ninety-third AGM on 10 December 1954, the breadth of BSA's holdings were mightily impressive, with a vast range of divisions and products, not just in Great Britain, but in Eire, France, Canada and the USA.

According to a June 1951 advertisement 'BSA Predominates', going on to say 'One out of every four motor cycles in service throughout the world is a BSA'. The 1950s was a decade when the Birmingham marque really did rule the motorcycle industry.

Giant Birtley earth scrapers building a dam at Cossey's Creek, New Zealand, mid-1950s.

For historical purposes these are listed in a separate section within this chapter. I have also taken the liberty of recording the directors as at 10 December 1954:

- Sir Bernard Docker, KBE, Chairman and Managing Director (Chairman and MD of the Daimler Co. Ltd, the Lanchester Motor Co. Ltd, Chairman of Hooper & Co. (Coachbuilders) Ltd and Carbodies Ltd);
- Sir P.J.H. Hannon, Deputy Chairman;
- Lewis Chapman (Managing Director of William Jessop & Sons Ltd, and J.J. Saville & Co. Ltd, Chairman of the Birtley Co. Ltd);
- Noel H. Docker;
- James Leek, CBE (Managing Director of BSA Motorcycles Ltd, BSA Cycles Ltd, BSA Guns Ltd, Ariel Motors Ltd);
- H.J.S. Moyses, OBE (Chairman of BSA Tools Group Companies);
- H.P. Potts (Managing Director of BSA Tools Ltd);
- J.E. Rowe, ACA (Financial Director and Group Chief Accountant);
- J.Y. Sangster (Chairman of Triumph Engineering Co Ltd);

- Sir Frank E. Smith GCB, GBE, FRS (Chairman of Group Research);
- Secretary: F. Ellinghouse FCIS.

The net profit from all group activities for the year ending 31 July 1954 was £1,428,688, before providing for tax.

Daimler buses were a major export success for the BSA Group, being sold in every part of the world.

BSA Group (November 1954)

Birmingham	BG Machinery Ltd	**Sheffield**
	Leo C. Steinle Ltd	
Motor Cycles and Bicycles, Guns and	Cardiff Foundry & Engineering	*Special Steels*
Rifles	Co. (1947) Ltd	
	Precision Alloy Castings (Birming-	William Jessop & Sons Ltd
BSA Motor Cycles Ltd (including	ham) Ltd	J.J. Saville & Co. Ltd
Sunbeam Motor Cycle Division)		Bromley, Fisher & Turton Ltd
BSA Cycles Ltd		
New Hudson Ltd	**Coventry**	**Newcastle upon Tyne**
Sunbeam Cycles Ltd		
Ariel Motors Ltd	*Motor Cars and Buses*	*Heavy Engineering*
Triumph Engineering Co Ltd		
BSA Guns Ltd	The Daimler Co. Ltd	The Birtley Co. Ltd
Monochrome Ltd	The Lanchester Motor Co. Ltd	
Metal and Plastic Compacts Ltd	Transport Vehicles (Daimler) Ltd	**London**
	Barker & Co. (Coachbuilders) Ltd	
	Carbodies Ltd	*Motor Vehicle Bodies*
Machine Tools and Small Tools		
		Hooper & Co. (Coachbuilders) Ltd
BSA Tools Ltd		
Burton, Griffiths & Co Ltd		**Also subsidiaries in:**
		Eire, France, Canada and USA

In 1953 BSA Motor Cycles Ltd and BSA Cycles Ltd had been formed into separate divisions – underlining the increasing importance of motorcycles to the overall group position. James Leek was the Managing Director not only of these two companies, but also Ariel Motors and BSA Guns.

The Rot Sets In

In BSA motorcycle history 1956 has to be seen as a bad year – even though on the surface there were near record sales and a double Clubman's TT success by Bernard Codd. But behind the scenes the storm clouds of unrest were bubbling up.

First James Leek was forced to retire with ill health. Then Sir Bernard Docker was ousted by Jack Sangster in an AGM chairmanship battle. And unfortunately in many ways, Edward Turner succeeded James Leek as Managing Director of the automotive side of BSA. These moves effectively started BSA's decline as a motorcycle manufacturer, and caused in the author's opinion by Sangster and notably

Turner putting Triumph first with BSA a very poor second in the priorities list.

When one looks at the following year, 1957, the problems had already started, with the BSA Cycles Division being sold off to Raleigh, BSA and Daimler Cars sold to Jaguar Motors and a lack of support for other companies in the group – including Ariel. Okay, there was a profit of £2.1 million, but a good slice of this was down to selling off the family jewellery, so to speak, rather than increasing profitability.

But at least Jack Sangster was still there, and even though he had been responsible for introducing his pet man Turner to the board, Sangster did know how to show a profit for shareholders, as Owen Wright says: 'With a strong smell of asset stripping in the air, the mighty BSA machine was steadily and systematically dismembered.' The sell-off continued, with the industrial engine side sold to rivals Villiers.

Other signs of problems to come were that the BSA transmission chain was axed (1956), whilst sidecar production followed (1958). Even the Redditch complex was progressively wound down, although at this time Small

The world famous "piled arms" Trade Mark is the symbol of all that is best in British Gun and Rifle making. Manufacturers of the World's Champion Martini International .22 Match Rifle and other superb sporting weapons.

Left to Right:
B.S.A. Martini International .22 Match Rifle
B.S.A. Hunter Short Action Rifle
B.S.A. Air Rifle

BSA Guns: Manufacturer during the mid-1950s of the World's Champion Martini International .22 Match Rifle and other sporting weapons.

Heath (BSA), Meriden (Triumph) and Selly Oak (Ariel) continued as centres of respective motorcycle production.

But much worse was to come. On 7 June 1961, BSA published a special centenary issue of the in-house *BSA Group News*, a copy of which was presented to all existing employees of the corporate giant. Then later that year came the firm's balance sheet, published at the AGM. This showed a record profit of some £3 million, which was to mark the high point in the Group's finances. A canny Jack Sangster chose this moment to retire (a more appropriate term in the author's opinion would have been to 'abandon ship'). And from that exact moment things began to slide.

For a start, the BSA Group was saddled with the twin problems of Edward and Eric Turner (as it happens no blood relationship to each other). The former was the autocratic appointed promoter of Triumph Engineering and, as events were to prove, openly hostile to any other marque that was in the same 'family', which really signalled problems for both Ariel and BSA. Additionally, Edward Turner, at least by then, was a designer well past his best (as proof of this I offer in evidence expensive failures to come which included the Triumph Tina Scooter, BSA Beagle 75cc lightweight motorcycle and the Ariel Pixie 50cc).

But at least as bad was the other Turner, Eric. As Owen Wright says: 'That other Mr Turner had already made his indelible mark on BSA's product range. Whilst the centennial news was being read from cover to cover, plans were already in advance to replace the long-lived and highly acclaimed A7 and A10 twins.' And this was only the beginning. Recruited by Sangster from Blackburn Aircraft, Eric Turner was essentially an accountant. So perhaps it will come as no surprise to learn that the famous B Group singles were in the process of being, like the A7/A10 twins, killed off, including the legendary Gold Star. Even the new C15/B40 unit-construction singles were in reality Triumph (Edward Turner) influenced models.

Edward Turner Visits Japan

In the 11 August 1960 issue of *The Motor Cycle* it was reported that: 'Edward Turner, Managing Director of the automotive division of BSA, left for Japan where he intends to spend seven or eight weeks studying the Japanese.' In the same news report, *The Motor Cycle* stated: 'Reports indicate that no fewer than 62,000 motorcycles *per month* are being produced.' This

meant that even before he left, Turner knew that Japan was manufacturing some three-quarters of a million machines a year!

So what did Edward Turner's lengthy (and no doubt expensive!) visit achieve? The answer is very little, at least to benefit the BSA Group or the wider British motorcycle industry. The hard facts are that when he visited Japan Turner should have been able to see clearly the potential dangers threatening the British industry. Certainly, he was there long enough to carry out an extensive overview of the Japanese manufacturing potential and the quality and design of its products. Yet upon his return nothing seemed to change, when clearly as the Managing Director, Edward Turner was in a position to effect a change if he had seen fit, even though he did prepare a long and detailed report upon his return.

Arrogance or Incompetence?

So was it arrogance or incompetence, or a mixture of both? I believe, sadly, that the simple fact is that Turner was the wrong man for the job. It should have been someone who could look at the Japanese with an unbiased view, whereas Edward Turner was a man used to getting his own way. Owen Wright described him as: 'Tyrannical, dictatorial and a master of office psychology, Turner considered only his own designs as worthy of being pursued.' And this clearly was the heart of the problem – a man so blinded by his own self-importance, that he could see no further than the end of his nose! And when one looks closely at Edward Turner the 'great designer' one uncovers that the truth was somewhat different from the legend that has been built around his name over the years.

The facts are that Edward Turner came up with the concept of the Ariel Square 4, which led him into the industry in the first place, from humble beginnings as a small motorcycle agent in south London during the late 1920s. After being recruited by the Ariel factory, he formed a closeness to the owner Jack Sangster that was to survive the test of time. This meant that when Sangster took over Triumph in the mid-1930s, he chose Turner as design chief for his new purchase. There Turner transformed the somewhat dowdy Triumph singles into the excitingly styled Tiger 70, 80 and 90 models. These were followed by what are, without doubt, Turner's greatest achievements, the Speed Twin (1937) and Tiger 100 (1938). Turner was also instrumental in setting up Ariel and later Triumph sales in the USA (through his friendship with Californian businessman Bill Johnson). Other Turner successes were mainly limited to clever marketing (notably of Triumph motorcycles) and styling cues such as the headlamp nacelle, tank-top grid and tank badges (again on Triumph machines).

Now we come to the failures. The first of these concerns the much-publicized Triumph Sprung Hub rear suspension of the late 1940s. Next, for the lack of any significant designs in the 1950s (except variants of the Speed Twin-based vertical twin formula and the 150 Terrier/200 Cub unit singles) and, as already mentioned, the development of the Triumph Tina scooter, BSA Beagle and Ariel Pixie. Finally, the ill-fated BSA Fury/Triumph Bandit, which were 350cc ohc twins that are generally agreed to have been badly engineered and a major cause in the BSA Group's subsequent downfall in the early 1970s.

The first signs that the Turner & Turner double act wasn't working came in September 1962, with the news that the Ariel works in Selly Oak was to close, with production being switched to Small Heath. At the time, the press put a gloss on the move, *The Motor Cycle* even going as far as to say that the move was caused by lack of space in the Ariel plant.

But of course the truth was somewhat different, and it was a case of cutting back, not of expanding.

Edward Turner Retires

Towards the end of 1963 Edward Turner decided to retire; he was then sixty-two years old but didn't retire completely and still remained in a consultancy capacity. The man who was chosen to replace him was Harry Sturgeon (then in his early forties), who had originated from the de Havilland aircraft factory in Hatfield but had then spent a short period with the Churchill machine tool company, another BSA subsidiary. Actually, perhaps against all the odds, Sturgeon was a success in his new role. Well, for one thing the staff now had someone who would listen and take on board their ideas.

As Owen Wright says: 'He brought into Small Heath a new mood of optimism and motivation. Sturgeon was a brilliant salesman, whose driving hand was behind many of the new lavish posters and snappy one-liner advertising catchphrases that played up to the so-called "swinging sixties".'

The American Market is All-Important

By now, the American market was by far BSA's most important customer, a situation that would remain for the rest of the marque's life. Summed up by Owen Wright: 'By the mid-1960s, the American influence was beginning to show itself, with an influx of "flamboyant" colour schemes, high-rise handlebars and a never-ending quest for more performance to be squeezed out of designs that had really gone beyond their safety boundary.'

Unfortunately, these changes were largely to go untaken. For one thing, this once great company was beginning to lose its way. The engineers, craftsmen, designers, salesmen and motorcycle enthusiasts were being replaced by cost accountants, paper chasers, whizz-kids and asset strippers.

To make matters worse, the board of directors had made a series of wrong moves. For example, there had been a continuing number of sell-offs, including the steel-making and machine-tool arms – quite often at well below their true market value.

All this had not been helped by a long illness that had struck down the one man who

BSA Power Units manufactured mobile and stationary power units for agricultural and industrial applications.

just might have pulled things around, Harry Sturgeon, who finally died in April 1967 from a brain tumour. That same year saw what has become known as the 'money-no-object think-tank', Umberslade Hall.

Lionel Jofeh

Lionel Jofeh arrived in February 1967 to replace the stricken Harry Sturgeon. Actually, Sturgeon's deputy, Bert Hopwood, should have been the man to succeed him, but Eric Turner (then BSA's Chairman) recruited yet another outsider. Jofeh had formally been Chairman and Managing Director of the Sperry Gyroscope Company. Although Eric Turner tried convincing Hopwood to remain, Jofeh's appointment was the final straw. And, quite frankly, I don't blame him, as by now the situation at least at senior management level was becoming serious.

Rather perversely, the BSA Group won the Queen's Award for Industry in 1967 and again in 1968. But these awards masked what was really going on behind the scenes. An example of how bad things really were is contained in the development history of the BSA Rocket 3/Triumph Trident 750cc three-cylinder superbike; this took a massive *six years* to progress from planning to production, not being helped by the bitter in-fighting between BSA and Triumph.

Lionel Jofeh's arrival was supposed to be 'a new broom', but unfortunately, if anything, things got worse, as there was not only a larger marketing department, with more staff, but also more management consultants, market researchers and accountants.

Steve Wilson describes the position as follows: 'What now followed Jofeh's February 1967 arrival at Small Heath resembled a silent Charlie Chaplin film, with Charlie struggling with increasing frenzy to master the inexorable cogs of some infernal machine that grinds on faster and faster, regardless of his desperation. More and more high-level, high-salary jobs with cars were created.' And 'Meetings, including those at which decisions were to be made, grew bigger and bigger.' BSA was by now effectively being run by committees!

Umberslade Hall

Purchased by Eric Turner in 1967, Jofeh's baby was the Research and Development Centre at Umberslade Hall. The latter was an imposing country house (more like a mansion!) situated near Henley-in-Arden and Solihull, midway between the Meriden, Small Heath and Redditch works. But although it was purchased in mid-1967, it was not fully completed for its new task until the end of 1968, and as Steve Wilson has commented, 'thereafter the establishment was run by a staff of 300 at an estimated annual cost of around £1,500,000 a year'.

But Umberslade Hall did not solve the intense BSA–Triumph rivalry. In fact, it made things even worse. It also spawned horrors such as the oil-in-frame models and the 50cc Ariel 3 trike, to say nothing of the 350cc ohc Fury/Bandit twin.

The Great Computer Bungle

Another great problem for the BSA Group at the time was computers. When interviewing Bert Hopwood for *Classic Legends* magazine during the early 1990s, Ted Ulrich asked Bert: 'Since the book came out [Hopwood's *What Ever Happened to the British Motorcycle Industry?*] have you had any second thoughts on the best times, the worst of times? Proud of this, sorry about that, if only … that sort of thing?'

Bert Hopwood's reply was as follows:

> You know I don't waste time patting myself on the back for the things that went right, or losing sleep over those that went wrong. In retrospect, neither I, nor anyone else, could really have done anything about the big issues at the time. Like the damned management consultants who rushed BSA into computers, turning the industry's best spares and service department into a shambles pretty well overnight.

Unfortunately, it wasn't just the spares and service that suffered. For example, months after the company quickly discovered that the Ariel 3 trike was a non-seller, the BSA computer system continued ordering thousands of engines from the Dutch-based Anker concern, ultimately costing the British firm millions of pounds.

Even today, it's quite common for government-funded computer systems to cause problems. But back in the early days of the computer industry just consider additional problems such as the sheer size of the hardware, huge purchase costs (compared to current day levels) and the fact that computers then took hours or days to achieve what is now possible in seconds on a home PC! Yes, BSA was an unfortunate guinea pig for the fledgling computer industry – yet another nail in Small Heath's coffin.

The Final Months

By 1970 BSA was losing vast sums of money, and industrial strife was rife. By July 1971 after a loss of £8.5 million, Lionel Jofeh parted company with BSA; Eric Turner followed a few months later in November 1971. This saw Lord Shawcross, a senior executive since 1968, being elected as Chairman. But all this was far too late; the problems were too big, the losses too great.

The Shawcross regime tried hard enough, but even with a £10 million cash injection could make little headway. Eventually after suffering a £3 million loss for the 1972 trading year, BSA neared bankruptcy. The result was a political deal and a take-over by Manganese Bronze Holdings chaired by Denis Poore, who had already swallowed up both AMC and Villiers Engineering.

The original plan called for Meriden to be axed and to transfer both Triumph and Norton production to Small Heath. But the Meriden workers rebelled, and, backed by a new incoming Labour government with Tony Benn as Industry Minister, the result was that the last batch of bikes to leave the Small Heath production lines on a Wednesday night in the summer of 1973 were a batch of white-painted Triumph Tridents for Saudi Arabia.

The Triumph Workers Co-operative had ultimately won, and attempts to restart engine production at Small Heath in 1974 failed. This resulted in the vast factory site being sold to the Birmingham Corporation. In 1977 the Small Heath factory was demolished. But Triumph's victory didn't do them any good, as it lost a pile of money from several government handouts over the years and finally closed in 1983, with the name alone being sold to Midlands businessman, John Bloor.

So in the final analysis it was Triumph which helped to kill off BSA – after the 'management' had tried everything it knew to achieve the same result. A truly sad end to what had been, for over half a century, Great Britain's largest motorcycle company.

11   Rocket Gold Star

The Rocket Gold Star (often simply referred to as the 'RGS') is without doubt the most sought after, coveted and lusted over of all the BSA twin-cylinder models described in this book. And this is despite being added, almost as an afterthought, only a few months prior to the ending of production for the A7/A10 series of pre-unit twins.

Hitting the Headlines

When the Rocket Gold Star was launched in the first week of February 1962 it certainly hit the headlines. *Motor Cycling* commented: 'By the inspired process of taking a 650cc twin Super Rocket engine and fitting it to a "Gold Star" specification frame, BSA have produced

The Rocket Gold Star in home market guise, with siamezed exhaust pipes, low 'bars and rear-set footrests. Although only offered for a few months during 1962 and 1963, the RGS has nonetheless become one of BSA's most glamorous and sought-after models.

The Rocket Gold Star was also built for the American market, with separate exhausts, touring handlebars and forward-mounted footrests.

a new machine for the super-enthusiast – the "Rocket Gold Star".' *The Motor Cycle* in its 8 February 1962 issue carried the headline: 'A Rocket Goes into Orbit' … 'New Clubman's Six-Fifty twin from BSA'. In a subsequent road test later that year, *The Motor Cycle* said: 'Scintillating high-performance road burner: good brakes, excellent rider comfort [the test bike had handlebars upturned to provide a more upright stance] and docile traffic manners.'

Eddie Dow's Rocket Gold Star

The Rocket Gold Star had in fact been the idea of former racer and leading Gold Star specialist dealer, Eddie Dow, whose dealership in the Oxfordshire town of Banbury had already built up an enviable reputation with owners of the Gold Star single-cylinder series. Worried that supplies of the GS were drying up, Dow, who was in constant contact with the Small Heath factory, suggested to BSA managers that a combination of the 646cc (70 × 84mm) A10 Super Rocket engine and Gold Star chassis would fill the gap between the demise of the single and the introduction of more sporting versions of the soon to be announced new unit-construction twin-cylinder family (*see BSA Unit Twins – The Complete Story*, The Crowood Press).

But as Steve Wilson was to recall in his six-volume 1980s series *British Motorcycles Since 1950*, 'It could be said that the scheme succeeded all too well, for the RGS was the ultimate, and one that made the forthcoming Rocket and Lightning look somewhat underwhelming.'

BSA engineers began the project in mid-1961. The engine was essentially the existing A10 to Super Rocket specification – which meant a light alloy cylinder head, sports camshaft, but with the compression ratio upped from 8.25 to 9:1 to provide greater punch. The ignition was courtesy of a Lucas magneto (with manual control) and the electrical supply came by way of a DC dynamo – this set-up being very similar to the Gold Star itself. However, in place of the GS's pukka racing Grand Prix carburettor, the RGS employed a single Amal 389 Monobloc of 1⁵⁄₃₂in (29mm) choke diameter, BSA not choosing to go the twin-carb route of the Triumph Bonneville.

A BSA 650 Rocket Gold Star brochure, with revised price from 10 April 1962 of £309 13s 6d, including £52 19s UK purchase tax.

Close Ratio Gears

Like the Gold Star, the RGS featured a close ratio gearbox, with ratios of 4.52, 4.96, 5.96 and 7.92:1, whilst the cam plate was of the reversible type, so that the method of operation (that is, up for down) could remain the same whether the gear pedal was pointing forward or rearward, for use with conventional or rear-set footrests. The frame was identical to the Gold Star except for the omission of the customary kink, demanded by the presence of the single-cylinder engine's oil pump.

The Front Fork Assembly

The front fork assembly too was genuine Gold Star, which supported its QD headlamp on brackets from the chrome-plated shrouds; in addition dust-excluder rubber bellows (gaiters) were often fitted. The lamp itself featured a plug-and-socket connection to the main wiring loom, thus making it easy to remove for competition events. The fork shrouds (headlamp brackets) could be removed to facilitate the fitment of clip-on handlebars,

the clip-ons being a cost option. Another cost option was the large Smith tachometer, driven from the timing chest and matched with the 120mph (193km/h) speedometer from the same source. These instruments were mounted on rubber-mounted brackets from the top fork yoke.

The Option List

It was a fact that the option list for the Rocket Gold Star was a lengthy one. It included alloy wheel rims, clip-on handlebars, rear-mounted foot controls and separate exhausts (a siamezed system was standard). These separate pipes could only be used with forward mounted footrests. Yet another 'extra' was the 190mm (7.8in) full-width front drum brake.

In standard guise, BSA claimed 46bhp at 6,250rpm, but in track configuration it was 50bhp. The latter was with a special racing megaphone exhaust.

Testing the RGS

As previously mentioned, *The Motor Cycle* carried out a comprehensive, three-page road-test

The optional 190mm front brake, which looked pretty but was not as powerful as the standard 8in single-sided type.

Although most of its contemporary rivals boast twin carburettors for maximum performance, the Rocket Gold Star had a single Amal Monobloc. This is perhaps one of the prime factors in the sweetness of carburation at the lower end of the scale. From tickover at 800rpm, the engine answered the throttle crisply and instantaneously, provided the ignition lever was used intelligently. From 1,500rpm, beefy, usable power was on tap right up to the manufacturers' recommended ceiling of 6,800rpm, at which 46bhp is developed.

The test bike – equipped with the standard siamezed header pipes, plus a Burgess style, BSA-manufactured silencer – made for a quiet exhaust note for such a sporting mount. According to *The Motor Cycle* tester:

> The delightfully subdued drone from the siamesed exhaust system allowed full use of the performance without fear of causing offence. Because of the wide spread of power, upward gear changes were normally made at 5,400rpm rather than the ceiling of 6,800 – equivalent to a corrected 50mph [80km/h] in bottom, 66mph [106km/h] in second and 80mph [130km/h] in third. The speedometer read a constant 4mph [6km/h] fast. Tweaking the twistgrip halfway continued the rush of the speedometer needle round to the 85mph [137km/h] mark. A further tweak of the grip at ninety unleashed a fresh surge of power until the needle was hovering near the magic 100.

Other Plus Points

Another facet of the November 1962 test was that: 'While not in the turbine-smooth category, the power unit was no rougher than one would expect of a vertical twin with high-kick pistons, and was commendably free of any noticeable vibration period.' Other plus points included:

• Acceleration, 'exceptionally rapid – guaranteed to satisfy the most hardened enthusiast'.
• Gear change, 'light and crisp in movement and positive at all times'.

report in its 22 November 1962 issue. With aforementioned sit up and beg riding position and the tester wearing a two-piece suit and overboots, a highest one-way speed of 105mph (169km/h) was recorded. Weather conditions were a slight tail wind and heavy rain.

But as the test revealed 'An 85mph [137km/h] top-gear speed speaks volumes for the tractability of a sporting engine. And on top of this the 646cc BSA Rocket Gold Star has effortless, surging acceleration through the gears and a tireless 90mph [150km/h] cruising gait. The maximum of 105mph [169km/h] obtained on test could certainly have been bettered had the November weather been co-operative.

The Motor Cycle had a favourable opinion of the machine's carburation:

- Brakes, 'both light in operation and extremely powerful'.
- Comfort, 'Well shaped and deeply uphol-stered, the dual-seat provided exceptional comfort no matter what mileage was being covered'.
- Fuel consumption, 'at 70mph, 61mpg [110km/h, 4.6ltr/100km]'.

But like every vehicle there were features which attracted criticism:

- Mudguards, 'It did not need a very long run in the rain, however, to prove the drawback of a narrow sports front mudguard – the amount of road filth that blows back on the machine and rider.'
- Steering, 'Straight-ahead steering was pre-cise up to 90mph [145km/h] but then became progressively lighter until at maxi-mum speed on a wet road, the front wheel tended to wander slightly. Tightening down the steering damper effected a partial cure.' And although 'Roadholding and stability under normal conditions allowed high aver-age speeds to be maintained safely, stiffening the action of the front fork would probably eliminate a tendency for slight rolling on a fast corner.'

- Lighting, this was described as 'adequate for mile-a-minute cruising after dark'.
- Horn, 'loud enough for jaunts about town, the horn would have to be more penetrating to be of much use during fast, open-road touring'.
- Roll-on centre stand, came as standard equipment and 'required only moderate effort to operate, but its feet were too sharp; parking places had to be carefully chosen, for the legs would gradually dig into tarmac.' A prop stand was a cost option.

But overall the test was positive, rather than negative, concluding: 'The Rocket Gold Star, then, is that rare bird, a high-performance motorway express which is almost equally at home in less exciting urban surroundings.'

Adding a Third Wheel

Rivals *Motor Cycling* also carried out a test of the RGS. Published in the latter's 13 March 1963 issue, it was notable because the test machine was fitted with a glass-fibre-bodied Watsonian Monza Super Sports sidecar. The *Motor Cycling* test began:

When BSA announced the A10 Rocket Gold Star last year, it was not difficult to predict that the

RGS in touring trim, with optional 190mm front brake and alloy wheel rims.

engine of a hot 650 roadster twin married to the frame of a famous Clubman's racer would produce something exceptional in the way of solo road-burners. Less obvious, perhaps, was the fact that this machine could also be the ideal prime mover for the sidecar enthusiast who wants an outfit that will top the 80mph [130km/h] mark at a pinch, cruise at 70 [110] all day, offer scalding acceleration – and combine all this with low-speed docility.

Modified Gearing

For chair work, the RGS's gearing was lowered by using a twenty-tooth engine sprocket and a forty-three-tooth clutch sprocket. These, together with the stock nineteen-tooth gearbox and forty-six-toothed rear wheel sprockets, gave an overall gearing of 5.2:1 instead of the standard 4.74:1.

As with the solo test bike, *Motor Cycling*'s RGS and Monza chair came in for considerable praise. In fact, beside the change of gearing there were surprisingly few other changes. Upturned handlebars (as on *The Motorcycle* test bike) were employed and the front tyre was studded rather than ribbed (in other words, the same pattern front and rear). Of the variety of optional extras that BSA listed for road and competition work, the test bike only made use of the tachometer.

An Easy-Going Nature

As *Motor Cycling* said:

Any fears about the incidental penalties of a 9:1 compression ratio proved to be unfounded. A single, almost effortless, kick invariably spun the crankshaft for a first-time start provided that the manual ignition control, mounted on the left bar, had been moved about three-quarters of the way towards 'retard'. Tickover and slow running were uneven on full advance, but intelligent use of this control made the 80-plus outfit sufficiently flexible for 28–30mph [45–48km/h] top-gear town travel. It was also necessary to retard the ignition slightly to avoid pinking when the machine was pulling hard uphill in top gear. In second gear, the outfit, weighing more than a quarter of a ton and carrying the rider and a lightweight passenger or sidecar ballast, would accelerate up to 50 [80] like a shot.

The tester continued:

Eric Cheers with the Rocket Gold Star that he rode in the 1962 Thruxton 500-mile race. The bike sports some BSA options including alloy rims, Lyta alloy tank and 190mm front brake.

About 70mph [110km/h] in top was the speed best suited to main road cruising. Then, the turbo-like smoothness of the engine, with the crankshaft turning over well below the 6,250rpm ceiling, was a perpetual source of pleasure. This standard of performance could be relied upon whenever traffic and other circumstances permitted.

Braking

The additional weight of the sidecar could, reasonably, have been expected to show up deficiencies of the brakes. However, the Monza chair came with not only a sprung wheel, but also its own brake. This no doubt was the reason why the *Motor Cycling* tester said:

> The rider had the comforting knowledge that all three brakes were well up to their job. The sidecar brake pedal – better adjusted than that of quite a few outfits tested previously – could be applied readily in conjunction with that of the rear wheel

brake, helping to pull up squarely without the chair slowing to the left. The 8in-diameter [203mm] front brake was excellent.

It should be realized that this brake was the stock BSA single-sided assembly, not the optional 190mm [7.8in] unit listed as a cost option.

Prices

Basic price on the British market at the time of launch in February 1962 – in standard form – was £244 10s, with a total price including UK taxes of £300.

The Motor Cycle test machine in November 1962 was listed at £323 8s – but this included the cost option rev counter. Then again, when *Motor Cycling* carried out its test (with Watsonian Monza sidecar) in March 1963, the machine alone (again with rev counter, but otherwise stock) was priced at £328 18s (including taxes).

A beautifully restored Rocket Gold Star in the National Motorcycle Museum, spring 2005.

Best in Show

When the Earls Court Show was staged in November 1962, *The Motor Cycle*'s editor, Harry Louis, said 'I reckon that Rocket Gold Star is the best-looking bike around.' And here are a few of the comments made at the time by visitors to the show, as recorded by Harry: 'Well, it has everything you want but no frills,' said twenty-two-year-old Jim Symes of Nottingham. 'That tank, with all its curves [the show bike was fitted with a 5gal (23ltr) Lyta component], fits in the general scheme of things; the bike looks nicely balanced, somehow, and I like that big front brake and the alloy rims. Yes, that Gold Star version's for me – when I can afford to change. Maybe early next year.'

Another admirer was twenty-year-old Mike Howard, of West Croydon, and his girlfriend, Wendy Cattell. They also owned another BSA twin, a 1960 Super Rocket. As Harry Louis said in his Show Report: 'Both coveted the RGS on its plinth.' But 'Nobody seemed to notice that that particular model was sporting about £50 worth of extras!'

With production of the Rocket Gold Star only lasting a few months (early 1962 to spring 1963) one has to wonder just how many show-goers actually got to own their dream bike, as only 2,200 examples were manufactured.

More Replicas than Genuine Examples

With what amounted to a very limited production life, and given the huge popularity of the machine, the Rocket Gold Star has unfortunately become the subject for a large number of fakes. In fact, most agree that there are actually more fakes than genuine examples! Some of

1962 Rocket Gold Star in production-racing guise – Mallory Park Post TT meeting, June 2004.

1962 Rocket Gold Star Specifications

Engine	Air-cooled, ohv vertical twin, 360 degree crank, single camshaft at rear of crankcase, alloy cylinder head and cast-iron barrel, bottom rocker covers
Bore	70mm
Stroke	84mm
Displacement	646cc
Compression ratio	9:1
Lubrication	Dry sump with oil pump featuring worm drive, a pressure-relief valve screwed into crankcase
Ignition	Magneto
Carburettor	Amal 389 Monobloc $1\frac{5}{32}$in (29mm)
Primary drive	Simplex chain
Final drive	Chain
Gearbox	Separate, four-speed gearbox, foot-change
Frame	All-steel construction, double front downtube
Front suspension	BSA telescopic, oil-damped forks
Rear suspension	Swinging arm, with twin Girling shock absorbers
Front brake	8in (203mm)
Rear brake	7in (178mm)
Tyres	Front 3.25 × 19; rear 3.50 × 19

General Specifications

Wheelbase	56in (1,422mm)
Ground clearance	6in (152mm)
Seat height	30in (762mm)
Fuel tank capacity	4gal (18ltr)
Dry weight	418lb (190kg)
Maximum power	46bhp @ 6,250rpm
Top speed	111mph (179km/h)

these, of course, have been built because of a particular enthusiast's love of the bike, but since the development of the classic scene from the beginning of the 1980s and the subsequent vast rise in value for the RGS, many individuals have cobbled together lookalikes to fool the unwitting and in the process have made a handsome profit.

There are, however, several checks that the would-be buyer can make before handing over the cash. The first concerns the frame. As already explained, the single-cylinder Gold Star frame had a kink in the offside (right) tube under the engine (for oil pump clearance); the Rocket Gold Star did not. At least this will tell you if someone has attempted a Gold Star-framed/Super/Road Rocket hybrid.

Next, you can check the large diameter wheel spindle (and matching fork legs) needed for the optional 190mm (7.8in) full-width front brake. But of course the required legs might have been retro-fitted.

Another item on the checklist is the chrome-plated mudguards. These were unique to the RGS and are distinct from either the Gold Star itself or the later A65 sport range such as the Spitfire, Lightning Clubman or Rocket. These can be identified by a beaded line on the lower edge of the six-stay front mudguard, and the trailing edge of the rear assembly where the registration plate and light fitting are open-sided, as on the Bantam.

Yet another detail is the silver/chrome 4gal (18ltr) petrol tank, with its butterfly nut quick-action racing filler cap; the badges should of course be the circular ones found on the Gold Star and some years of the A7 Shooting Star.

Summary

In the author's view, the history of the Rocket Gold Star shows all that was wrong with BSA during the 1960s. Here was a bike that should – and could so easily – have been built during the boom years of the 1950s, but wasn't. And when it was finally authorized, production came on the very eve of the launch of the new A50/65 unit construction twins. But as was evident at the time and has been proved over the subsequent forty-plus years, customers wanted this bike. Sadly, BSA didn't listen too much to these valuable people and so the group built bikes that it *thought* people would buy, instead of what they largely wanted. No wonder events turned out the way they eventually did!

12 Today's Old Bike Scene

There has always been a fascination with old motorcycles amongst enthusiasts. First it was vintage and veteran models and runs such as the London to Brighton and the Banbury event.

VMCC

Then during the 1960s the VMCC (Vintage Motor Cycle Club) came into prominence. Founded by Titch Allen, this organization is still very much in existence, with a huge membership, many local branches, its own comprehensive magazine and events such as the annual Founders Day at Stanford Hall, near Lutterworth. Since the late 1960s the VMCC has also had a popular racing section, which stages road races on British short circuits. This is now called the Historic Racing Championship and in 2005 staged meetings at Mallory Park, Pembrey, Lydden Hill, Cadwell Park and Anglesey. But, as with other old bike clubs, the biggest emphasis is with the normal road rider – except of course where these specialize in racing, scrambles or trials.

The Classic Boom

But the really big change in the old bike scene came just over a quarter of a century ago, when the historic motorcycle movement witnessed what can only be described as a major lift. It was during the latter part of the 1970s when almost overnight interest in motorcycles, particularly British ones, suddenly boomed. What had once been the preserve of specialist engineers and amateurs lovingly rebuilding pre-war machines, changed course.

Post TT races, Mallory Park, June 2003, plunger-framed A10 c.1951–52, with aftermarket screen, topbox and carrier.

30 July 2003, VMCC Founders Day, Stanford Hall, Leicestershire: an immaculate 1960 A10 Super Rocket and Watsonian sidecar. The bike has optional rev counter (with separate headlamp brackets) and chrome-plated mudguards.

The latter part of the 1970s had seen the release of a vast stock of British bikes from the 1940s, 1950s and 1960s, which had been put to one side as newer, more hi-tech roadsters left the by now mainly Japanese factories and also large numbers of obsolete competition machines that were no longer winners on the circuit became available.

At that time, the machines were available at reasonable cost and the generations that had been young men during the times when these motorcycles were new, found themselves in the fortunate position of having the money to spare to indulge their need to recapture the dreams of youth. And so the classic boom got under way.

Classic Bike Magazine

The British publishing company EMAP (East Midland Allied Press) had the foresight to judge this burgeoning trend, the result being that in March 1978 it launched the world's first magazine catering for this new breed, *Classic Bike*. Its first editor was Peter Watson and there were articles on side-valve models, vintage racing, Ducati singles, dustbin fairings, Edward Turner and War Department motorcycles.

That first issue also tested a Model 7 (500cc) Norton Dominator. Published monthly, it retains a position as one of the two-wheel industry's best-selling journals.

Through demand for classic machinery and increased press coverage, the value of this new breed of 'classic' machine rose steadily

Unrestored A10 Golden Flash, c.1955. With nacelle, swinging-arm frame and single-sided hubs. Essentially an ideal restoration project, as the machine is still largely stock specification.

throughout the early 1980s, before finding a level in the middle of that decade. In hindsight, this was probably the golden era of the classic motorcycle, with the market in a healthy state, but with prices still relatively low, except for genuinely rare and exotic models.

The Speculators

As the 1980s drew to a close, the dealers and speculators who were active in the historic car scene began to move into bikes and this inevitably unbalanced the previously stable market platform. There was a surge in values generally, although the greatest rises were confined to the prestige models, notably Vincents, Brough Superiors and Italian MV Agustas, which in the autumn of 1989 were changing hands for £25,000 upwards, with Broughs commanding even more.

Quite simply, the market moved away rapidly from its enthusiast base to an investment-oriented one. The day of the 'bank vault' motorcycle had arrived. In Britain, hundreds of motorcycles – notably British and Italian, were being exported to Japan, where the yen-rich could afford to pay often double the price that could be realized in Britain. Often these machines ended up being sold in Tokyo antique shops. The classic craze was sweeping Japan to such an extent that not only were genuine classic machines becoming much sought after, but there was also a booming business developing for modern-day classic styling exercises. These included models such as Yamaha's SRX 600 and Honda's XBR 500 being dressed up to look like a Norton, AJS, MV Agusta or a BSA Gold Star.

However, every boom has its bust, and in the autumn of 1990 certain factors led the classic motorcycle market into decline. The worldwide recession felt in countries such as the United States, Great Britain and Japan resulted in many potential buyers becoming extremely wary, and those who had speculated in many cases found that they had overstretched themselves.

As happened in the classic car world (to a much greater and more costly extent!), this

period saw a glut of machines being unloaded onto a depressed market, and the result was a giant fall in prices. In the twelve months from September 1990 to September 1991, Vincents, Broughs and MV Agustas lost an average of at least a third of their value, in fact wiping out at a stroke much of the 'paper' profits recorded during the late 1980s boom years.

Good Old 'Beeza'

But mainstream marques such as Triumph and BSA had generally not been affected in the same way. Not only were motorcycles such as the Triumph Speed Twin and Bonneville, plus the BSA A7 and A10 models in much greater supply, but their owners were almost exclusively genuine enthusiasts, not someone trying to get rich quick.

The motorcycles covered in this book, except perhaps the interwar V-twins, are in reality the staple classic diet of British motorcycles of the late 1940s through to the 1960s. Not only have these bikes given reliable service for many years to their countless owners, but they have grown in value at more sustainable rates – with fluctuations in price in either direction. This is for a number of very good

BSA Owners' Club stand at a classic bike show during the early 1980s, with a Rocket Gold Star as the central attraction.

Concours winner at an Owners' Club rally; a superbly restored 1956 plunger-framed A10.

reasons. Foremost is the fact that so many A7 and A10 series machines have survived. Another factor is that parts are generally still available and at reasonable costs, which in turn makes restoration more attractive and ensures the continued use of the motorcycle.

BSA also has an excellent owners club, with local branches not just in the UK but around the world.

A Popular Choice

BSAs have always been a popular choice, both when they were new, and still today as a classic bike. In November 2001 *Classic Bike* published a special BSA issue. Interestingly, it also published in the same issue an entirely unrelated twenty-four-page supplement of what it considered the world's 'Top 100 Road Classics'.

This A10 was still being used as regular everyday transport in the mid-1980s.

The list of BSAs was as follows:

- 1   Rocket Gold Star   1963
- 6   DBD34 Gold Star   1955
- 12   A10 Golden Flash   1959
- 32   A7 Star Twin   1951
- 52   A65 Lightning   1965
- 73   S29 Sloper   1929
- 85   Bantam DI   1948
- 92   Model B Round Tank   1924

This was a pretty impressive total of eight models. Only Triumph scored more (nine entries); the next highest was Norton with six. And BSA, with the RGS, had the honour of being number one. Of course, as *Classic Bike* said: 'Motorcycles are so subjective, so emotive, that choosing the top 100 road classics in an entirely dispassionate manner is an almost impossible task.' The priorities were 'technical merit, build quality, aesthetics, performance, practicality and impact in as objective a manner as possible'.

Specialists

The classic scene also had the advantage of creating specialists who carried out a wide range of services, including not only sales of the motorcycles themselves, but also engine rebuilds, full restoration, parts supply and remanufacture, and in some cases modifications and improvements using modern technology.

One such specialist is the Welshman, Steven McFarland, the proprietor of SRM Engineering, originally based in Pembroke Dock, but now located in Aberystwyth, Dyfed. He had purchased his first BSA at the age of thirteen – a Bantam two-stroke. By the time he was seventeen he had owned four Beezas and later went on to own a whole collection of Small Heath-built machinery.

Steven purchased his first A10 when he was 'about eighteen' and used it as his daily transport. However, he liked it so much that he restored it to Rocket Gold Star specification. Then in 1978 he purchased another A10 and an A7 that were used for daily transport for many years thereafter.

As he told the author in 1984: 'I cover approximately 25,000 miles a year, of which about 15,000 are on one A10 and found that it was necessary to strip the engine every year to replace the main bush.' He continued 'After a few years of this, I decided to do something

1960 Golden Flash with its proud owner at Snetterton, Norfolk, summer 1985.

RIGHT: Gary Anderson with his 1951 A10 racing sidecar outfit, Bob McIntyre Memorial meeting, East Fortune, 18/19 June 2005. The front brake is a modified 2LS assembly from a late 1960s BSA unit twin; the wheel size is 16in.

BELOW: The sidecar of the Gary Anderson 1951 A10 racing outfit began life as a standard BSA sports chair.

to extend the life of this bearing which also affects the oil supply to the big-ends. Since other A10 owners had the same problem, I thought that I could overcome this inherent problem of the wear of the timing side bush and start a business to offer this service to other owners.' Steven McFarland looked at various ways of replacing it with a needle roller, but in the end came up with one suitable combined needle ball bearing, available at that time. However, it 'did not have sufficient load capacity and not having the facilities to perform the various machinery operations required, I decided to devise my own "super bush" precision engineered large bearing conversion'.

He achieved this by regrinding the main bearing to accept a larger diameter hardened and tempered nickel-chrome steel sleeve, specially made by Steven for both the A10 and unit construction A65. This, he said, 'increases

the diameter of the bearing and loading area by 25 per cent'. This sleeve is pressed on to the crankshaft and holds a hardened steel thrust washer onto the crank web. A special hi-grade bore phosphor-bronze bearing incorporates special lubrication channels for the thrust surface. The bronze bearing was made slightly undersize and then machined out after fitting to ensure perfect alignment, close tolerance fit and removed any ovality which may be transmitted through the bearing from the crankcases. This bearing arrangement reduced friction, which in turn reduced wear, as the co-efficient friction was far less between hardened steel and phosphor-bronze than that of the softer steel of the crankshaft and phosphor-bronze, and with the increased load capacity of the bearing, this, in Steven's words, 'dramatically increased the life of both the timing side main bearing and big-ends'.

In May 1984 he was able to report 'Many owners who have had this conversion, together with Tufftrided crankshafts, have covered well over 30,000 miles with no main bearing problems. My own bike had covered 35,000 miles, including two trips to Europe.'

Needle Roller Bearing Conversion

By the mid-1980s Steven McFarland's company SRM Engineering had obtained the necessary equipment to perform a needle roller bearing conversion on the timing side. With this conversion, the timing side bush was replaced by a needle roller bearing and a separate narrow series ball bearing – which he claimed had 'a combined load capacity 10 per cent greater than the drive side roller bearing'. Bearing manufacturers had by the mid-1980s managed to increase the load capacity of the combined needle roller/bearing and it now had sufficient load capacity to do the job, so, Steven McFarland commented, 'We might use this bearing in the future. We use a ball bearing with the needle roller to positively locate the crankshaft and eliminate end float.'

Performing the Conversion

To perform the conversion described above, the crankcases were set up on a jig borer and machined out to accept the needle roller and ball bearing, which were then retained in the timing side crankcase. The oil was now to be end-fed to the big-ends, which was done by machining an oilway in the crankshaft and the fitment of a stainless steel quill into the end of the crankshaft, which was then machined true. An oil seal ran on this quill which was housed in a special casting, which in turn was fitted to the outer timing side casing.

The oilways were altered in the crankcases and oil supply to the bush blocked off. Oil was redirected through a pipe in the crankcase and into the inner timing side casing, then to the outer timing side casing to which the aluminium casting was fitted. The crankcases were bolted together with both timing side castings, then a special shaft with a cutter fitted was inserted through the two main bearings, ensuring the oil seal housing was machined directly in line with the crankshaft. As the oil pump no longer had to feed the main bush and all the lubricant was fed to the big-ends this resulted in a 'substantial' increase in oil pressure to the big-ends.

Steven McFarland also commented: 'I have found that crankshaft Tuftriding both increased

SRM's conversion for the A7/A10 series described in the main text.

wear resistance of the big-ends by up to 1,000 per cent and also improves fatigue resistance. This can be done to all plain bearing crankshafts.'

SRM also offered the following parts/servicing for pre-unit BSA twins:

- finned aluminium magnetic sump filters;
- taper roller steering head bearings;
- crankshaft spline repairs;
- journals built to standard size;
- alloy welding;
- inserts, rebores, crank grinding etc.;
- forged alloy con-rods for A10;
- Mikuni carb kits, jetted and set ready to fit;
- dry belt drive kits with front cush drive for pre-unit twins.

An Owner's View

Another Welshman with ideas on how to modify an A10 successfully is Mike Rowlands. When interviewed in March 2003 Mike had owned his A10 for twenty-three years. It was comprehensively rebuilt in the late 1980s (using an engine from a Super Rocket), with modifications that included a needle roller timing-side main bearing conversion, and the fitting of an oil pump from the unit construction A65 engine and a feed-side cartridge oil filter.

The latter was neatly housed at the front of the crankcase where the dynamo used to be. The electrics had also been revised with a crankshaft-mounted alternator and Rita electronic ignition with a magneto flange-mounted trigger unit, which Mike purchased second-hand.

Finding it impossible to find an alternator-type primary chaincase on the used market, he got one from a small trial batch manufactured by SRM (who had carried out his bottom-end conversion). This cover features an A65-type inspection cover, which ensures that ignition timing with a strobe light is a simple task.

An Amal 930 Concentric carburettor replaced the original Monobloc instrument, whilst there were also new larger 1½in (38mm) inlet valves, together with a Spitfire camshaft. But seeking to maintain reliability, Mike chose a relatively low 8.25:1 compression ratio.

A major failing on Mike's A10 was, he felt, the stock 1960 type cast-iron full-width brake hubs. These were ditched in favour of a 1968-type BSA twin leading shoe drum, with A65 fork legs at the front and an earlier (*circa* pre-1956) A10 single-sided hub at the rear.

Another modification, made in the 1990s, was that the entire primary drive was replaced with a belt drive conversion by Fair Spares – originally for the Norton Commando. The firm manufactured a pulley to match a pattern mainshaft supplied by Mike and the optimum drive ratio was calculated by Paul Dewhurst, SRM's resident A10 modification expert. Running dry and with a sealed bearing for the clutch, the drive is cooled by perforations made in the chaincase.

Mike Rowlands' experiences show just how far one man will go to make his pre-unit BSA a viable machine that can give, as he puts it, service which 'keeps going and going. I don't even carry a screwdriver.'

Heavily modified A10 Café Racer. The basis of the machine is a 1957 model, with Ariel type full-width alley rear hub. Although the basic engine and chassis are original, just about everything else is new or modified.

Index